HELPING FAMILIES HELP CHILDREN

HELPING FAMILIES HELP CHILDREN

Family Interventions With
School-Related Problems

By

LARRY B. GOLDEN, Ph.D.

University of Texas at San Antonio
San Antonio, Texas

and

DAVE CAPUZZI, Ph.D.

Portland State University
Portland, Oregon

CHARLES C THOMAS • PUBLISHER
Springfield • Illinois • U.S.A.

118914

Published and Distributed Throughout the World by

CHARLES C THOMAS • PUBLISHER
2600 South First Street
Springfield, Illinois 62717

This book is protected by copyright. No part of it
may be reproduced in any manner without written
permission from the publisher.

© *1986 by* CHARLES C THOMAS • PUBLISHER

ISBN 0-398-05237-9

Library of Congress Catalog Card Number: 86-1484

With **THOMAS BOOKS** *careful attention is given to all details of manufacturing and design. It is the Publisher's desire to present books that are satisfactory as to their physical qualities and artistic possibilities and appropriate for their particular use.* **THOMAS BOOKS** *will be true to those laws of quality that assure a good name and good will.*

Printed in the United States of America
SC-R-3

Library of Congress Cataloging-in-Publication Data

Helping families help children.

Bibliography: p.
Includes indexes.
1. Problem children—Counseling of.   2. Problem
children—Education.   3. Home and school.   I. Golden,
Larry B.   II. Capuzzi, Dave.
LC4801.5.H44   1986   371.93   86-1484
ISBN 0-398-05237-9

This Book is Dedicated to Two Great Mothers:
Avellino Malloy Capuzzi and Trudy Zadan

CONTRIBUTORS

DONALD R. ATKINSON, Professor and Director of Training, Department of Education, University of California, Santa Barbara, Santa Barbara, California.

BERT BENNETT, Administrative and Clinical Director, St. Mary's Center, Norton, Virginia.

GORDON L. BERRY, Professor, Educational Psychology, Graduate School of Education, University of California, Los Angeles, Los Angeles, California.

PATTI BOSWELL BLOOMER, Treatment Specialist, Fayette County Drug and Alcohol Commission, Uniontown, Pennsylvania.

MICHAEL L. BUNDY, Counselor, Willow Brook Elementary School, Oak Ridge, Tennessee.

DAVE CAPUZZI, Professor and Coordinator, Counselor Education, School of Education, Portland State University, Portland, Oregon.

DAVID L. FENELL, Assistant Professor, Department of Guidance and Counseling, School of Education, University of Colorado, Colorado Springs, Colorado.

IRENE C. GAFNEY, Masters Degree Candidate, Family and Child Development Department, Virginia Polytechnic Institute and State University, Falls Church, Virginia.

LARRY B. GOLDEN, Assistant Professor, Counseling and Guidance, Division of Education, The University of Texas at San Antonio, San Antonio, Texas.

RUTH K. GOLDMAN, Professor, Psychology Department, San Francisco State University, San Francisco, California.

ROBERT G. GREEN, Associate Professor, School of Social Work, Virginia Commonwealth University, Richmond, Virginia.

JAMES GUMAER, Associate Professor, Counselor Education, Virginia Commonwealth University, Richmond, Virginia.

ED JACOBS, Associate Professor, Department of Counseling Psychology and Rehabilitation, West Virginia University, Morgantown, West Virginia.

LINDA F. LITTLE, Assistant Professor and Program Director, Family and Child Development Department, Virginia Polytechnic Institute and State University, Falls Church, Virginia.

ARMANDO LIZARDI, Graduate Student, Graduate School of Education, University of California, Los Angeles, Los Angeles, California.

JAMES E. MARTIN, Assistant Professor, Department of Special Education, School of Education, University of Colorado, Colorado Springs, Colorado.

KATHLEEN MAY, Supervisor of Special Education, Elwyn Institutes, Davidson School at Upsal, Philadelphia, Pennsylvania.

JOHNNIE WORD MEDINA, Program Development Specialist, North East Independent School District, San Antonio, Texas.

GARY MILLER, Associate Professor, Department of Educational Psychology, University of South Carolina, Columbia, South Carolina.

DENNIS E. MITHAUG, Dean, School of Education, University of Colorado, Colorado Springs, Colorado.

MICHAEL S. NYSTUL, Associate Professor, Department of Counseling and Educational Psychology, College of Education, New Mexico State University, Portales, New Mexico.

ALLEN J. OTTENS, Acting Director, University Counseling Center, Villanova University, Villanova, Pennsylvania.

AMY OTTENS, Workshop Coordinator, Elwyn Institutes, Davidson School at Upsal, Philadelphia, Pennsylvania.

DENNIS M. PELSMA, Assistant Professor, Counseling Psychology, University of Kansas, Lawrence, Kansas.

WILLIAM A. POPPEN, Professor, Department of Educational and Counseling Psychology, University of Tennessee, Knoxville, Tennessee.

ROBERT REARDON, Director, Curricular-Career Information Service and Professor, Department of Human Services and Studies, Florida State University, Tallahassee, Florida.

LOU C. TALBUTT, Information Manager, Virginia VIEW, College of Education, Virginia Polytechnic Institute and State University, Blacksburg, Virginia.

ROSEMARY A. THOMPSON, Director of Guidance, Oscar Smith High School, Chesapeake Public Schools, Chesapeake, Virginia.

PAUL D. WARNER, Coordinator of Counselor Education, Brigham Young University, Provo, Utah.

PRISCILLA N. WHITE, Professor, Department of Child and Family Studies, University of Tennessee, Knoxville, Tennessee.

G. SCOTT WOODING, Coordinator of Student Services, Elboya Junior High School, Calgary, Alberta, Canada.

PREFACE

There is no need to convince anyone of the importance of including families when we attempt to intervene with a misbehaving child. The family is in a powerful position to support or sabotage the best efforts of any professional helper. Nevertheless, families tend to be ignored when behavioral problems surface at school. Perhaps school authorities believe that they should be able to solve problems on an in-house basis, contacting parents only as a last resort. It's also possible that school authorities have become demoralized in their attempts to work with families. A meeting is arranged and parents don't show up. Parents can be hostile and even inclined towards litigation. Some parents are totally lacking in parenting skills and some are just too tired and discouraged. Consequently, the school pays lip service to the importance of families and otherwise keeps them at a safe distance.

This book is intended for the professional who works with children and adolescents—school teachers, counselors, administrators, social workers, and psychologists. The professional's time, energy, and expertise are regarded here as precious commodities. Our assumption is that one must make shrewd decisions about how to involve families in resolving school problems.

Our book is divided into three distinct sections. Part One, "Specific Behavioral Problems," describes many of the problem areas that professionals confront everyday, including school phobia, suicide, giftedness, child abuse, alcoholism, truancy, stress, and pregnancy. Each chapter attempts a "family" orientation in accounting for both etiology and treatment.

Part Two, "Non-Traditional" Families," presents a sociological perspective on the forces that shape today's families. With amazing suddenness, family life doesn't look the way it did in the Fifties! Stepfamilies? There was something about stepfamilies in the Cinderella story—a miserable situation but everyone lived happily ever after! Divorce? A tragedy that happened in that house down the block. Dual career families? In the good old days there were "Moms" who took care of everybody.

Part Three, "Interventions in the School," provides the information one needs to go forward with confidence, well, at least with something that feels better than trepidation, in helping kids and families with school related problems. One chapter is devoted to the special problems faced by racial and ethnic minority families in our schools. Another chapter introduces the reader to an innovative classroom management system. The last chapter provides a ready-to-use assessment tool for evaluating the suitability of a family for brief counseling interventions.

We all know that the family is a tough institution, the basic human unit that goes back into prehistory, the essential ingredient of civilization that is treasured by all of the world's religions. The school, for its part, enables every generation of children to make preparations for leaving their families and to make a new, hopefully, important contribution to the human enterprise.

All of us who work in the helping professions have made a personal investment in helping families survive these particularly hard times. When we help families help their kids adapt to the social and educational requirements of schools, we bring a note of harmony out of fearful chaos!

We wish to acknowledge the help with editorial work received from Valerie Ranegar and Sharon Wofford, graduate students at the University of Texas at San Antonio.

Larry B. Golden
San Antonio, Texas

Dave Capuzzi
Portland, Oregon

CONTENTS

118914

PART III Interventions in the School

Chapter

HELPING FAMILIES HELP CHILDREN

PART I SPECIFIC BEHAVIORAL PROBLEMS

THE SCHOOL PHOBIC CHILD
THE SUICIDAL ADOLESCENT
THE GIFTED CHILD
THE ABUSED CHILD
THE CHILD OF ALCOHOLIC PARENTS
THE TRUANT CHILD
THE MENTALLY RETARDED CHILD
THE CHILD UNDER STRESS
THE UNWED ADOLESCENT MOTHER

Chapter 1

THE SCHOOL PHOBIC CHILD

GORDON L. BERRY AND ARMANDO LIZARDI

Most child specialists would agree that it is common for children to experience fear about a number of things or objects in their environment. Fear is a natural response to real or imaginary danger because it is related to those elements in a child's world that he or she cannot understand or feels powerless to control (Ambron, 1975). Fears, while their meaning can be simple or complex, seem to be a natural part of the developmental process of children. In most cases youthful fears come and go quickly, cause little anxiety, and do not interfere very much with a child or young person's life (Weiner, 1982).

Concern for the fears that children are experiencing becomes necessary however, when they produce the type of irrational anxiety condition that disturbs the child's normal functioning. Such a concern is important because persistent fears may become transformed into a phobia, which is a severe and excessive fear aroused by a particular object or situation, and characterized by an extreme desire to avoid the object (Sutton-Smith, 1973; Ambron, 1975; Harris and Tiebert, 1984).

Weiner (1982) pointed out that about 5 percent of children are likely to develop an excessive, incapacitating fear of some object or event; such phobic reaction can begin any time after age 2 and most commonly start between age 4 and 7. An estimated 77 people per 1000 (7.7 percent), according to Weiner, have some kind of phobia, but only 2.2 cases per 1000 (0.22 percent) might be severely disabling (p. 304).

The children who do develop a phobia at an early age and are pressured to deny or hide their real fears may then attribute all of the fears to one situation or object, while older children who hold on to irrational fears frequently develop school type phobias which can render them incapable of attending school (Sutton-Smith, 1973). The focus of this chapter will be on this anxiety disorder known as school phobia.

School phobia, also referred to as school refusal is well known to child psychiatrists, school psychologists, counselors, school social workers and many teachers. It is an anxiety disorder that is especially troublesome for the parents of the school phobic child because his or her irrational behavior in connection with school attendance frequently disrupts the natural functioning of the entire family.

The purposes of this chapter are: (1) to provide a summary of selected psycho-social characteristics of school phobia, (2) to provide a summary of selected etiological theories and treatment modalities for school phobia, (3) to provide selected procedures for the early identification of school phobia, and (4) to provide selected intervention strategies that special services providers (i.e., counselors, school psychologists, nurses, and social workers) can utilize to assist school phobic children and their families.

The chapter is structured so that the first two purposes are covered in summary fashion in order to establish a point of departure for discussing intervention strategies for the families of school phobic children. It is important that the major focus be placed on the problems of identification of school phobia and family intervention because it is this social unit where most of the early psycho-social adjustment of the child takes place. There is also general agreement among authorities that inadequate parental and family relationships are among the precipitating factors in the development of school phobia in children.

CHARACTERISTICS AND DEFINITION OF SCHOOL PHOBIA

Literature discussions of school phobia tend to call attention to the fact that there has been some historical confusion over the use of the term, and the psychological traits associated with it. A part of that confusion stems from the use of such terms as "school avoidance," "reluctance to go to school," and "school refusal" inter-changeably with school phobia to describe this condition in children (Shapiro and Jedede, 1973). Beyond the general problem of what conceptual term to use for school phobia has been the more important issue of the disagreement regarding its psychological traits as they are related to both the child and his or her family. It appears to us and some others that the diverse views related to the name and the traits have emerged throughout the early studies of school phobia because of the differences in the various psychological orientations of those who treat it, and the fact that it is a rather complicated psycho-social condition that is not uniform in etiology and structure

(Shapiro & Jegede, 1973; Waldron, Shried, Stone and Tobin, 1975). School phobia, like a variety of other behavior disorders, must be viewed from a number of psychological and socio-cultural factors for understanding the origin of the problem, and school professionals must be prepared to employ diverse treatment modes to remediate it.

We fully appreciate the diverse issues and views surrounding this behavior disorder, but choose to use the term, school phobia, because it is the most prevalent one recognized by the psychoanalytic community, psychologists, and the professionals in the schools. Simply stated, therefore, school phobia refers to an irrational fear, extreme reluctance, or severe anxiety on the part of the child to some aspect of the school. It is accompanied invariably by selected somatic symptoms that the children use as a device to convince their parents that they should remain at home, but their problems often disappear once they are assured that they do not have to attend school (Waldfogel, Collidge, & Hahn, 1957; Kelly, 1973; Atkinson, Quarrington, Cyr, 1985). Some of these same notions of this disorder were advanced by Bert, Nicholas and Pritchard (1969) when they described school phobias as:

> ...a disorder affecting children who have some difficulty in attending school, severe emotional upset at the prospect of going to school as shown by such symptoms as excessive fearfulness, undue tempers, misery, or complaints of feeling ill without obvious organic cause, a tendency to remain at home with the knowledge of parents and an absence of significant anti-social problems such as stealing, lying, wandering destructiveness, and sexual misbehavior (p. 131).

Weiner (1982) divides school phobia into those reactions that are acute and chronic. According to Weiner, the symptoms of acute school phobia can occur suddenly at any age from elementary school through high school and even among college students. Acute school phobic children tend to be happy as long as they are permitted to remain at home, and can even maintain peer relationships and complete school assignments within the home environment. Chronic school phobia, according to Weiner, involves adjustment difficulties that go beyond the attendance problems. Weiner points out that these children "tend to withdraw not just from school but from previously enjoyed activities; they mope around the house; their fears of school often become generalized to the environment; and they consequently grow increasingly uncomfortable in interpersonal or unfamiliar situations" (p. 340).

Kennedy (1965) contends that four symptoms are common to school phobia: (1) morbid fears associated with school attendance; (2) frequent somatic complaints: headaches, nausea, drowsiness; (3) symbiotic relationships with mother, fear of separation; and (4) anxiety about many things such as darkness, crowds, and noises. The description of school phobia from the **Quick Reference to the Diagnostic Criteria, DSM III** (1980) supports the concepts advanced by Kennedy and others by identifying school phobia as a persistent reluctance or refusal to go to school in order to stay with the major attachment figures or at home.

It is important at this point in the chapter to contrast the differences between truancy and school phobia, since both problems have "school absence" as a common characteristic. A truant is usually thought of as a child who is absent from school without his or her parent's or the school's permission. Often, this type of truant may be kept at home by parents because the child can be of some direct help by his or her presence within the family (Kahn, Nursten, & Carroll, 1981).

Perhaps the most appropriate way to distinguish between the truant and school phobic child is to look at their behavior. It has been repeatedly pointed out in the literature that, unlike truant children, the school phobic child does not have severe antisocial problems such as stealing, destructiveness, or wandering from home (Berg, Nicholas, & Pritchard, 1969). A major difference between the two groups may be, therefore, that truants' problems frequently take the form of a conduct disorder, while that of the school phobic child is reflected more by an underlying anxiety disorder.

We do find some common elements within the many definitions and descriptions of school phobia. The pupils with this problem do not, however, represent a homogeneous group. For example, Coolidge, Hahn, and Peck (1957) identified two types of school phobia, neurotic and characterological. These two types share some symptoms in common and differ widely in others. The "neurotic" groups show an acute and dramatic onset with clinging behavior, but they continue to function well in non-school areas. The "characterological" groups reveal a more insidious onset and indications of character disturbance from an earlier age and are more deeply disturbed and severely crippled. The "neurotic" group is comprised mostly of children in grades kindergarten through the fourth, whereas the "characterological" group is made up mainly of young adolescents.

Kennedy (1965) moved the classification system of Coolidge and others

to the next stage of development by specifying the differential characteristic of the neurotic crisis (Type 1) and way-of-life (Type 2) school phobias.
Children with the Type 1 disorder tend to be younger, have more
cooperative parents, and make a comparatively rapid response to intervention; while, in contrast, children with Type 2 school phobia are older,
have less cooperative parents and respond slowly to even intensive
treatment, such as hospitalization (Clarizio & McCoy, 1983).

Incidence of School Phobia

Some of the recent literature has pointed out that school phobia and
the professional recognition of it may well be on the increase. In 1962,
Leton reported 2 per 1000 pupils might be school phobic, while Lall and
Lall (1979) suggested that school phobia had risen from 3 to 17 cases per
1000 during the period in which they were studying it.

It has been reported that the incidence of school phobia peaks between
third and fifth grades. Some studies have shown that it is detected more
frequently in girls than boys (Lall & Lall, 1979). Later reports suggest
that school phobia occurs about equally in males and females (Weiner,
1982). School phobia also tends to be more common among children
from higher socioeconomic levels, with parents who hold professional or
managerial jobs. Clarizio and McCoy (1983) present the argument that
this apparent incidence level among high socioeconomic groups might
be explained because they have fewer children; have more time to
become involved in the reciprocally dependent relationship with the
child, which is frequently observed in school phobia; and school phobia
is a costly treatment that would be more available to children from such
families, with the consequent greater likelihood of identification of
problems in this group.

We should point out that there is no agreement among the researchers
on the significance of social class, occupation of parents, intelligence,
and the sex of school phobic children. It is, therefore, important for
helping professionals to assess children based on the symptoms and
problems manifested by them rather than one set of socioeconomic or
personality characteristics.

For the purpose of having a working set of concepts of school phobia
for this chapter, the school phobic child can be considered an emotionally
disturbed boy or girl between the ages of 5 and 12 whose disturbance
involves anxiety that leads to prolonged absences from school, and who

exhibits irrational fear and anxiety about going to school. In addition, the child has great anxiety about life at school which is compounded with an exaggerated, illogical fear of becoming separated from his or her home and mother (Berry & Lazardi, 1985). The reader will note that the age span of school phobics suggested here is limited to the early grades, but it is our belief that many of the behavior problems of secondary school pupils can be traced to the inability of parents and school professionals to identify and treat the school phobic child during the elementary years. It should also be noted, that while our definition focuses on the anxiety and fear related to the school setting, we fully recognize that acute school phobic children might, if examined closely, have a wide range of situations and places that would provoke irrational fears.

ETIOLOGICAL AND TREATMENT ORIENTATIONS ASSOCIATED WITH SCHOOL PHOBIA

The general theories associated with causes of school phobia are numerous and complex. Because of the complexity of this behavioral disorder, both its etiology and treatment approaches seem to grow out of the particular personality theories subscribed to by the professionals studying the subject. Therefore, school phobia is not a concept that is easily explained by a single etiological theory, nor is treatment always explained by a single theoretical orientation. This section of the chapter will, however, attempt to cover in summary fashion, four of the major causal and treatment orientations.

Psychoanalytic Orientation

Much of the literature has focused on the explanation of school phobia as seen from a psychoanalytic perspective. Virtually all of psychoanalytic theories subscribe to a concept that school phobia and chronic school refusal are related to a form of separation anxiety, resulting from an unresolved, overly dependent relationship between the child and his or her mother. Within the framework of the psychoanalytic model, the mother is considered to be overly protective out of her own feelings of inadequacy, and she makes the child dependent to the point where the overdependence breeds mutual hostility and resentment (Berg & McGuire, 1971; Atkinson, et al., 1985).

The treatment of school phobia from a psychoanalytic framework focuses on working with individuals or the family on the unresolved dependency relationship between mother and child. Treatment generally requires a lengthy process of uncovering underlying and unconscious dynamics in order to improve family relationships and to consequently resolve the school phobic disorder (Boyd, 1980; Harris, 1980).

Psychodynamic Orientations

Some disagreement with the basic concept of the separation anxiety notions advanced by the psychoanalytic model has come from writers who have proposed a psychodynamic explanation of school phobia (Radin, 1968). Kelley (1973) referred to the psychodynamic perspective as a nonpsychoanalytic explanation of school phobia. According to Radin (1968), the psychodynamic model involves the following: (1) a fostering of the child's infantile omnipotence where the distinction between ego and ego-ideal is obscured because of faulty parental attitudes, (2) a threat to the child's omnipotent self-image through the evaluation of realistic school performance, (3) the child's avoidance of school and his treatment in the home, where he reestablishes his omnipotent self-image and security, and (4) the further inflation of the child's ego and false pride resulting from parental succor and affection.

The psychodynamic treatment approach generally involves the therapist focusing on the child's unrealistic self-image and power beliefs, as well as the application of an appropriate degree of pressure to ensure the child's early return to school. In addition, the complicity of the family and other significant people in the child's life, such as school personnel, is assessed and these people are activated in counteracting the excessive power maneuvers of the child (Leventhal, Weinberger, Stander, & Sterans, 1967; Weinberger, Leventhal & Beckman, 1973). A desire of this therapeutic approach is that the child and parents will develop insight into their problem, reduce their fears, and eventually the child will return to school.

Learning and Behavior Orientations

Learning theories and other behavioral orientations have occupied much of the literature in the last twenty years. Simply stated, the learning models see general phobias as maladaptive learned responses, and school phobia as a series of anxiety related concerns on the part of the child of being separated from or losing his or her mother, and fear of going to school as a potential place of failure (Atkinson, et al., 1985).

Behavioral explanations of school phobia also draw on broad learning principles which view the child as learning maladaptive behavior, as well as experiencing separation anxiety problems related to home and family. There is some variance among behaviorists on selected issues involving school phobia, and this is partly related to the specific circumstances contributing to the nature of learning maladaptive behavior (McDonald & Shepard, 1976). At the same time, the behaviorally oriented explanations of school phobia utilize the theoretical learning models of both classical conditioning (learning via the pairing of stimulus and response) and operant conditioning, learning via the subsequent reinforcement of responses (Kelley, 1973; Herbert, 1978).

Treatment approaches within the framework of the learning and behavioral model foster those learning principles which involve reinforcement techniques, counter-conditioning, desensitization, and the actual teaching of some skills which help the child to have confidence to return to school (Herbert, 1978). Counselors can help the child through systematic desensitization in a relaxed, nonthreatening atmosphere, (e.g., the counselor walks the child to the school, they stand on the playground, and they walk into an empty classroom). The counselor can help the teacher by assisting him or her to eliminate any inappropriate teacher response to the child.

Psychopharmacological Orientations

Drug therapy should be a major step for all parties to consider in the management of school phobia. This approach might only be used after other treatments have failed.

It is important to point out in connection with the psychopharmacological orientation that none of the advocates of drug therapy argue that there is a biochemical defect which perpetuated the school phobia, even though the drugs are sometimes efficacious (Shapiro and Jegede, 1973). In addition, accompanying psychotherapy with drugs is always recommended. Researchers mainly suggest drug therapy because it expedites the child's return to school.

Both the etiology and treatment modalities, while frequently diverse in their approach to school phobia, all seem to agree that it is important to begin treatment early with the child, and to involve the parents and total family in the helping process. The next section of the chapter will focus on the early identification of school phobic children and selected intervention strategies that can be used by school professionals to assist their families.

IDENTIFICATION AND FAMILY INTERVENTION STRATEGIES FOR SCHOOL PHOBIA

Throughout the chapter we have emphasized the fact the school special services professionals have a very important identification and intervention leadership role to play in assisting school phobic children and their families. The potential for a vigorous program of identification and intervention is possible because the school is a social institution that is involved with children, parents, their families and the community in an organized way. From their vantage point, special services professionals function as (1) a mental health leader, (2) a family/community consultant and (3) an intervention agent as they plan programs that will focus on the problems and assistance for school phobic children and their families.

Identification and Intervention Model: A Proposal

Identification and intervention procedures involving school phobic children can be complex because both of them are dependent on the specific and unique aspects of the child's problem, as well as the techniques and theoretical commitment of the professional treating the problem. We have attempted to address some of the complexity of the school phobia problem by structuring our identification and intervention strategies within the framework of a practical model. This identification and intervention model is designed to provide professionals with a series of functional action stages that are broad enough to be applicable to the many diverse psychological orientations associated with the intervention and treatment of school phobia. The model is also built around the notion that its content should be useful to (a) reduce the incidence of emotional distress or disturbance for members of a designated population; and (b) to promote "emotional robustness" in members of the target population (Bower, 1963). The proposed model is therefore proactive and focuses on anticipating potential disorders, as well as offering strategies for assisting those individuals who have a problem. In addition, the model is based on the assumption that the major participants: (1) the child, (2) the parents and family, (3) the professionals in the school, (4) the mental health professionals outside the school, and (5) the forces within the child's community are all necessary ingredients in the identification, intervention and treatment process.

The Identification and Intervention Model is viewed as having four major stages. These stages are the following: Stage One—In-Take/Information; Stage Two—Identification; Stage Three—Intervention; Stage Four—Referral/Treatment (some level of referral or treatment might begin at Stage Two and continue throughout the process).

Stage One—In-Take Information: The initial stage of the model is called the In-Take/Information stage because the counselor actively becomes involved in seeking out the potential problems. The counselor checks with the attendance personnel in order to look for the first indicator of possible school phobia, which is a high level of absenteeism for a given student. This may be accomplished by a routine evaluation of all reported absences. The counselor may wish to open a file on all children with absences, re-evaluating it on a monthly basis to see if the absences indicate a need for further inquiry.

It is during this stage that the counselor makes the initial contact with other school personnel, the potential school phobic individual, and the parent or guardian. The purposes of these contacts are to gather information and open channels of communication through which the counselor can proceed smoothly to the second stage.

Stage Two—Identification: Stage Two is a point where the counselor might actively be involved in using the intake information to accurately assess the possibility of having a school phobic child. Using information gained from personal contacts and school records, the counselor may find strong indications that a child is exhibiting signs of school phobia. It is during this stage that the counselor could use some of the socio-psychological indicators contained in the **School Phobia Identification Guide** developed by the authors in their previous work (Berry & Lizardi, 1985). While this guide will not be discussed here, its purpose is to provide mental health professionals with a brief, easily used, and tentatively objective method of identifying the school phobic person. Related to this stage in the identification process, some of the school, personal, and family indicators contained in the guide are summarized as follows:

(1) **School Behavior Indicators**—characteristics which the school phobic individual is likely to exhibit during the school day. For example, increased excused absences; frequent requests to leave classroom activity; and displayed unexplained fear of school events; (2) **Personal Behavior Indicators**—characteristics that are negative and self-defeating which the school phobic individual manifests physically or psychologically, during the school day. For example, somatic complaints; exhibiting some form of anxiety; depression; feeling worthless; and being highly critical of self; (3) **Parent/Family Indicators**—characteristics which the school phobic individual's family appears to exhibit, either observed directly or indirectly. For example, traumatic home situation—divorce or a death; mother or father overly protective; child experiences clinging behavior with parent; and parents who have limited involvement with school activities.

Stage Three—Intervention: Once the child has been assessed or identified as school phobic, the counselor can initiate the programs needed to formulate the interventions. Since intervention also indicates some form of involvement, it is highly suggested that the counselor become knowledgeable concerning the various types of intervention (Bower, 1962). In consideration for this model, it is suggested that the counselor initiate involvement in the following areas: (1) **Primary Intervention**—dealing with the entire school population in the assessment and dissemination of information regarding school phobia. The counselor can be actively involved in the following: (a) developing school phobia information pamphlets for distribution to all parents; (b) developing in-service programs for teachers and school personnel on the characteristics of school phobia; (c) providing lectures and discussions at "back to school night" or at parent meetings on the subject of school phobia; (d) providing an "Orientation Day or Week" for kindergarten pupils, first graders and newcomers, not only to show them the physical plant of the school, but to meet teachers and other school personnel in order to learn about the expectations regarding playtime, lunch, general school activities; and (e) establishing involvement programs for parents that will make them feel a part of the school. (2) **Secondary Intervention**—These interventions would be focused on groups or individuals that are manifesting early symptoms or school phobia, or are particularly vulnerable due to some of the causative aspects of the disorder. At this point, the counselor may wish to provide intervention procedures by doing the following: (a) providing more time in the schedule to counsel first graders and newcomers to insure that they are making positive adaptations to the school environment; (b) encouraging school personnel to be more sensitive to the psychological development of children; (c) providing social skills evaluations to pupils in order to seek out those experiencing possible problems relating to others; (d) providing potential problem oriented students opportunities for involvement with positive peer role models; and (e) providing procedures that would allow the counselor to have some level of involvement in pupil absences, as opposed to relying only on an attendance office. (3) **Tertiary Intervention**—while these interventions are identified as tertiary, our intention is only to convey a level, not their degree of importance. On the contrary, since school phobia must be treated within the context of the home and family, this level of intervention is most important because it focuses directly on the child and his or her family relationships. Significantly, this phase of the intervention process is usually carried on simultaneously with the other intervention levels previously mentioned. In fact, even those parents who are receiving assistance from an outside agency for problems associated with school phobia can gain from an organized program that is carried on by the school and coordinated with the other professionals providing support to the family.

Special services professionals who do provide assistance to parents must always be guided by their knowledge of the family needs, involvement from other professionals, and their own codes of ethics related to the level of therapeutic support they can and should provide. With these understandings in mind, specific interventions with the family might include: (1) educational-information group meetings, focusing on child development, psychological, and/or medical aspects of the school phobic child's problem or other information that can be given by any specialist in that field (who should have some understanding of group dynamics); (2) training meetings such as those to teach parents behaviors that will help them to understand how to help the child with his or her problem, as well as to help themselves practice the proper parental responses and behaviors; (3) group counseling meetings which emphasize effective communication with the child, given by school guidance counselors, social workers, psychiatrists, or psychologists; (4) individual parent conferences with the school staff (teachers, psychologists, or social workers); and (5) the utilization of films, video cassettes and other media aimed at teaching effective parenting skills. Briefly stated, the overall goal of the intervention strategies conducted cooperatively between school professionals and the families of school phobic children are to help them discuss their feelings with a supportive group of professionals and other parents; to learn about the developmental needs of their children; to deal with their own children constructively and objectively in view of these needs; to get specific techniques and ideas for dealing with their children's problem behavior and disabilities; and to learn about materials, community resources, and activities available for them and their children (Swanson & Willis, 1979).

Stage Four—Referral: This stage actively focuses on the counselor utilizing his/her integration abilities. The counselor continues, if needed, referral to appropriate community health agencies and checks network of feedback from agencies back to counselor, school personnel, child, family and community. The counselor acts as the agent in finding appropriate treatment facilities/programs for the severe school phobic individual.

The four stages described in the School Phobia Identification and Intervention Model are not intended to be seen as "lock-step" phases of the process. Rather, each stage is flexible, fluid and interrelated as the counselor and the various participants move through them. Figure 1 illustrates the interrelatedness of the model's process.

Finally, it should be noted that an intervention plan involving school professionals and families is a cooperative effort. Within this cooperative process, counselors and school psychologists must provide information to parents about the needs of their children, as well as to offer support to them concerning their own needs and goals. Stewart (1978), drawing on the work of Jordan (1972), offers the following suggestions for school professionals to utilize when intervening with parents concerning the needs of children with special problems.

(1) Be honest in your appraisal of the situation and explain it without unnecessary delay.
(2) Deal with both parents, since they are a natural unit.
(3) Be precise, but do not be unnecessarily technical in your explanation.
(4) Point out who must be responsible ultimately.
(5) Help the parents grasp the issues.
(6) Keep in mind the referral agencies that can be of assistance.
(7) Avoid precipitating ego-defensive reactions in the parents.
(8) Do not expect too much too soon from the parents.

(9) Allow parents their quota of concern and uncertainty.
(10) Try to crystallize positive attitudes at the onset by using good counseling techniques.

Figure 1
SCHOOL PHOBIA IDENTIFICATION AND INTERVENTION MODEL

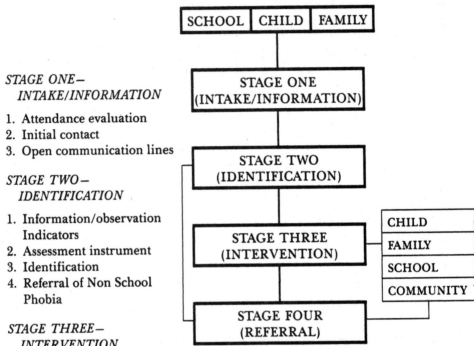

STAGE ONE—
 INTAKE/INFORMATION

1. Attendance evaluation
2. Initial contact
3. Open communication lines

STAGE TWO—
 IDENTIFICATION

1. Information/observation Indicators
2. Assessment instrument
3. Identification
4. Referral of Non School Phobia

STAGE THREE—
 INTERVENTION

1. Initiation of intervention strategies
2. Use of intervention forms
 A) Primary intervention
 B) Secondary intervention
 C) Tertiary intervention
3. Dissemination of information
4. Data collection

STAGE FOUR—REFERRAL

1. Development of referral network
2. Feedback agent

SUMMARY:
SPECIAL SERVICES PROFESSIONALS AS TEACHERS

School phobia, like so many problems of children and youth, impact negatively on the individual and the entire family. Our approach in this chapter was to identify some of the psycho-social characteristics of school phobia and to indicate how the special services professionals in the school can have a leadership role in assisting the school phobic child, as well as to provide intervention strategies involving the family. In advancing some of our notions, we are fully aware that many teachers, counselors, school psychologists, nurses, social workers and other professionals in our schools are faced not only with children who have special needs, but they also have a large number of other tasks that take their time and challenge their energies. In many school districts elementary school counselors are not even available to help the young child who is in need. At the same time, we are also aware that these same professionals, when they are available, are looking for ideas, concepts, and tools that will assist them in being more effective in bringing their services to children and their families. It was our attempt to structure this discussion to meet the needs of these concerned professionals, and in so doing, to help them to better serve the children and families in their charge.

School phobia is an individual and a family problem. We conclude that the school is one social institution that has a role in assisting both groups. Counseling and the related psychological services are by definition involved in functioning within the broad meaning of the word intervention, which is that process designed help others to develop new points of view, to create alternative life style strategies, to acquire new learning while questioning old ways, and to practice different behaviors. We submit that after all the literature is reviewed and all of the psychological orientations evaluated, a major goal of the counselor and other mental health professionals, like teachers, is to develop effective and cooperative intervention programs that will teach children and parents constructive ways to handle their problems.

REFERENCES

Ambron, S. R. (1975). *Child development.* San Francisco: Holt, Rhinehart and Winston.
Atkinson, L. B., Quarrington, B., & Cyr, J. J. (1985). School refusal: The heterogeneity of a concept. *American Journal of Orthopsychiatry, 55,* 83–101.

Berg, I., & McGuire, R. (1971). Are school phobic adolescents overdependent? *British Journal of Psychiatry, 119,* 167–168.

Berg, I, Nicholas, K., & Pritchard, C. (1969). School phobia—Its classification and relationships to dependency. *Journal of Child Psychology and Psychiatry, 10,* 123–141.

Berry, G. L., & Lizardi, A. (in press). The school phobic child and special providers: Guidelines for early identification. *Special Services in the Schools,* Fall, 2, 1.

Bower, E. (1963). Primary prevention of mental and emotional disorders. A conceptual framework and action possibilities. *American Journal of Orthopsychiatry, 33,* 837.

Boyd, L. (1980). Emotive imagery in the behavioral management of adolescent school phobia: A case approach. *School Psychology Review, 9,* 180–189.

Clarizio, H. F., & McCoy, G. F. (1983). *Behavior disorder in children.* Cambridge: Harper and Row.

Coolidge, J. C., Hahn, P. B., & Peck, A. (1957). School phobia: Neurotic crisis a way of life? *American Journal of Orthopsychiatry, 27,* 296–306.

Harris, J. R., & Tiebert, R. M. (1984). *The child development from birth through adolescence.* Englewood Cliffs, NJ: Prentice-Hall.

Harris, S. R. (1980). School phobic children and adolescents: A challenge to counselors. *The School Counselors, 27,* 163–269.

Herbert, M. (1978). *Conduct disorders of childhood and adolescence: A behavioral approach to assessment and treatment.* New York: John Wiley.

Jordan, T. E. (1972). *The mentally retarded.* Columbus, Ohio: Charles Merrill.

Kelly, E. W. (1973). School phobia: A review of theory and treatment. *Psychology in the Schools, 10,* 33–42.

Kennedy, W. A. (1965). School phobia: Rapid treatment of fifty cases, *Journal of Abnormal Psychology, 74,* 263–279.

Lall, D. R., Lall, B. M. (1979). School phobia, it's real and growing. *Instructor, 89,* 96–98.

Leton, D. A. (1962). Assessment of school phobia. *Mental Hygiene, 46,* 256–264.

Leventhal, T., Weinberger, G., Stander, R. J., & Sterns, R. P. (1967). Therapeutic strategies with school phobics. *American Journal of Orthopsychiatry, 37,* 64–70.

Mc Donald, J. E., & Shepard, G. (1976). School phobia: An overview. *Journal of School Psychiatry, 14,* 291–306.

Radin, S. S. (1968) Psychotherapeutic considerations in school phobia. *Adolescence, 3,* 181–193.

Shapiro, T., & Jegede, R. O. (1973). School phobia: A bable of tongues. *Journal of Autism and Childhood Schizophrenia, 3,* 168–186.

Stewart, J. C. (1978). *Counseling parents of exceptional children.* Columbus Ohio: Charles E. Merrill.

Sutton-Smith, B. (1973). *Child psychology.* New York: Appelton-Century-Crofts.

Swanson, B. M., & Willis, D. J. (1979). *Understanding exceptional children and youth. An introduction to special education.* Chicago: Rand McNally.

Waldfogel, S., Coolidge, J. C., & Hahn, P. B. (1957). The development, meaning and management of school phobia. *American Journal of Orthopsychiatry, 27,* 754–776.

Waldron, S., Shrier, D., Stone, B., & Tobin, F. (1975). School phobia and other childhood neuroses: A systematic study of the children and their families. *American Journal of Psychiatry, 132*:8, 802–808.

Weinberger, G., Leventhal, T., & Beckman, G. (1973). The management of a chronic school phobic through the use of consultation with school personnel. *Psychology in the Schools, 10,* 83–88.

Weiner, I. B. (1982). *Child and adolescent psychopathology.* New York: John Wiley and Sons.

Chapter 2

THE SUICIDAL ADOLESCENT

DAVE CAPUZZI AND MICHAEL S. NYSTUL

The list of famous suicides is long—Cleopatra, Ernest Hemingway, Adolph Hitler, Jim Jones and his People's Temple victims, Jack London, and Marilyn Monroe (Rosenhan and Seligman, 1984). Suicide ranks among the top 10 causes of death in the United States, outnumbering murders (Weiten, 1983). Many people who commit suicide disguise it as an accident so survivors will not be embarrassed and can collect life insurance. Experts have estimated that there are five to eight times as many suicides as are actually recorded (Weiten, 1983).

One of the most alarming facts about suicide is that the rate of recorded suicides per 100,000 persons has steadily increased over the past 30 years; this is particularly true for young people 15–24 years in age. In 1950—4.2 suicides/100,000; 1974—10.9 suicides/100,000; and 1984—12.8 suicides/100,000 (Shneidman, 1984).

Gifted students appear to be at high risk, and gifted girls in particular. In 1979 Taylor reported that gifted girls commit suicide at the highest rate of any girls nationally. Schools are often not sensitive to the needs of the gifted—resulting in underachievement, depression, high drop out rates, and suicidal tendencies (Webb, Meckstroth and Tolan, 1982).

The tragedy of suicide transcends the statistics and its victims. This tragedy is also experienced by the family, the friends, the school, and the community. Frequently, survivors of someone who has committed suicide feel ashamed, guilty, resentful, confused, remorseful, and depressed (Weiten, 1983). These facts when taken together indicate that suicide has become a major mental health problem, warranting careful attention. This chapter will explore the suicide phenomenon—its causes, myths, and treatment strategies.

CAUSES

Theoretical Perspectives

Shneidman (1984) identified four major theoretical perspectives for understanding why a person of any age would commit suicide. They are sociological, psychodynamic, psychological, and constitutional-biochemical.

1. **Sociological.** Durkheim (1897) described four reasons why a person would attempt suicide from a sociological perspective:

• Altruistic suicides can occur when a person believes in something so strongly that it becomes permissible to commit suicide for that belief (e.g., Japanese Kamikaze pilots).

• Egoistic suicides occur when the person doesn't feel a sense of belonging to the community and therefore doesn't feel needed.

• Anomic suicide results when the relationship between the individual and society has been shattered (e.g., the person is fired from a job).

• Fatalistic suicide can occur when an individual feels society offers no hope.

• Durkheim's theory appears to have withstood the test of time as it continues to be accepted by most sociologists today (Shneidman, 1984).

2. **Psychodynamic.** Sigmund Freud emphasized the importance of unconscious processes in behavior. He also described a death wish which may be related to suicidal behavior (Freud, 1969). Karl Menninger (1938) delineated the psychodynamic position by noting that suicide is the result of three wishes—the wish to kill, the wish to be killed, and the wish to die.

3. **Psychological.** The psychological approach differs from the psychodynamic in that unconscious forces are not emphasized. Shneidman (1976) provided a psychological view which contends that certain general psychologic features must be present for a suicide to occur:

• Acute perturbation—an increase in the individual's state of unhappiness.

• Heightened inimicality—an increase in self-hate, guilt, shame, etc.

• An increase of constriction of intellectual focus—a tunneling of thought process, a narrowing of the mind's content, an inability to see viable options.

118914

• The idea of cessation—the insight that it is possible to put an end to suffering by committing suicide.

4. **Constitutional-Biochemical.** The "medical-model" has identified a biochemical basis for many forms of depression and links depression to suicide. The medical perspective also notes that antidepressant medications have been useful in the treatment of severe depression and the reduction of suicide risk.

Motivational Perspectives

The causes of suicide can also be understood from the vantage point of the suicide attempter's explanation of motivation after the suicidal crisis has passed. Some examples of the typically reported motivations which have been reported to the authors by their clients are:

1. Wanting to reduce stress.
2. Wanting to escape an intolerable situation.
3. Needing to avoid a relationship conflict.
4. Wanting to take control of life by ending life.
5. Feeling that living is too difficult, tiresome and pointless.
6. Seeking revenge.
7. Hoping to attract the attention of others.
8. Wanting to control exactly how and when death will occur.
9. Wanting to become a martyr for a cause.
10. Seeking punishment for wrong doing.

MYTHS ABOUT SUICIDE

Shneidman, Farberow, and Litman (1970) identified five myths associated with suicide:

Myth 1: Suicide is Committed Only by People With Severe Psychological Disorders

Actually, only a small percentage of those who commit suicide have a diagnosed psychological disorder. Suicide rates are higher for depressed people, but most victims of suicide appear to be "normal" (Shneidman et al, 1970).

Myth 2: People Who Talk About Suicide Don't Actually Commit Suicide

Some people that talk about suicide don't kill themselves. Nonetheless, the highest risk groups for suicide are those that openly discuss the possibility (Shneidman et al, 1970).

Myth 3: Suicide Usually Takes Place With Little Or No Warning

The majority of suicides were preceded by some kind of warning. The nature of the warning may vary from a clear threat to a vague statement like, "you don't need me around anymore" (Shneidman et al, 1970).

Myth 4: People Who Attempt Suicide Are Fully Intent on Dying

Most of the people who attempt suicide do not actually want to die. They may be desperate and attempting to send out a dramatic distress signal. This might explain why one in eight suicide attempts actually ends in death (Shneidman et al, 1970).

Myth 5: People Who Are Suicidal Remain So Forever

The majority of people who become suicidal remain so for a brief period. If they manage to get through the crisis, their suicidal thoughts may never return (Shneidman et al, 1970).

TREATMENT STRATEGIES

Evaluating Suicidal Potential

The best treatment strategy for suicide would seem to be prevention. An initial step in prevention is to identify individuals in our schools and communities who are in the high risk category for suicide. Shneidman et al (1970) identified six factors which can help evaluate suicide potential.

1. **The Nature of Any Verbal Threat**—As previously mentioned, those who threaten to kill themselves are in the high risk category. A person who has a specific plan and the means to carry out the plan (e.g., has a gun and plans to use it) is especially prone to a suicide attempt (Shneidman et al, 1970).

2. **Emotional Tenor**—Young people who are depressed and talk of

hopelessness, helplessness, futility, and make irrational statements about the future may be particularly suicidal (Shneidman et al, 1970).

3. **Presence of Severe Stress**—Suicide is often precipitated by stressful life events such as marital breakup of parents, being fired from a job and serious illness (Shneidman et al, 1970).

4. **History of Self-Destructiveness**—Any history of self-destructive behavior (e.g., alcohol and drug abuse, engaging in dangerous activities, etc.) could suggest suicidal tendencies (Shneidman et al, 1970).

It is very important to determine if the person has attempted suicide before. Those who have a history of attempting suicide are more likely to try again than those who have never attempted suicide before (Shneidman et al, 1970). The chances that an individual will be successful with repeated attempts are high since each attempt becomes more lethal (Shneidman et al, 1970).

5. **Changes in Behavior**—Dramatic changes in behavior often occur several weeks before a person attempts suicide (Shneidman et al, 1970). Potential victims may drop out of school or quit a job they have held for a number of years. Potential victims may also have a significant change in mood—such as from a depressed and agitated state to one of serenity—since the decision, plan, time and circumstances connected with the intended suicide have been determined.

6. **Social Support**—People who have little or no support systems (e.g., family) are also in the high risk group for suicide (Shneidman et al, 1970) since they are not likely to ask for help or reach out to friends or family members during periods of stress.

CRISIS INTERVENTION

Crisis intervention often is necessary when a person is known to be planning to commit suicide or is actually attempting suicide. The goals of crisis intervention are psychological and medical stabilization. Medical stabilization is necessary if the individual has attempted suicide (e.g., an overdose). Psychological stabilization is required to help individuals overcome their suicidal ideations (thoughts) and preoccupation with death as the ideal solution to problems.

Crisis intervention strategies vary according to the situation. Those who have acute suicidal ideations but who are not actually attempting suicide can benefit from the following:

1. **Assess the Individual's Suicide Potential**—The school mental counselor,

social worker, school nurse, etc. may wish to use the six guidelines for evaluating suicidal potential previously described.

2. **Strongly Recommend Hospitalization** — If the person appears to be in a very high risk group for suicide, hospitalization should be recommended. This can provide a safe place where individuals can get rest and if necessary, drug therapy. Hospitalization would be especially important if the individual has a history of suicide or has indicated a specific plan to commit suicide and has a means to carry out that particular plan (e.g., plans to shoot him/herself and has a loaded gun in the car).

3. **Notify Relatives About the Family Member's Suicidal Tendencies** — Relatives and friends should be notified so they can help monitor suicidal tendencies. Even if the individual is hospitalized, he may leave a against medical authorization. When an individual is suicidal it is important to bring together family members or other people in the "support system" who can provide important background information on stress related issues such as a history of drug abuse and a recent relationship problem. These people should be encouraged to provide support. Family therapy may be valuable after the individual has had a chance to rest.

4. **Suggest Sleep Therapy** — Many who have suicidal ideations have difficulty sleeping. It is not uncommon for suicidal individuals to have suffered serious sleep deprivation for days or weeks. Sleep is therefore a very important part of recovery. Life will often look much better after a few good nights of sleep.

If the individual is hospitalized, professionals may suggest that relatives do not visit during the first few days of hospitalization. Visitors may interfere with the individual's sleep and may also contribute to anxiety.

5. **Consider Drug Therapy** — Drugs can be useful to help a suicidal person with physical or psychological problems. The main psychiatric uses of drugs include treatment of depression (many antidepressant medications also help the patient sleep); controlling psychotic reactions; and reducing anxiety.

The second type of situation occurs when individuals are **actually attempting to kill themselves** (e.g., are found after they have overdosed). In these situations, the following guidelines may be of use to the helping person:

1. Immediately notify the proper authorities (e.g., suicide prevention team, police, etc.).

2. Talk with the person and try to create hope that tomorrow will be a better day. Try to convey that you really care and want to help. Also,

stress that the attempter is an important person and identify ways s/he is needed and will be missed.

3. Avoid confronting or putting any "pressure" on suicide attempters before the authorities arrive. The suicide attempter may become hostile, aggressive, and more actively suicidal when confronted by relatives or people they are familiar with. Individuals will usually be more coopera-tive with the authorities. Suicidal people are in a life crisis and tend to be confused and in need of structure. Authority figures (with their uni-forms and badges) often symbolize "law and order" to the attemptee. These professionals have also received training to deal with crisis situations, and tend to react in a calm, or reassuring professional manner.

4. Notify the suicide attempter's relatives for the reasons previously described.

5. Consider hospitalizing the attempter to receive medical and psycho-logical treatment as well as sleep and rest.

6. Ask about medication to treat the medical and psychological prob-lems (as previously described).

POST CRISIS COUNSELING STRATEGIES

After the crisis has subsided, a referral for mental health counseling on an outpatient basis will be needed. Naturally, each counselor's approach will vary according to his or her personal orientation and the unique needs of the client. The following guidelines may be useful in develop-ing a counseling approach with someone who has been suicidal:

Step One: Determine What Caused the Person to Attempt Suicide

It is important to understand suicide from the attempter's perspective. This phenomenological understanding can help the client feel the counselor really cares (because the counselor is trying to listen and understand). This perspective can also provide the counselor with a realistic picture of how the attempter views the world. The attempter's reason for considering suicide will probably be reflected in one of the four perspectives previously described (i.e., sociological, psychodynamic, psychological, and constitutional-biochemical).

The second author of this chapter recently held the position of Psy-chologist and Chief of Mental Health at a U.S. Public Health hospital on the Navajo Indian reservation. During the three years he held that position he provided counseling services to over 100 patients who had attempted suicide.

During the initial counseling session, he would ask clients what made them want to take their own life. The following are 10 typical reasons clients gave for attempting suicide, and the circumstances associated with the suicide attempts.

1. "Why not?"

This was the response of a 16-year-old girl who had taken 10 times the leathal dose of aspirin and other medication. She seemed to be asking herself an existential question—"Is this what life is all about? I don't want it . . . "

2. "Who cares?"

An 18-year-old girl who felt no one loved her or cared about her made this statement. She also attempted an overdose.

3. "I'm just a burden."

The client was a 68-year-old grandfather who had heart problems and felt he was just a burden to his family. He tried to hang himself.

4. "My brother is really mad at me."

This statement was made by a 16-year-old boy just before he shot himself in the head and killed himself. The boy had a fight with his brother in the morning and later that day drank with his friends and shot himself.

5. "I don't want to wait for that test."

A 64-year-old man said this before he shot himself in the head and died. He was in an outpatient clinic of a hospital and was told he would have to wait for some test results.

6. "I'll just make a mess of everything."

This statement was made by an 18-year-old boy who had dropped out of high school and recently had been fired from his job. He overdosed on pills but did not die.

7. "I can't measure up no matter what."

An 18-year-old boy who was a star athlete said this before he shot himself to death. He felt no matter what he did, his parents wouldn't appreciate his effort.

8. "I just can't live with one hand."

A 20-year-old young man said this after he was caught trying to drown himself in a pond only 8 inches deep. The client died one year later after he became intoxicated and froze to death.

9. "I must of been crazy."

This statement was made by a 15-year-old girl who had a psychotic reaction to PCP–Angel Dust. She tried to stab herself with a butcher knife.

10. "I just felt so sad all the time."

A statement by a 36-year-old housewife who had suffered a long history of depression and tried to overdose on aspirin.

Step Two: Personality Assessment and Life Style Changes

As counselors explore the client's reason for considering suicide, they will also be formulating some understanding of the client's personality. The personality assessment can be formal or informal. An example of a formal assessment could be the Adlerian Life Style Analysis (Dinkmeyer, Pew and Dinkmeyer, 1979).

Assessment of the client's personality can help the counselor establish counseling goals with the client. In most cases, some life style adjustments will be required so the client can avoid future suicidal episodes.

Step Three: Develop a Regular Stress Management Program

Many clients who have experienced suicidal tendencies also have trouble with stress management. It is important for the client to learn to alleviate stress on a daily basis and not to wait for stress to build up and become overwhelming.

The counselor may need to help clients develop stress management procedures that can be incorporated into their life style. These activities should be something that the client enjoys so s/he will have a better chance of sticking with it (Nystul and Freidman, 1982).

CONCLUSION

This chapter provided an overview of the suicide phenomenon—its causes, myths, and treatment strategies. Herein were described four perspectives which can be used to promote understanding of the underlying causes of suicide (i.e., sociological, psychodynamic, psychological, and constitutional-biochemical). Five myths of suicide have been identified. Also suggested are specific counseling strategies which may be useful in the management and treatment of a suicidal patient.

Suicide rates appear to be increasing, especially among the 15–24 age range. This is a disturbing statistic. There is an old slogan that says our youth is our future. Perhaps a growing number of today's youth see no future. If this is so, there appear to be family, community, and societal issues which need to be explored. Future research may address these issues in an attempt to gain a better understanding of the dynamics of suicide.

REFERENCES

Dinkmeyer, D., Pew, W. L., & Dinkmeyer, D. C. (1979). *Adlerian counseling and psychotherapy,* Belmont, California: Wadsworth.

Durkheim, E. (1897). *Suicide: A study in sociology.* Glencoe, Ill.: Free Press.

Menninger, K. (1938). *Man against himself.* New York: Harcourt, Brace.

Nystul, M. S. & Friedman, D. (1982). A Youthful life-style for life. *Humanistic Education and Development,* 21, 2, 86–92.

Rosenhan, D. L. & Seligman, M. E. (1984). *Abnormal Psychology.* New York: W. W. Norton.

Shneidman, E. S., Farberow, N. L. & Litman, R. E. (eds.) (1970). *The psychology of suicide.*

Shneidman, E. S. (1976). A psychological theory of suicide. *Psychiatric Annals,* 6, 51–66.

Shneidman, E. S. (1984). Suicide, In R. Corsini (ed.) *Encyclopedia of Psychology, V. 3.* New York: John Wiley.

Taylor, R. (1979). *The gifted and the talented.* Colorado: Educational Consultant Agency Publishing Co.

Webb, J. T., Meckstroth, E. A., & Tolan, S. S. (1982). *Guiding the gifted child.* Columbus: Ohio Psychological Publishing Co.

Weiten, W. (1983). *Psychology applied to modern life: Adjustment in the 80's.* Belmont, California: Wadsworth.

Chapter 3

THE GIFTED CHILD

G. SCOTT WOODING AND PAUL D. WARNER

Modern interest in identification of gifted individuals began around the turn of this century with the collaboration of Binet and Simon (Tannenbaum, 1983), and interest in understanding their characteristics began with the extensive works of Terman (1925). No efforts were made to promote the counseling or guidance of the gifted until the 1950's (Perrone and Pulvino, 1979). This interest, heightened by the frantic search for talent which resulted from the Sputnik scare in 1957, culminated in an excellent chapter on pupil personnel services which appeared in the work of Gowan and Demos (1964) a few years later. Again there was a waning of interest in counseling of the gifted until a decade later when such authors as Hoyt and Hebeler (1974), Zaffrann and Colangelo (1977, 1979), and Ziv (1977) wrote extensively on this subject. Despite these recent efforts, little in the way of practical advice for the average school counselor is provided, as the writings tend to be highly theoretical and diffuse. Thus, the counselor who is faced with the task of attempting to solve the complex problems presented daily by this extremely valuable minority must read through entire books of separate articles before finding potential approaches to the difficulties. It is the purpose of this chapter to summarize the findings presented by the works of these and other authors in such a way as to suggest directions to be taken in the school when gifted students look to their counselor for guidance.

THE ROLE OF THE COUNSELOR

While the counselor's role within the school is always a complex one, and varies greatly from school to school, the counseling functions with regard to the gifted appear to fall within three broad areas: those involving the student; those involving the parents; and those concerned with the interaction between the student and the school. These areas will obviously overlap considerably, but they are sufficiently distinct to warrant their separate discussion.

Counseling the Student

While gifted children may suffer from the same wide range of academic and emotional problems as do their non-gifted counterparts, some of their difficulties stem directly from giftedness. Zaffrann and Colangelo (1977) identify three specific areas into which these problems fall: personal/social, educational, and career. The problems experienced by gifted students and their potential solutions will be discussed using this model.

Personal/Social Problems. Terman's monumental studies of gifted personality traits (Terman and Oden, 1940, 1947, 1951; Terman, 1954) implied that gifted students had fewer emotional problems than did the non-gifted. While this continues to be an area of controversy, several personality traits unique to the gifted have been identified by recent researchers which could result in more emotional problems developing in this group than in children of lesser talents. These problems include perfectionism (Roeper, 1982; Whitmore, 1980), unrealistic expectations of themselves (Van Tassel-Baska, 1983; Whitmore, 1980), supersensitivity (Cruikshank, 1963; Freeman, 1983; Van Tassel-Baska, 1983; Whitmore, 1980), and inability to relate to age peers (Davis and Rimm, 1985; Whitmore, 1980; Zaffrann and Colangelo, 1977). While all of these traits would rarely be found in one individual, just one emotional problem in any degree of severity could be enough to make that child's life miserable and interfere with the use of whichever gift is present. The counselor could take one of several approaches in dealing with a student who exhibits one or more of these traits.

1. In severe cases, as is often found in older children whose problems have gone unrecognized for a number of years, counseling techniques could be used such as Rational Emotive Therapy (Ellis, 1962), to help change the child's faulty belief system, or Cognitive Behaviour Therapy (Meichenbaum, 1977), to change the internal dialog which is causing the problem. For example, in dealing with perfectionism, the problem is that the student sets standards that are so high that, even with the gifts possessed, the standards cannot be reached, resulting in feelings of worthlessness and negative self-talk. The counselor must help the child to see that the goals are coming from

within, and that they can therefore be modified to a more realistic level. Helping the gifted child recognize counter-productive self-talk and then replacing that negative dialogue with positive and realistic self-talk will help overcome the non-productive cognitions.

2. Simulations and role playing activities may be useful in help-ing the gifted child to see personal behaviour manifested from without, in order to comprehend how the behaviour looks from a more objective standpoint. With bright students, this more objective representation of their behavior allows them to make choices about alternative ways to interact with their environment. For example, gifted children are often so eager to answer questions that they raise their hands vigorously most of the time, creating a non-response from the teacher, and negative peer reactions. Simulations and role-playing will help develop more effective strategies for answering questions and obtaining the information they are seeking.

3. Bibliotherapy (Frasier and McCannon, 1981) can be very use-ful with younger children who do not understand what it means to be gifted. These children usually realize that they are different, but often construe this to be a negative quality. Thus, reading stories about other gifted children, biographies of famous gifted adults, and books describing the traits of gifted children, can help them to understand themselves and to reduce their anxiety about being "different."

4. If there are a number of students in the school with similar problems, group counseling focussing on the affective needs of the gifted, can be very effective. Not only do such groups provide a forum where common problems can be shared and solutions discussed, but they are highly effective in providing true peers for gifted students. Thus a by-product of an effective group is the development of close friendships with students of similar abilities and interests, a situation that rarely develops in the regular classroom. Sharing inner feelings with others not only brings about greater awareness, but improves the gifted child's ability to accept self and others. Self-esteem is enhanced through this process.

In addition to the problems experienced by gifted children as a result of inherent personality traits, difficulties also occur frequently as a consequence of how others react to them. The fact that students are generally grouped in classes by chronological age results in gifted chil-dren having few, if any, true peers with whom they may communicate at the same level. Further, Coleman (1962) has shown that academic brilliance is not valued by young children. This may result in either the gifted child being socially isolated or the object of derision if that child does not also possess any of the skills that are valued in that classroom, e.g., athletic prowess, leadership ability. The counselor's function in this case is to structure situations in which the gifted student can associate with true peers. These include pull-out programs, where students of similar interests and abilities are taken out of the classroom to work on special projects, counseling groups or, if available, a referral to a school for the gifted. If none of these options is available, it is often helpful to show a film about children who are different in some way as a lead-in to a series of discussions about tolerance and understanding.

Another personal or affective problem which gifted children often experience occurs due to the expectation levels set by both parents and teachers. The intellectual maturity shown by these children at home and in the classroom results in adults expecting a similar degree of emotional maturity. When childish behavior occurs the result is often a scolding, despite the fact that the behavior would have been appropriate for any other child that age. This can lead to the development of a poor self-concept, as gifted children see age-mates not being punished for identical behaviors, and can only interpret this to mean that there is something wrong with themselves. Counselors must be aware of the potential existence of this problem and should initiate counseling with the parents, and they could speak at staff meetings, or to individual teachers, in order to remove the pressure from the child.

Educational Problems. The main educational problem experienced by the gifted student is that of underachievement. Once identified, academically gifted children are expected to do well scholastically, and when they do not, the result is great consternation on the part of parents and teachers. There are many theories as to the causes of underachievement (Hildreth, 1966; Taylor, 1964; Purkey, 1969; Zilli, 1971). Most appear to pinpoint low self-esteem as the primary cause. According to Davis and Rimm (1985), low self-esteem, resulting in part from not believing that one is capable of living up to parents and teachers expectations, can result in the masking of these feelings of inadequacy with bravado, rebellion, or other protective defense mechanisms. These often lead to the next step of academic avoidance behaviors, which then result in poor study habits, social and disciplinary problems, and low grades. The counselor's role is to assess the reason for the behavior. If low self-esteem is at the root of the problem, this can usually be determined by means of the counseling interview. If the student is not able to communicate directly, an excellent technique has been suggested by Pulvino, Colangelo, and Zaffrann (1976), who used essay writing as a means of clarifying inner feelings when students were uncomfortable in discussing personal problems with a counselor. Such topics as "My Place in the Future," or "My Place in the Family," can often be useful with students who write better than they communicate verbally. Once it is determined that self-esteem is a problem, rational and cognitive techniques can be utilized to change the student's thinking patterns. Parents and teachers will also have to be consulted to modify the demands placed on the child if these demands prove to be unrealistic.

A somewhat less complex educational problem occurs as a result of the lack of challenge in the curriculum of the early grades for gifted pupils. Since little effort is necessary to obtain high marks, the study habits required for the more difficult tasks of high school courses do not develop, and grades slip accordingly. Divergent thinkers have particular difficulty with organization and study habits for, even when they become aware of the necessity of good work habits, they cannot develop them on their own. Counselors who find gifted students receiving poor grades, but find no evidence of self-esteem problems, might teach appropriate organizational skills, e.g., how to take notes and keep notebooks, or how to keep track of assignments. This can be done on either an individual or a group basis, depending on the number of students experiencing the problem. Often it is useful to have the child report to the counselor for a few minutes at the end of each day for a two or three-week period to reinforce the concepts taught.

Career Problems. The realization that the gifted face special problems in the selection of a career has been one of the most recent focusses of gifted counseling. Although Gowan and Demos (1964) devoted almost three pages to the subject of "Vocational Adjustment," they recognize few actual unique problems, and most of their suggestions for counselors could as well apply to non-gifted students. The first major recognition of a special set of difficulties faced by gifted graduates appeared as a result of the National Invitational Seminars on Career Education for Gifted and Talented Students which was held at the University of Maryland in 1972 and 1973 (Hoyt and Hebeler, 1974). In these seminars four areas of problems were delineated. The first is that of multipotentiality. While aptitude tests can often help point a confused student in a career direction, the gifted will usually show an even pattern of subtest scores along the upper reaches of the scales being used by the test. It is of little help to counsel these students that they may choose almost any career they wish. When uniformly high scores occur on an aptitude test, the counselor can explain that since the student obviously has ability in most areas, further testing and probing is necessary. Interest tests should be given to determine which careers the student might enjoy. Short internship programs could be arranged so that the client can spend a few days observing adults in careers that seem challenging. Research projects should also be designed so that careers that showed potential on written tests can be explored in depth. When these steps have been taken, potential choices can then be rank ordered and choices made accordingly.

The second problem with regard to vocational choice is that of expectations. Parents and teachers of gifted students tend to expect such achievements as very high grades, academic awards, enrollment in prestigious universities, and entrance into high profile professions. These goals may run counter to those of the student who may have made sensible decisions based on knowledge not available to others. In this case a counselor is often required to help explain these decisions to others involved. The opposite problem develops when parents ignore the abilities and wishes of the gifted child, and apply pressure towards a family business, farm, or career not requiring the level of ability possessed by the student. Again counselor intervention can mediate a difficult situation by helping parents to understand the appropriateness of their child's goals.

The third problem area arises from the nature of the career or careers selected by the gifted. Even without parental pressure gifted children often choose careers involving long periods of training, usually in a university. For these major commitments of time, money and intellectual energy are required, with the result that many students become frustrated and switch to less demanding programs. If counselors are aware of these concerns, they can help students to prepare for them by discussing them along with the more informational aspects of a career program. Further, if the counselor helps parents to. be aware of the possibilities for frustration which may occur, the parents can be prepared for periods of depression and can empathize and encourage their child to continue.

The final area of difficulty with regard to career selections pertains to the difficulties female students face in selecting a career (Fox and Richmond, 1979; Zaffrann and Colangelo, 1977). As recently as 1964,

Gowan and Demos stated that "The standard procedure for gifted girls should be to prepare them for teaching unless they indicate some other professional goal" (p. 263). While the prejudice which once existed towards women in professional careers is no longer the insurmountable hurdle it once was, it is still found in the professional world and in traditional families. Even more difficult to overcome is the dilemma created when females appear to be faced with a choice between a career and having a family. Counselors can help prevent these problems by bringing in successful professional women to discuss their solutions to these dilemmas, and by making available the plentiful literature that indicates that all careers are open to both sexes.

Counseling the Parents. Many of the problems which develop between gifted children and their parents, such as low self-esteem in the child, are the result of the parent not understanding the personality traits which accompany giftedness. The counselor's role is to ensure that parents of a gifted child are in possession of as many facts as possible about their child in order that misperceptions do not occur. Obviously this requires early identification by the school, followed by a thorough parent interview. Parents will need reassurance that the behaviors that they consider unusual for a child are a result of the gifts present, and not of serious personality problems. The ability of the gifted child to become absorbed in a task is a good example. Parents often become very frustrated when they have called their child to dinner several times with no result. Often this is interpreted as defiance, when the behavior is actually the result of such complete concentration on the task at hand that the instructions did not register. It is up to the counselor to review these behaviors and to set the parents mind at ease. Often just understanding why their child is different is enough to prevent future difficulties in communication. The counselor can further aid this situation by directing the parent to readings which help explain giftedness in reasonably clear terms, e.g., DeHaan (1961), Munger, (1983).

Parents also need to know what opportunities are available for the education of their children. Counselors should be aware of what programs are offered, where they are offered, and what entrance criteria are involved. They also need to be able to assess which of the available programs would be the best for the particular child, based on the personality and learning characteristics shown both on standardized tests and on observations in the classroom. Parents of the gifted are often hesitant to "push" for proper educational programs for their children as they feel that, compared to parents of handicapped children, they have little to complain about (Ross, 1979). Counselors should encourage parents to be aware of their educational rights (see Davis and Rimm, p. 357), and not to be ashamed of their "problem."

Finally, parents may find the presence of a gifted child in the family disruptive to family harmony. This is particularly true when less gifted siblings are involved. The counselor may have to help teach parents strategies for explaining to non-gifted children why they cannot compete in the gifted area with their sibling. Often it looks to the others as if the gifted, child is favored when parents make special efforts to enrich that child's learning experiences. In this case the counselor can also help the parents look for the siblings' strong areas so as to provide parallel enrichment to them, thus making the division of parental attention more balanced.

The Counselor's Role in the School

The counselor's first task in ensuring that gifted students within the school are receiving the maximum benefits of the educational process is to see that a thorough identification program is in place. This can be done through a review of the files of students transferring into the school, through teacher nomination forms (see Davis and Rimm, p. 85), as well as through careful analysis of routine standardized testing results which are generally carried out yearly by most school districts.

Once the students are identified the next step for the counselor is to inform the staff members as to the identities and characteristics of the gifted children within the school. Like parents, most classroom teachers are not aware of the personality characteristics of gifted students, many of which can be very annoying. This results in personality conflicts which can have negative effects on the entire class. One example is the child who dominates the class with constant questions. This could be interpreted as a need for attention, "smart-alec" behavior, or as showing off, rather than as a genuine attempt to understand all ramifications of the concept being taught. Similarly, the student who begins reading a book in class, rather than doing the assigned task, is seen as defiant, rather than one who completely understands the task but does not see any reason why it should be completed when it is understood. Once informed, teachers can develop alternative approaches which do not involve confrontation, and which help the gifted child to get the most out of school.

Finally, the counselor should take the lead in the development of programs within the school for the gifted population. If special schools for the gifted are included within the district, the counselor should determine which students would benefit from the program offered and make the appropriate referral. Even if such a school does exist, many students will choose not to attend. In this case the options of pull-out programs, acceleration, and separate classes should be considered. If none of the above suggestions are feasible, the counselor could consider the establishment of clubs or groups which would allow these students to socialize with true peers. An example might be a chess or Dungeons and Dragons club to be held during the lunch hour, using volunteers as supervisors.

In conclusion, while counseling may have developed late in the history of gifted education, great strides have been made in the last thirty years in the understanding of what the counselor's role should be in the education of gifted children. Even though the gifted comprise only a small percentage of the student population, their potential contributions to society are of a magnitude far exceeding their proportion. If counselors can play a role in helping those who encounter problems to achieve their full potential, they will have more than justified the time required to learn about the gifted and to develop special programs.

REFERENCES

Colangelo, N. T., & Zaffrann, R. T. (1979). *New voices in counselling the gifted.* Dubuque, Iowa: Kendall/Hunt Publishing Co.

Coleman, J. W. (1962). *The adolescent society.* New York: Free Press of Glencoe.

Cruikshank, W. (1963). *Psychology of exceptional children and youth.* Englewood Cliffs, N.J.: Prentice-Hall, Inc.

Davis, G. A., & Rimm, S. B. (1985). *Education of the gifted and talented.* Englewood Cliffs, NJ: Prentice-Hall, Inc.

DeHann, R. F. (1961). *Guidelines for parents of capable youth.* Chicago: Science Research Associates, Inc.

Ellis, A. (1962). *Reason and emotion in psychotherapy.* New York: Lyle Stuart.

Fox, L. H., & Richmond, L. J. (1979). Gifted females: Are we meeting their counseling needs. *Personnel and Guidance Journal, 57,* 256–260.

Frasier, M., & McCannon, C. (1981). Using bibliotherapy with gifted children. *Gifted Child Quarterly, 25,* 81–85.

Freeman, J. (1983). Emotional problems of the gifted child. *Journal of Child Psychology and Psychiatry, 24,* 481–485.

Gowan, J. C., & Demos, G. D. (1964). *The education and guidance of the ablest.* Springfield, Ill., Charles C Thomas.

Hildreth, G. H. (1966). *Introduction to the gifted.* New York: McGraw-Hill.

Hoyt, K. B., & Hebeler, J. R. (1974). *Career education for the gifted and talented.* Salt Lake City: Olympus Publishing Co.

Meichenbaum, D. (1977). *Cognitive behavior modification.* Plenum.

Munger, A. (1983). The parent's role in counseling the gifted: The balance between home and school. In J. Van Tassel-Baska (Ed.). *A practical guide to counseling the gifted in a school setting.* Reston, VA.: The Council for Exceptional Children.

Perrone, P. A., & Pulvino, C. J. (1979). New directions in the guidance of the gifted and talented. In J. C. Gowan, J. Khatena, & E. P. Torrance (Eds.). *Educating the ablest (2nd ed.).* Chicago: Peacock.

Perrone, P. A., & Pulvino, C. J. (1979). A theoretical perspective for understanding the gifted and talented child. In N. Colangelo & R. T. Zaffrann (Eds.). *New voices in counseling the gifted.* Dubuque, Iowa: Kendall/Hunt Publishing Co.

Pulvino, C. J., Colangelo, N., & Zaffrann, R. T. (1976). *Laboratory counseling programs.* Madison, Wis., Dept. of Counseling and Guidance, University of Wisconsin.

Purkey, W. W. (1969). Project self-discovery. Its effects on bright but underachieving high school students. *Gifted Child Quarterly, 13,* 242–246.

Roeper, A. (1982). How the gifted cope with their emotions. *Roeper Review, 5,* 21–24.

Ross, A. O. (1979). The gifted child in the family. In N. Colangelo and R. T. Zaffrann (Eds.). *New voices in counseling the gifted.* Dubuque, Iowa: Kendall/Hunt Publishing Co.

Tannenbaum, A. J. (1983). *Gifted children: Psychological and educational perspectives.* New York: MacMillan Publishing Co.

Taylor, R. G. (1964). Personality traits and discrepant achievement: A review. *Journal of Counseling Psychology, 11,* 76–82.

Terman, L. M. (1925). Mental and physical traits of a thousand gifted children. In L. M. Terman (Ed.). *Genetic studies of genius (Vol. 1).* Stanford: Stanford University Press.

Terman, L. M. (1954). The discovery and encouragement of exceptional talent. *American Psychologist, 9,* 221–230.

Terman, L. M., & Olden, M. H. (1940). Status of the California gifted group at the end of sixteen years. In National Society for the Study of Education, *Intelligence: Its nature and nurture,* 39th Yearbook. Bloomington, Il.: Public School Publishing Co.

Terman, L. M., & Oden, M. H. (1947). *Genetic studies of genius (Vol. 4): The gifted child grows up.* Stanford: Stanford University Press.

Terman, L. M., & Oden, M. H. (1951). The Stanford studies of the gifted. In P. Witty (Ed.). *The gifted child.* Boston: Heath.

Van Tassel-Baska, J. (1983). *A practical guide to counselling the gifted in a school setting.* Reston, VA.: Council for Exceptional Children.

Whitmore, J. R. (1980). *Giftedness, conflict, and underachievement.* Boston: Allyn and Bacon.

Zaffrann, R. T., & Colangelo, N. (1977). Counseling with gifted and talented students. *Gifted Child Quarterly, 21,* 305–331.

Zilli, M. J. (1971). Reasons why the gifted adolescent underachieves and some of the implications of guidance and counseling to this problem. *Gifted Child Quarterly, 15,* 279–292.

Ziv, A. (1977). *Counseling the intellectually gifted child.* Toronto: University of Toronto.

Chapter 4

THE ABUSED CHILD

Lou C. Talbutt

Child abuse and neglect continues at an alarming rate in this country. Breezer (1985) reported that "estimates of the actual number of incidents [of child abuse] range between one and two million per year" (p. 435). Borgers and Woodmancy (1985), citing a report of the Joint Commission on Mental Health of Children, found that "the mental health field is not meeting the needs of children" (p. 173). Child abuse and neglect is of special interest to educational and mental health professionals because they have both a legal and professional obligation to treat and protect victims of child abuse and neglect. In order to deal effectively with child abuse, educators and mental health professionals need to: (1) understand the seriousness of the problem; (2) identify child abuse; (3) be aware of the reporting laws and legal implications; (4) possess intervention strategies for working with individuals and families; and (5) educate others regarding the prevention and treatment of child abuse.

Educational and mental health professionals are urged to become advocates for children. Child abuse generally includes minors or individuals eighteen or under in age. Thus, teenage abuse should not be ignored. Borgers and Woodmancy (1985) gave several reasons why mental health professionals should be advocates for children.

> One important reason is that those in the helping professions understand the importance of childhood in human development; and this understanding makes them a natural, concerned, and articulate group to help children reach their fullest potential.
>
> ... Counselors can protect the rights of students, educate board members, administrators, and teachers about the issues and create a more humane and responsive climate in schools based on an awareness and respect for the rights of youth ...
>
> The underlying beliefs of the helping profession also thrust mental health professions into advocacy positions. ... This respon-

sibility is derived from the commitment of those in the profession to individuality and human dignity . . . (p. 174).

Educators and mental health personnel, then, are in a position to advocate for children due to the nature and commitment of their profession. Further, they are able to appreciate the importance of childhood in one's total development and be committed to the dignity of each individual.

Definition of Child Abuse. The child abuse Prevention and Treatment Act, Public Law 93-247, of 1974, defines child abuse as:

> the physical or mental injury, sexual abuse, negligent treatment, or maltreatment of a child under the age of eighteen by a person who is responsible for the child's welfare under circumstances which indicate that the child's health or welfare is harmed or threatened thereby.

Child abuse may be: neglect (failure to provide for a child's basic needs), emotional maltreatment, abandonment, physical and sexual abuse. Fischer and Sorenson (1985) classified child abuse and neglect into four categories: (1) physical abuse; (2) physical neglect; (3) sexual abuse; and (4) emotional maltreatment (pp. 185–187). Their examples of physical abuse included such things as burns, fractures, bruises, and lacerations. Physical neglect included characteristics such as inappropriate dress, consistent hunger, and unattended medical problems. Physical indicators of sexual abuse included bruises or bleeding of the genital areas, venereal disease, and other problems. Emotional maltreatment included such characteristics as speech disorders and lags in overall development.

While the definition of child abuse may seem clear, it is often difficult to get individuals to agree on particular cases of child abuse. The American Humane Association (1981) described this situation.

1. People often disagree about when interaction patterns, once considered to be normal, become either physically or emotionally abusive.
2. They may disagree about the dividing line between normal, acceptable physical discipline and abuse.
3. People may disagree about what constitutes abuse or neglect. The court, the society as a whole, and the culture of which the child and family are part may have different standards for judging behavior (p. 56).

The most obvious signs of abuse include physical injuries such as bruises, welts, and burns. Emotional abuse is less obvious, with symptoms including depression, withdrawal, and aggression. The American

Humane Association (1981) defines emotional abuse as occurring "when parents are responsible for an impairment of a child's intellectual, psychological or emotional capacity or an impairment of a child's capacity to view himself as a separate individual with dignity and self worth" (p. 56–57). Grigg and Gale (1977) listed characteristics of child abuse as "silence, withdrawal, fear, submissiveness, anger, hostility, and aggression" (p. 192). The other side of the issue concerns the characteristics of abusing parents. According to the American Humane Association (1981), "abusing parents are much like any representative sample from the general population" (p. 54).

a. They come from every socioeconomic class.
b. They come from all educational levels.
c. They come from every cultural or racial subgroup.
d. Their average personality profile scores based on descriptive psychological tests show that they are much like a representative sample of the general population (p. 54).

Educators and mental health professionals need to be aware that because abusing parents come from every socioeconomic and cultural group, keen observations of children are necessary to detect child abuse. Following are some possible reasons why parents abuse children.

1. Parents may have been abused themselves and may lack good parenting skills.
2. Parents may suffer from stress or have other emotional problems.
3. Parents may have drug or alcohol problems.
4. Parents may be too immature or may hold unrealistic expectations of children.
5. Parents may have children with special needs who require more time and energy than the parents are prepared to give.

Legal Implications Regarding Child Abuse. An understanding of the reporting laws and legal implications are important for counselors. Fischer and Sorenson (1985) reported that California was the first state in 1962 to require the reporting of child abuse and that by 1964 twenty states had similar laws (p. 190). Camblin and Prout (1983) completed a survey which showed that all states and the District of Columbia now have mandatory reporting laws for child abuse and that all state laws grant immunity from civil or criminal liability for those reporting in good faith (p. 360). Immunity means that if individuals make an honest mistake in reporting child abuse, they can not be held liable for civil or criminal charges. While all states have a reporting law, those in the helping professions should be aware that the wording of state laws vary. For example, Camblin and Prout (1983) found that all states require certain school personnel to report suspected cases of child abuse, but that state laws differ regarding the professionals named in the law (p. 360). Fischer and Sorenson (1985) reported that some state statutes required school counselors to report child abuse, while other laws include them among "educators," "other school personnel," or "employees or officials of any public or private school" (p. 188). First, school personnel and mental health professionals should become familiar with the laws on child abuse for their state(s) of employment. Secondly, professionals should act in good faith. Hummel, Talbutt, and Alexander (1985) wrote "An honest error in judgment would not result in litigation against the reporter unless the person making the report had acted with malicious intent" (p. 145).

Court Cases. Because state laws are clear regarding immunity, educators and mental health professionals should not hesitate to report suspected cases of child abuse. The following court cases illustrate times when immunity for school guidance counselors was upheld by the courts. In **Dick v. Watonwan County** (1982), a U.S. District Court in Minnesota upheld the counselor's right to report child abuse according to the law of the state and ruled that the counselor was not liable when acting in good faith. The court offered the following explanation:

> McCarthy [the counselor] had a duty under Minnesota law to
> report the suspected neglect or abuse. . . . In addition, McCarthy
> is entitled to good faith immunity under federal law (p. 996).

In **Dick** (1982), the case centered around a student who told the counselor that she was interested in foster care due to parental drinking and violent arguments at home. The counselor reported the situation to the county welfare department, which resulted in the parents being committed to a detoxification center. The parents had not been drinking at the time of their placement in the detoxification center, leading them to bring suit. Several factors were in the counselor's favor. First, the student introduced the topic of foster care, not the counselor. Secondly, the counselor followed the state law and there was no evidence that the counselor had not acted in good faith. Thirdly, in reporting the matter, the counselor talked to the welfare officials about foster care, not the commitment of the parents to the detoxification center.

In another case, **Roman v. Appleby** (1983), a U.S. District Court in

Pennsylvania reached a similar conclusion. The court found that the counselor had acted in good faith and had consequently maintained immunity. The court determined:

> that the high school guidance counselor was entitled to immunity under provisions of Pennsylvania Child Protective Services Law with respect to referral of student to county children's services . . . (p. 449).

Roman (1983) involved litigation against a school counselor by parents for violation of their first amendment rights to manage private family matters. The counselor asked the student about his parents and their attitudes about sex, masturbation, and religion. Again in this situation, the student initiated the first counseling session. The mother was aware that the sessions were taking place, although she never authorized the counselor to ask questions about the family's attitudes about sex or religion. During counseling, the counselor told the student that

> his parents were too strict; their religious views were too rigid and conservative; he could not function in reality; he was possibly psychotic; his fears of being a homosexual were normal for his age . . . (p. 453).

The guidance counselor then held a conference with the parents and recommended mental health counseling because she believed that the student had serious psychological problems. When the parents failed to follow through with counseling, the guidance counselor reported them to the county children's services to have the student declared a dependent under Pennsylvania's Juvenile Act. The judge denied the petition. However, the court determined that the counselor had followed the state law, had acted in good faith, and consequently had immunity. In this situation, the counselor also checked with the parents to see if they had followed through with counseling prior to making the report to the children's services.

These cases reveal several important points for counselors and mental health personnel.

1. Immunity is upheld by the courts when professionals act in good faith; thus, counselors should not fail to report child abuse for fear of litigation.
2. Counselors may not be liable even if the court decision is in favor of the parent(s) against the counselor.
3. Counselors should use professional judgement, including

checking with other appropriate professionals, before reporting child abuse, especially if the situation is not clear.

On the other hand, professionals may be liable for failure to report child abuse. In **Landeros v. Flood** (1976), the Supreme Court of California ruled that a physician was liable for failure to report child abuse. The same could be true for other mental health professionals required to report child abuse. Some state laws require the penalty of a fine for failure to report. Other state laws indicate that a person may be guilty of a misdemeanor and may also face civil liability (Hummel, Talbutt, and Alexander, 1985, p. 145).

Reporting procedures vary among states. Many states require oral reports within a specified period of time followed by written reports. Fischer and Sorenson (1985) found that twenty-four states follow this procedure with other states requiring oral reports only and some states requiring oral reports to be followed by written reports when requested (p. 323). Fischer and Sorenson also reported that a number of states have toll-free "hotlines" to facilitate the reporting of child abuse and neglect.

Clearly, the laws and court cases support the professionals' duty to report child abuse. Breezer (1985) reported that "educators might help save some of the 2,000 children who die each year under circumstances that suggest abuse and neglect" by reporting suspected child abuse (p. 436). Now that the seriousness of child abuse has been examined and the professionals' responsibilities have been clarified, the next section will deal with intervention strategies for successfully dealing with the treatment and prevention of child abuse.

Interventions

The Team Approach. Of all the current problems facing the school and society, child abuse is an area in which the interdisciplinary team approach should be utilized. Because the problems of child abuse are so complex, it is necessary that parents, agencies, school personnel, and mental health professionals work together to prevent and treat child abuse. Jenkins (1985) gave the following definition of the interdisciplinary team approach.

> [It] is a systematic means of coordinating the expertise of various school personnel and outside consultants to deal effectively with complex and typical problems of students with special needs (p. 205).

While Jenkins was writing about the special needs population, the same intervention strategies can be applied to child abuse.

Professionals involved in the team approach to child abuse problems should include:

1. School teachers and administrators
2. Guidance counselors
3. School psychologists and social workers
4. School nurses
5. Parents
6. Social service and mental health professionals

Teachers are often the first individuals in the school setting to see and suspect symptoms of child abuse. Consequently, they are key professionals in reporting child abuse. By consulting with administrators, guidance counselors, and school nurses, teachers are more likely to feel secure about reporting child abuse. The problem, then, becomes an investigative matter for social service professionals. Depending upon the nature of the problem, parental training, relocation of the child, and follow-up treatment for the child and family by mental health professionals are possible interventions. Mental health personnel, then, in turn need to work with the school staff to help the abused child settle into the school setting and get appropriate support.

The team approach is also recommended for child abuse prevention. If child abuse is to be reduced in this country, prevention is the key. Talbutt (1981) recommended a series of three child abuse workshops for schools using an interdisciplinary team approach. In phase one, Talbutt suggested that public schools involve other professionals to present programs on the recognition of and legal responsibilities of child abuse. Parent and teacher associations should involve physicians, psychologists, public health nurses, and attorneys to raise the consciousness of parents, society, and school personnel regarding child abuse. In phase two, Talbutt suggested that schools deal with the handling of child abuse. In-house policies and referral programs for dealing with families and child abuse should be established and explained by teachers, administrators, and counselors to parents and the public. In phase three, Talbutt recommended that there be:

an ongoing committee composed of parents, teachers, administrators, curriculum specialists, and counselors to write and update child abuse policies for the school and to plan and incorporate programs on parenting and family life into the school curriculum (p. 145).

The purpose of the third phase was to educate future parents regarding family life and parenting. By helping students understand family life and how to be effective parents, educators can help students become better prepared for parenting.

Professionals involved in the recognition, treatment, and prevention of child abuse have various roles. School personnel not only have reporting responsibilities, but they have responsibilities for educating parents and the school community. The following suggestions summarize some activities for school counselors to use in dealing with child abuse and neglect in conjunction with parents and other mental health professionals.

1. In-service training should be conducted within the school setting by guidance counselors for teachers and others on the recognition of child abuse. The school nurse, school psychologists, and others should be included in the program.
2. Programs in the form of information and awareness regarding child abuse should be planned for parents and school professionals at school events. Mental health professionals, medical, and legal personnel should be included in the programs.
3. Social service personnel should be invited to speak to school staffs on the procedures for investigating child abuse and to address the procedures used in handling the child and family in various types of abuse situations.
4. In-house policies should be established by school administrators in collaboration with counselors and others in the school system regarding appropriate reporting procedures.
5. Teachers, school counselors, parents, and administrators should work together to include parenting skills and information on family life in the curriculum.

Specific Interventions and Case Studies. With the team approach to child abuse, mental health professionals and school personnel may employ a variety of strategies including counseling, consultation, and teaching. These strategies may be classified as either direct or indirect interventions. Counseling (individual, group, or family) is an example of direct intervention. Indirect interventions include consulting and teaching.

Professionals must consult both within and between agencies. Just as school counselors have a responsibility to work with personnel employed within the school system, social workers, psychologists, and others employed within the same agency need to coordinate their professional skills to provide effective child abuse programs. Schools have responsibilities for reporting child abuse, educating parents and students, and providing support for victims of child abuse while the investigative procedures and follow up should be conducted by social service agencies. Coordinators for school pupil personnel services and social welfare administrators need to plan and work together regarding available child abuse programs.

Once a potential child abuse case has been reported by the guidance counselor, teacher, school administrator, police, physician, or others, it is the function of the social service agency or assigned department within that agency to investigate and make recommendations. Working in conjunction with the legal system, the social service professional assigned the case takes steps, if necessary, to relocate the child.

Whether the child remains in the family or is relocated, counseling is an essential technique used by mental health professionals if the abused child is to become a well-adjusted member of society and if the parents are to change their behaviors. Individual counseling (working with each person privately), group counseling (including parents or children with other group members having similar problems), or family counseling (working with the family unit together) may be utilized separately or in combination.

Once counseling has begun, either as a part of the counseling process or through classes, effective parenting and communication skills should be taught. Such skills are necessary for parents during the process of recovery, especially if the child remains with the family. Classes should include topics dealing with stress, discipline, anger, parental roles, and realistic expectations. The important point is that these strategies or some part of them are effective if used together by a team of professionals, rather than in isolation.

The following three hypothetical open-ended cases are presented for readers to review and discuss. Based on the previous information in this chapter, readers might like to discuss the appropriate professional roles and intervention strategies for each situation. Also, the three cases deal with clients of different age levels and different situations, allowing readers to compare the three cases.

Case #1. Judy is a member of your kindergarten class in a public school setting. Judy's attendance is irregular; she is dirty and inappropriately dressed; she is often tardy and appears hungry. No physical abuse is present. Judy reports that she is responsible for getting up in the mornings, getting herself dressed, and walking to school. At a school picnic, she ate continuously. Your state law names "all school personnel" as responsible for reporting child abuse and neglect.

- Can this situation be classified as child abuse and neglect if the child is not being physically harmed? Explain.
- Do you have enough evidence to report child abuse and to whom would you make the report? Explain.
- What resources might be available for food and clothing? Is this the school's responsibility? Why? Why not?

Case #2. Sam is a teenager in the eighth grade. He keeps to himself, has limited social skills, and seems uncomfortable in class discussions. He was absent last year for two weeks. He explained that "he was in a bike accident." He had a broken arm and bruises on his face. Recently, he has been absent from your eighth grade English class. When he returned to class, he appeared nervous when you asked about the unexplained bruises on his face. You have heard from other students that his stepfather drinks and that Sam and his mother do what the stepfather says. Your state requires "teachers" to report child abuse.

- Would you visit the home to get a closer look before reporting the case? Why or why not?
- Would you report the case immediately? If not, what are some resources you might use for additional information?
- Would you have any responsibility for Sam's social development at school? What interventions could you take at school?

Case #3. Alice and her mother are present in your guidance office early one morning to talk with you. Both report that they are being abused by the father. The mother is being physically abused, minor bruises appear on her face, and Alice is being sexually abused. Both appear upset and nervous. They are afraid to return home.

- How would you proceed, and with whom would you confer?
- How is this case different from the first one, and how does that difference determine the procedures you follow?
- Does the mother's presence and report to you make a difference in your handling of the case?

Implications For Professionals. The following statements summarize some major implications for school and mental health professionals.

1. School personnel and mental health professionals have legal and moral responsibilities for reporting child abuse. Failure to report child abuse can result in litigation against the

professional. Immunity is granted when professionals act in good faith and make an honest mistake in judgment. For specific details, professionals should become acquainted with and follow their state statute on child abuse.

2. Because child abuse is a complex issue, the team approach is one way of involving numerous professionals with varied strategies on different facets of the same problem.

3. Education and prevention is an important aspect of the problem if child abuse is to be reduced. Thus, programming and educational opportunities should be emphasized to better prepare students for parenting and family life.

4. The schools, society, and mental health agencies have unique roles in dealing with child abuse. Each group should understand its role and the roles of others.

5. Reporting, treating, and preventing child abuse are three facets of the problem. Dealing with one area without the others leads to an incomplete solution.

6. Reporting, however, is the most important link if child abuse is to be treated. For this reason, school personnel who see millions of children daily should be active in observing and reporting cases which might otherwise go unnoticed.

Because school personnel come into contact with so many children, they have opportunities to be exposed to child abuse. A section from the American School Counselor Association's "Position Statements" (1983, 1–2) on child abuse (adopted January 1981) provides some guidelines for reporting child abuse.

School counselors who suspect a child is being abused or neglected should report the following information to the appropriate authority as soon as possible:
1. Name and address of the child and parent (or guardian).
2. Child's sex.
3. Nature and extent of the child's injuries, abuse or neglect.
4. Any evidence of prior injuries, abuse, or neglect.
5. Action, if any, taken to treat, shelter or assist the child.
6. Name of the person or persons making the report.
7. Other pertinent information. . . .
The following sample procedures may be used in referring suspected child abuse/neglect:
1. Any school counselor who suspects that a child has been abused shall report this as soon as possible to the principal (designee) on the day of observation.
2. The principal (designee) will review the report and school information with appropriate staff members within two days of

the referral; reasonable cause must be determined before informing the appropriate referral agency.

    3. The school principal or designee shall call the appropriate referral agency (telephone number) and notify them of the alleged child abuse.

        a. You may request that the agency case worker maintain contact with a specific staff member.

        b. You may ask that the specific identity of the reporter remain confidential (instead, the referral agency, if asked, would state that the referral came from the _____ School Department)...

Limitations. A major limitation to the team approach in dealing with child abuse includes failures in communication among the necessary parties resulting in important aspects of the problem being neglected. For example, when school personnel fail to work with social agencies or fail to understand the investigative process, they are more likely to avoid reporting child abuse out of fear or misunderstanding. Likewise, social agencies might not always be aware of the support and counseling groups available in the schools for children with unique problems. A lack of knowledge can lead to inappropriate or no action. Also, failure to understand the state law on immunity in one's place of employment can lead to failure to report child abuse.

Limitations also exist for each intervention strategy. Individual counseling is an essential support for parents and children. Yet, as a strategy alone, it is not sufficient. Without the home investigation, improved parenting skills, and family counseling, the solution is incomplete. Likewise, the home investigation and recognition of the child abuse problem cannot be solved unless additional steps are taken by mental health professionals to educate the parents and improve family communication. The reporter is the first important link. Yet, the reporter is often not the person responsible for investigating or recommending solutions to the problem. For this reason, it is important that the reporter, as in the case of the teacher, understand the importance of the first step. Then, the school becomes an important agent for bringing about change. The school also plays an important role in acting as a change agent by educating future parents. Again, educational and preventive measures cannot solve immediate problems requiring treatment.

The interdisciplinary team approach provides a solution for dealing with the complex problems of child abuse. Mental health professionals and school personnel must be aware of their responsibilities to the abused child, to parents undergoing treatment, and to future parents and children in society. Society, in turn, through governmental funding, public awareness, and the legal system, must support professionals working together to solve the problems of child abuse. Professionals in conjunction with society have the difficult and important task of observing, reporting, treating, and preventing child abuse.

REFERENCES

American School Counselor Association. (1983). Position statements. *The School Counselor*, 20, 1–8.

Breezer, B. (1985). Reporting child abuse and neglect: Your responsibility and your protection. *Phi Delta Kappan*, 66, 434–436.

Borgers, S. B. & Woodmancy, M. (1983). Children and their rights. *Elementary School Guidance & Counseling*, 17, 170–176.

Camblin, L. D. & Prout, H. T. (1983). School counselors and the reporting of child abuse: A survey of state laws and practices. *The School Counselor*, 30, 358–367.

Child Abuse Prevention and Treatment Act, Pub.L. No. 93-247, 388 Stat. 4, 4–5 (1974).

Dick v. Watonwan County, 551 F. Supp. 983 (Minn., 1982).

Fischer, L. & Sorenson, G. P. (1985). *School law for counselors, psychologists, and social workers*. New York: Longman, Inc.

Grigg, S. A. & Gale, P. (1977). The abused child: Focus for counselors. *Elementary School Guidance & Counseling*, 11, 187–194.

Hummel, D., Talbutt, L. C., & Alexander, D. M. (1985). *Law and ethics in counseling*. New York: Van Nostrand Reinhold.

Jenkins, D. E. (1985). Ethical and legal dilemmas of working with students with special needs. *Elementary School Guidance & Counseling*, 19, 202–209.

Landeros v. Flood, 551 P.2nd 389 (Calif., 1976).

Roman v. Appleby, 558 F. Supp. 499 (Penn., 1983).

Talbutt, L. C. (1981). Child abuse: A team approach for elementary counselors. *Elementary School Guidance & Counseling*, 16, 142–145.

The American Humane Association. (1981). *Helping in child protective services*. Englewood, CO: The American Humane Association.

Chapter 5

THE CHILD OF ALCOHOLIC PARENTS

PATTI BOSWELL BLOOMER AND ED JACOBS

The interventions discussed in this chapter are the initial interventions with children of alcoholics (COA's). Long-term counseling with addicted families is only alluded to since we feel that addiction counseling should be done by someone who has extensive knowledge and training in the field of addiction. In writing this chapter, we present basic information about alcoholism and COA's since we assume that the reader is not a certified addiction counselor.

We will be using the term "alcoholic" and "alcoholism," however, since we want to stress that we are referring to the disease of addiction which includes alcohol and/or any other drug addiction. Since the disease of addiction affects both men and women, we will use the terms "he" and "she" and "his" and "her" interchangeably to remind the reader of this point.

We will primarily address the psychological and behavioral dysfunctions due to living in an addicted environment. Although we recognize the growing problem of teenage alcohol and drug addiction, we did not feel that it should be covered in this chapter since our emphasis is on working with COA's. The purpose of this article is to inform the reader about COA's and to discuss the education and counseling interventions that are helpful in treating COA's. Three interventions discussed are: education, initial treatment, and long-term family intervention.

INTRODUCTION: THE PROBLEM

There are at least fifteen million school-age American children with parental alcoholism (Booz-Allen and Hamilton, 1974). According to the National Association for Children of Alcoholics' Charter Statement, children of alcoholics left untreated will develop an inability to trust, an extreme need to control, excessive sense of responsibility, and denial of feelings. These will result in low self-esteem, depression, isolation, guilt, and difficulty maintaining satisfying relationships. They are prone to experience learning disabilities, anxiety, attempted and completed suicide, eating disorders, and compulsive achieving.

Given this prognosis and the numerous research findings that approximately 50% of children of alcoholics either become or marry alcoholics, we believe that treating COA's is equally as important as treating the alcoholic. Too often, therapists focus on treating the addicted person and not the children. Certainly we think that the addicted person should be treated, but we also feel that counselors, depending on their expertise, should provide initial or long-term treatment for the children. In order to provide the treatment, the first thing that has to occur is the identification of the COA's. Presenting programs to students explaining the effects of addiction on the family members can result in some students identifying themselves as a COA. Also, the counselor can educate the teachers in the school about the characteristics of COA's since the child of the alcoholic comes to school exhibiting the effects of living in an addicted home. A number of authors have described these effects (Ackerman, 1983; Deutsch, 1982; Lawson, Peterson, and Lawson, 1983) Their lists include:

Characteristics, Attitudes, and Behaviors of COA's

Poor physical appearance
Bruises, burns, broken bones, blackened eyes
Aggressiveness
Withdrawn behavior
Morning tardiness
Lack of trust
Inability to identify feelings
Compulsive need to achieve
Secretiveness about the family
Avoidance of involving parents in school related activities
Feelings of no control in their lives
Poor academic performance
Sleepiness (especially on Mondays due to parent's weekend binges)
Anxiousness (especially on Fridays due to fear of weekend binges)

Sharon Wegscheider (1979), in her classic article, "Children of Alcoholics Caught in the Family Trap," describes four roles often assumed by COA's. These include the Family Hero, the Scapegoat, the Lost Child, and the Mascot. It is important for the counselor to be aware of these roles and how they are exhibited in school age children. Although these roles are discussed separately, a COA can manifest symptoms from more than one role.

The Family Hero

This person is the super achiever in most areas of their life. Their function is to make the family look good to the outside world. They are generally excellent students. This person is rarely identified as a COA because they are so good at playing their role. (Certainly it is fine to do well in school, but the Family Hero is achieving for inappropriate reasons.)

The Scapegoat

This person is the one who is the target of the parents' frustration, anger, and confusion. The scapegoat presents the family's anger to the world by acting out (fighting, stealing, unplanned pregnancies, alcohol and other drug abuse) and takes the focus off the family. This is often misunderstood by teachers, counselors, and administrators in that they focus on the student's behavior rather than the motivation of the behavior.

The Lost Child

This person is generally lost within the family, as well as, within the school system. This is the "relief" child in the family because they do not seem to need attention. They stay to themselves, suffer loneliness and feelings of isolation. They, too, are often not identified as COA's by teachers, counselors, and administrators because they tend to do their school work and function without appearing to need any help.

The Mascot

The mascot is the child who provides comic relief and tries to diffuse explosive situations. They often are hyperactive, learning disabled, and have short attention spans. These children are relatively easy to identify due to their attention getting behaviors.

These four roles are important to be familiar with since most COA's will portray one or more of them. The counselor must understand that it is the motivation for the role rather than the behavior that needs to be focused on.

If a counselor sees a child who exhibits any of these aforementioned characteristics and/or roles, it may be an indication that the child is from an addicted home. Do realize that many kids who are not from an alcoholic family will exhibit these behaviors. The counselor will want to look for patterns of behavior and not just one behavior. Once the problem is identified, it is important that an intervention is made or the psychological effects can be carried into adulthood.

INTERVENTIONS

There are a number of interventions that can be effective in helping COA's. The intervention that is most useful and yet the most difficult is that of getting the entire family including the alcoholic into treatment with a trained addiction counselor. Although getting the entire family into treatment is the ideal situation, we feel it is important to point out that getting just one family member into the recovery process is valuable. This helps the individual and the recovery of that person often impacts the family system in such a way that other members of the family will seek help. (For those not familiar with the disease of addiction, it may need to be mentioned that usually every member is affected and needs to recover in some way, not just the alcoholic.)

Education Intervention

Usually the first intervention that is made with the COA is education. As was mentioned previously, this is done through programs, films, and various reading material. Professionals often reach COA's by somehow letting them know that they are being affected by the disease and that there is help and support groups available.

Initial Treatment Intervention—Rapport Building

COA's either seek out treatment due to a crisis at home or a program at school, or they are identified because of the symptoms they are exhibiting. Once contact is established, building rapport with the COA is crucial and often very difficult because of the family messages of "Don't talk!

Don't trust! Don't feel! (Black, 1982). The counselor will want to be very aware as she probes into intimate family matters, the COA may begin to deny the problem to protect the family. If the counselor senses the denial, she may say something like:

"I do realize that it may be hard to talk about these things since you may have been told not to talk about family matters outside of the home. Also, it is probably painful to think about some of the things that I am asking. From what you are saying, it does sound like there **may be** a drinking problem and I want you to know that although you are talking about it, this does not mean you are being disloyal to your family."

The counselor will also need to be aware that questions like "How do you feel about that?" may interfere with rapport building due to the fact that COA's are often not in touch with their feelings. Instead the counselor may tentatively suggest the appropriate feeling. For example:

Joey: "My typical weekend is cleaning the entire house and taking care of my brothers and sisters."

Counselor: "That's a lot responsibility for a thirteen year old. That must seem unfair?"

Joey: "Yea it does."

Counselor: "I imagine it would make you angry at times."

Joey: (Hesitantly) "I do get mad."

Counselor: "Are you allowed to talk about that in your family?"

Joey: "No, this is the first time I have ever said this to anyone."

Counselor: "I am glad that you are feeling like you can tell me those kinds of things."

During the initial contacts, the counselor should be aware that the COA may have more difficulty opening up or trusting than other clients due to the lack of trust in authority figures. Also, the counselor needs to be sure not to imply during the rapport building stage that the child's recovery will have any effect on the family. Comments like "Joey, if you come and talk to me, there is a good chance we'll be able to help your family" should be avoided.

History Gathering

As early as possible, the counselor will want to gather information regarding the family. This may come after ten or fifteen minutes of the initial contact. Asking questions about the family may need to be done in a sensitive manner since many COA's will be very uncomfortable with the questions. The purpose for gathering history is to determine the extent of the disease, the roles of the different family members, and if any treatment has occurred.

COA History Gathering

It is important to obtain history specifically concerning the COA to determine the role played, the level of impact sustained and the behavior patterns used. Brooks (1981) has developed a list of some questions to ask COA's.

1. Do you worry about your mom's and/or dad's drinking?
2. Do you sometimes feel that you are the reason your parent drinks so much?
3. Are you ashamed to have your friends come to your house and are you finding more and more excuses to stay away from home?
4. Do you sometimes feel that you hate your parents when they are drinking and then feel guilty for hating them?
5. Have you been watching how much your parent drinks?
6. Do you try to make your parents happy so they won't get upset and drink more?
7. Do you feel you can't talk about the drinking in your home — or even how you feel inside?
8. Do you sometimes drink or take drugs to forget about things at home?
9. Do you feel if your parents really loved you they would not drink so much?
10. Do you sometimes wish you had never been born?
11. Do you want to start feeling better?

The answers to these questions will help to understand how the COA is viewing his world.

Family History Gathering

Along with gathering COA history, it is important to gather family history to form a broader picture of the alcoholic environment. Some good questions to ask are:

1. Who lives in the home?
2. What is your mom like? (stepmom)
3. What is your dad like? (stepdad)

 4. What are the others in the home like?
 5. Who talks to whom? In what manner?
 6. How long has your parent(s) been drinking?
 7. Does your parent's mood change when drinking?
 8. How often do they drink?
 9. Where do they drink? Home, bar, etc.
10. Have either of your parents ever sought treatment? (therapy, ALANON, or AA)
11. Is there any physical or sexual abuse in your home? (You may want to preface this question with a comment like: "Many times children living in an alcoholic family experience physical or sexual abuse. Sometimes this is real difficult to talk about but this really seems to be a common problem."

Short-Term Therapy Intervention

After gathering the history, the counselor may find it necessary to call the appropriate agency, such as Protective Services, if there is suspected abuse and/or neglect. If the history indicates that the family is receiving treatment, then no intervention may be necessary. However, a phone call to the primary therapist may be helpful to establish lines of support and communication. If therapy intervention is indicated, we advocate that the counselor intervene using the two step model outlined below. The two steps are:

STEP I: Seeing the COA for short-term therapy
STEP II: Seeing the COA and a significant adult.

STEP I: Seeing the COA for Therapy

The goal of this short-term therapy (We think this should be short-term therapy unless the counselor is well versed in drug and alcohol therapy.) is to help the COA understand the addiction so that they no longer feel responsible for causing and/or curing it. A second goal is to get the COA to cope with the chaotic situation in which they live so that they no longer need to feel angry and resentful. A third goal is to get to the second step which is seeing the COA and some significant adult.

Accomplishing Goal 1: Helping the COA Understand Addiction

The counselor needs to present an explanation of addiction. We suggest using the disease concept of addiction to accomplish this. (The disease concept is the prevailing model in the drug and alcohol field). By using the disease concept, it allows the COA to begin understanding that alcoholism is a disease that they are not responsible for. Help them to learn the three C's: "I didn't cause it"; "I can't control it"; and "I can't cure it."

It is important for the counselor to go over the various roles (Family Hero, Scapegoat, Lost Child, and Mascot) and help the child understand that the roles are a function of disease and that he no longer has to play that role. The counselor will also want the child to understand that the role the family gave him does not come from who he is, but rather what the family perceived that they needed from him. For example, the scapegoat is led to believe that he is a bad person, whereas in reality the family needs someone to look bad and take the attention away from the family dysfunction. In the case of the Hero, she needs to come to understand that the family needed someone to save them and to present accomplishments to the family.

The counselor would also want to give COA's age-appropriate literature and to urge them to attend self-help groups such as ALATEEN or therapy/support groups for COA's.

Accomplishing Goal 2: Coping With the Chaos

Often it is very difficult to get the COA to let go of his anger and resentment because the pain and chaos is immense. To help bring about acceptance, the youngster needs to be encouraged to speak freely and honestly about the pain. In cases where the child is not able to talk about his pain, the therapist may want to encourage alternative means of expression such as art, photography, or poetry. This helps reduce the magnitude of the pain so that the counselor can begin to work towards helping the COA cope with an extremely chaotic home situation. The counselor may use such theories as Ellis's (1975) ABC model where the youngster looks at the self-defeating sentences that he is telling himself about his particular situation. The counselor can also use Transactional Analysis (T.A.) to teach the child how to step out of the chaos by using his

Adult ego state (James and Jongeward, 1971). If you are not familiar with these theories, we urge you to investigate them.

Accomplishing Goal 3: Getting to STEP II

During short-term therapy with the COA, the counselor will want to assess whether some significant adult is available to help move the family towards treatment. Preferably, this adult will be one of the COA's parents. However, it can be anyone who can impact the family. The counselor would want to explain the reasons for this request which is to help support the COA in his recovery and to discuss the possibilities for treatment. This may be the time to suggest to the child that she may be able to help the family by getting a significant adult to come talk to the counselor. (The counselor needs to be aware that by making this suggestion, he may be "hooking into" the child's role in the family, especially the hero.)

To accomplish this, the counselor would ask questions like:

1. Do either of your parents acknowledge a drinking problem or any problem?
2. Would either of your parents be willing to come and discuss this problem in the home?
3. Is there anyone 17 or older who would come in? (There are two reasons for asking if there is anyone older. The first is for adult input about the situation. The second is for transportation of the COA to treatment when he is referred to a drug and alcohol counselor.)

If the COA feels that some significant adult will readily come in, the counselor would ask the COA to invite that adult to the next session. If the child felt that the adult may resist coming in to discuss addiction, the counselor may suggest using some secondary problem, such as a school or social issue. If the child felt that it would be best for the counselor to make contact, the historical data will be helpful in determining how to go about getting the adult to come in. The counselor may call the person and ask if he/she would come in and discuss the drinking problems in the home. If the child indicates that the adult denies the drinking problem, the counselor may again resort to a secondary problem.

When contacting the significant adult, the counselor may want to use such leading phrases as:

"We need your input in this problem."

"I would like you to come in because I think you could shed some light on this problem."

"I need you to help me figure out the child's problem."

"I am not sure if I am getting an accurate picture of the situation and feel that your clarification would be extremely helpful."

It is important that the counselor realize that the goal is to make a successful referral. Use whatever it takes to get a significant adult involved in the helping system. However, the counselor must also be aware that once child's treatment is exposed, the parents may sabotage his recovery. If the COA believes that no one would come in or that it is not in his best interest to contact anyone, and the counselor agrees, the counselor would skip STEP II and make an appropriate referral for the COA.

Step II: Seeing the COA and a Significant Adult

The purpose of this step is to discuss treatment plans. If the adult is coming to the session to discuss the addiction problem, the adult may need time to express feelings and concerns. The counselor will want to give adequate time for this prior to discussing further treatment planning. It is important to realize that the session is not meant to be a therapy session per se but rather it is for support and referral.

If the adult thinks he is coming in to discuss a problem regarding the child, certainly the task of shifting the focus to the alcoholism is much more difficult. The counselor will want to spend time building rapport by discussing the secondary problem. When trust is established, the counselor will want to shift the discussion to possible causes of the secondary problem. He may spend some time suggesting possible causes (financial, medical, emotional) keeping in mind that the final suggestion of drinking in the home is to be the attempted focus of the session. The suggestion of drinking in the home must be done in a tentative, non-threatening manner so as to not frighten the adult into not returning or not following through with the referral. Once this topic is broached, the counselor will then begin to put the referral process into action. This may entail educating the adult about the disease, the kinds of services available, and the importance of seeing a drug and alcohol expert.

A second way to introduce the problem of family addiction is to draw out and support the child in revealing his concerns about the addiction. The counselor may or may not want to inform the child that he is going to do this. This will depend on the child, the rapport built, the historical data, and climate of the session.

Once the adult and the COA have met with the counselor and have discussed the problem of addiction, the next step is to make the referral to the drug and alcohol specialist. It is important that the counselor have available the name and phone number of a good drug and alcohol counselor. The phone call for an appointment should be made during the session.

This concludes the two step model for initial treatment intervention. The next intervention would consist of long-term treatment of the individual and/or the family by a trained addiction therapist. As we said in the opening of this chapter, long term therapy should only be done by a drug and alcohol specialist.

IMPLICATIONS, LIMITATIONS, AND WARNINGS

There are millions of COA's presently in the school system. School personnel are the professionals who have the greatest potential for reaching this population. We feel that our model will enable school counselors to reach out because it is designed with the understanding that the school counselor and mental health professional will have limited knowledge concerning family addiction and COA issues. For this reason, we have repeatedly stressed the importance of referral after initial treatment intervention.

We advocate that professionals reach out to COA's, in spite of the risk of having angry parents calling administrators. It is therefore necessary to have the proper support of the program. Implied in our model is the belief that anyone seeking help should be afforded that help. This may contradict some theories that advocate that the entire family must be seen together. We firmly believe that COA's should be helped even if they are the only family member seeking treatment.

Finally, it is important to realize that to work effectively with COA's the counselor should not have any "unfinished business" regarding alcoholism. If he does, he may become enmeshed in the family and ineffective in the helping process.

Concluding Comments

We hope this chapter has provided you with information about COA's and the necessary steps of intervention. It is important that helping professionals realize the magnitude of this problem and by focusing on and successfully treating COA's, the chain of addiction may be broken!

REFERENCES

Ackerman, R. J. (1983) *Children of alcoholics.* Holmes Beach, FL: Learning Publications, Inc.

Black, C. (1982) *It will never happen to me.* Denver: M.A.C.

Booz-Allen, & Hamilton, Inc. (1984) *An assessment of the needs of and resources for children of alcoholic parents.* Rockville, MD: National Institute on Alcohol Abuse and Alcoholism.

Brooks, C. (1981) *The secret everyone knows.* San Francisco: Operation Cork.

Deutsch, C. (1982) *Broken bottles broken dreams.* New York: Teachers College Press.

Ellis, A., & Harper, R. A. (1975) *A new guide to rational living.* Englewood Cliffs, NJ: Prentice-Hall.

Lawson, G., Peterson, J. S., & Lawson, A. (1983) *Alcoholism and the family.* Rockville, MD: Aspen Publications.

James, M., & Jongeward, D. (1971) *Born to win.* Reading, MA: Addison-Wesley.

Wegscheider, S. (1979) Children of alcoholics caught in family trap. *Focus on Alcohol and Drug Issues,* 2, 8.

Chapter 6

THE TRUANT CHILD

Linda F. Little and Irene C. Gafney

Each day in the United States, between two and three million children do not attend school. Since no national figures are available on the rate of truancy, it is unclear how many absent children are actually truant (Vance, 1985). For example, illness can be feigned, or parents may at times legitimize absences for their own needs or to protect children from experiencing punishment in the school setting.

Truancy, defined here as any unexcused absence from school, has in the past been conceptualized both in research and intervention efforts as lineally caused and single system focused (e.g. individual traits, family pathology, school ineffectiveness). By those with a psychodynamic orientation truancy is seen as arising from past events and trauma usually inflicted by the parents or resulting from biochemical imbalances, imperfect genes, or internal deficits in the child, and by those with a sociological orientation as due to environmental stresses and variables (Galloway, Ball & Seyd, 1981). In this chapter we will review these approaches to investigating the truancy problem, and present an alternate approach which conceptualizes truancy from a meta systemic or ecological perspective. A case study and intervention strategies suggested by such an approach are also presented.

The Literature Suggests . . .

Numerous studies have sought to link truancy to individual character or emotional problems. Amatu (1981) reported on several studies attempting to correlate truancy and conduct disorder; Ollendick (1979) investigated the association of truancy with anxiety, low intelligence, and poor behavioral adjustment; Nielson and Gerber (1979) linked truancy to delinquency, poor peer relations, and academic and behavior problems; while Emery, Weintraub and Neale (1972) correlated truancy with fighting, stealing and related delinquent activities.

Longitudinal studies have dealt with the long term effects of truancy upon the individual. Nielson and Gerber (1979) found adults who had been truant as children, experienced higher school dropout rates, drug use, criminal behavior and psychological problems in later life than non-truants, and Kandel, Raveis, and Kandel (1984) found higher cigarette use and lower general health in adults who had been truants. These studies focused upon the consequences of truancy employing a lineal causality model of reasoning and in effect extricating the individual from the environment.

Other studies, focusing on the environment of the truant child, have sought to link truancy to particular types of families and levels of family functioning, and have generated statistics on the demographics of truant families. Nielson and Gerber (1979) found that in 57% of truants' families one parent had not graduated from high school, and in 25%, neither parent had graduated; 78% of truant families had at least one other truant child; 76% of the families were experiencing multiple stresses at the time of truancy; 40% of parents of truants were separated and 41% had experienced a recent serious illness. Emery et al. (1982) found truancy associated with marital difficulty.

Attempts have been made to explore the problem of truancy from a single systems perspective by evaluating the interaction patterns that exist within truant families which might encourage the development of a symptom (e.g. truancy), and the symptom's maintenance. Amatu (1981) reported parents of truants less likely to become involved in or actively assist with their child's school work. Galloway, Ball and Seyd (1981) found parental apathy a characteristic of truants' parents, finding, in fact, many truants had the active consent of their parents to miss school. Amatu (1981) reported on a pervasive attitude among truants' parents that suggested truancy was necessary and unavoidable when there was a need in the home for the child's help. Little and Thompson (1980) found in self reports of parents of truant children that they were more overindulgent and overprotective and less accepting of their children than parents of non-truants, and Galloway (1983) found 80% of truants' parents were inadequate in controlling the behavior of their children.

Still attempting to deal with past or individual causes of truancy, many self-report studies hoped that the truants themselves could answer the question of why they do not attend school. Nielson and Gerber's (1979) study indicated that 73% of truant children disliked school and found no one in the school they could go to for help. In Reid's (1983) study, truants associated teachers with failure and conflict. Eaton's (1979) study found truants more dissatisfied with school staff than non truants. In Nielson and Gerber's (1979) study teachers were seen as unfriendly, authoritarian and unresponsive with 70% of truants viewing school as the major cause of their truancy, and 75% admitting that teachers were the worst aspect of school.

Reynolds (1974) shifted the focus from students' self reports of how school contributes to truancy to evaluating the school's role from a systemic perspective. He found that, when ability range and socioeconomic background of pupils were held constant, schools did vary dramatically in rates of truancy.

Reconceptualizing the Problem

To approach the problem of truancy effectively, a shift must be made from defining it as an individual, a family, or school problem to a perspective encompassing the entire ecology of the child as a continuously changing context of relationships between whole systems (Keeney, 1983). Of course each of these systems, family, school, and community has its own internal structure, rules, and roles, but it is in the person of the child that these independent systems come together (Aponte, 1976). Shifting to this more complex perspective new dimensions of the truancy problem emerge giving rise to new solutions.

Thus truancy leaps from an isolated bit of behavior to part of an interlocking sequence of behaviors between systems. In this approach we are drawing the boundary of truancy not only around the individual, family, or school, but around the individual and the relevant environment. In doing this, we reorient the very way we think about truancy from a view that someone, some system or some cause is to blame, to the view that the presence of the truant is vital for the maintenance of stability within /between/and among participating systems (Hoffman, 1981).

A Meta View: Systems Touching. To more fully understand the chains of behavior maintaining the truant behavior, it is helpful to consider the concept of homeostasis: "... sequences of behaviors... out of a finite repertory of possible behaviors are combined into different sequences, but leading to identical outcomes (Watzlawick, Weakland & Fisch, 1974 p. 17)." Each system assumes its role and takes its stance at problem resolution. It is as if each has been set in motion on a path with limited behavioral options, and the options are played out, regardless of the latest input, so that any changes are aborted by the system.

With the majority of literature on truancy focused on the family or individual as repository of the cause of problem behavior, it is not surprising that the school's response has been to view the child as a victim of an unresponsive family and a hostile environment. Rescue fantasies, attitudes of blame and recrimination, or the view that the family of the truant is having insurmountable problems for which there are no remedies, certainly none by the school, are common. Rarely do school administrators look within the school system for the contribution of the school to the truant behavior (Nielson & Gerber, 1979). The battle is felt to be lost once the student's truancy becomes persistent and habitual and a typical escalation of punishments is instituted against the child which range from changing teachers, visiting guidance counselors, or detention, to legal action and involvement of juvenile court (Gallaway et al., 1981; Nielson & Gerber, 1979; Reid, 1983). As punishment escalates and more of the same is seen as ineffective in dealing with the truancy, parents are contacted. But the attitudes each party brings to their meeting is predetermined. Parents, often school truants themselves, may become defensive and hostile to what is perceived by them as an inflexible and unreasonable attitude toward their child's truant behavior (Amatu, 1981; Emery et al., 1982; Galloway, 1983; Gallaway et al., 1981; Nielson & Gerber, 1979). Contacting the school might be perceived as risk taking for the parents, and if their attempts at intervention are ineffective, their already existing attitude of helplessness, hopelessness or hostility may become exaggerated. The school authorities experience these attitudes as uncaring behavior. Parents and school system are thus locked in conflict maintained by past experiences, histories, and exaggerated stereotypes. As each system sees only its position as important and struggles for power, an escalation of behavior occurs resulting in fixed and inflexible positions with each side scapegoating the other (Tittler & Cook, 1981). This results in further alienation and confrontation (Tucker & Dyson, 1976). In this atmosphere of recrimination and blame, the child takes on a position as power broker between adversaries, with communication between each system through the child (Haley, 1976). This role, a powerful one, exacts a price academically, emotionally, and physically (Tucker & Dyson, 1976). Because children may manifest symptomatic behaviors when placed between strongly competing systems where the adults adhere to greatly differing values and expectations, it is evident that a child's truancy may indeed become a function of the relationship of the adults within systems in conflict.

> **The Case of Judy, Mother, and the School.** When Mother sought the help of a family system's therapist, Judy had missed thirty days of school during that academic year. Mother, a single parent holding a professional position, had "tried everything" to influence Judy's school attendance. At first, she allowed Judy to stay home, thinking she would get bored, lonely, and want to return to school. Mother allowed Judy to sleep late on mornings she refused to attend school, and then delivered Judy to school when she felt ready to attend.

In this example, Mother is in a covert alliance with Judy, helping her miss school, she is the "enabler," the "co-truant." Also illustrated is a power reversal in the family. It is Judy deciding when and if she will attend school.

> School personnel, who at first were accepting of Mother's solutions to Judy's transition to the new school and new classroom, began to apply pressure for regular school attendance. At a conference requested by the school counselor Mother was persuaded to take a forceful approach to alleviating the absences.

The boundaries between systems begin to blur as school personnel advise Mother. This defines Mother as ineffective, in need of the school's help to parent successfully. Mother is in a "one-down" position. At this point the power balance between the two systems is unequal and dysfunctional.

> For several days Mother used the help of a strong male friend to physically force Judy into school attendance. Struggling all the way, they dressed Judy, carried her to the car, locked her in the back seat, and carried her into the classroom where, prior to their leaving, she repeatedly vomited on her desk and the floor surrounding it.

Although Mother takes charge of the child, assuming her normal position of power in the family hierarchy, it is under the direction of the school. Mother also receives the secondary gain of help and support of her male friend.

> When Judy's strong reaction to forced school attendance did not abate, Mother decided that she was not going to "go through that charade again." The school was told that, "someone else would have to drag Judy to school." Mother had quit and was no longer

going to be responsible. Judy was more determined not to return to school.

By not forcing the child to remain in school, Mother's position collapses. She abdicates her power to the child. At the same time the school is put in a powerless position, unable to affect the truant behavior. The power between both systems has been equalized by the truancy. Both adult systems are in a helpless position and the child has claimed the power in both.

> The "someone else" who would have to force Judy's school attendance appeared in the form of a court official with a subpoena, making Judy's school attendance a legal issue, and the mother's failure to deliver Judy to school a punishable act.

The school begins to escalate its response, blaming mother and placing responsibility totally upon her.

> Judy was a physically mature sixth grader, who had gained 30 pounds over the course of the academic year. She was bright, verbal, assertive, sophisticated, and determined not to live in the mid-south town to which her mother's job had brought them. She was not going to make friends with the "stupid southern kids who were still playing jacks and learning stuff she knew as a third grader in southern California." She was angry, and had no intention of budging from her position.

Judy's stance is a metaphor for mother's position. Her dramatic school difficulties are helping mother avoid facing job and transfer decisions.

> Mother's venom about the family's current living arrangements was equally as strong as Judy's. She had never dealt with such "inflexible, rigid people" as the school officials she had contacted. In her opinion they cared nothing about individual needs of children and parents, and were teaching sub-standard academic material. "Judy could miss a whole year of that damn school," she spewed, "and would not be a day behind any of those immature brats she has to be with in class."

Mother gives conflicting messages to the child: Go to school—The school is worthless. Mother and Judy are in a coalition against the "sub-standard" school.

> If only she had known the cultural differences she would be faced with, she would never have been lured to relocate from friends and family by the promising professional opportunities her new position offered. Mother was clear. If Judy's behavior continued,

she would leave her position and return home to less promising professional opportunities, but the support of friends and a school system that knew how to work with kids.

Mother's leaving her job is a metaphor for Judy's leaving school. Judy's school refusal becomes functional behavior that allows mother to return to family and friends and a secure less demanding job.

> Judy's teacher was angry as was Judy's principal. They had been quite patient with these newcomers, and had "bent over backwards" to facilitate Judy's adjustment to the school. The teacher had planned a party to welcome Judy to the classroom. Judy was not impressed and refused to join any of the celebrations. The teacher had prepared lesson plans and get well cards. With Judy's repeated absences, arriving in the middle of the morning, and creating scenes that needed to be cleaned up, the teacher had been increasingly "put out by the family's demanding special treatment." She was convinced Mother just needed to be more firm and consistent in her demands that Judy attend school, and stop treating the child like royalty.

The teacher puts herself in a position to advise and judge mother, unbalancing power between systems and blurring boundaries. She takes no responsibility for maintaining the truancy problem.

> The school personnel came to believe that both Judy and her mother held condescending attitudes toward the school and the staff. They became determined not to push their limits in further attempts to accommodate. If regular school attendance was not forthcoming, Judy would be retained in the sixth grade. The principal announced, "This is war. They'll do it our way or they won't do it."

War on the Boundaries. Unclear hierarchies within systems often reflect power struggles between systems. Bowen, Haley, and Minuchin among others, use the triangle as a way to conceptualize power in family system interactions (Hoffman, 1981). The triangle represents the way communication between two persons in dysfunctional systems will involve a third. Just as Bateson (1971) believed that two persons in a dysfunctional system could not communicate without involving a third, it can be seen that two systems in conflict bring in a third system as a power tactic in what Bateson refers to as "the infinite dance of shifting coalitions (p. 241)."

In the case of truancy, a natural triangle emerges with power and hierarchy issues clearly paramount. To exemplify, the parents are naturally more powerful then the child in the family hierarchy. The child with problem behavior is defined as needing help and therefore is in a "one down" position to the parents. But, as the parents attempt to get the child to return to school and their attempts fail, the child claims the power in the hierarchy of the family system (Madanes, 1980). As provider of education the school system is in the power position to the child in the school hierarchy. The child's task is to follow the directions of the school and thus become an educated person. Yet, as the school hierarchy, i.e. first the teacher, then the guidance counselor, then the principal, fails to get the child to attend school a shift occurs in who holds the power. It is the child who rises to the position of power and the school is placed in a helpless position. In these ways, the disturbances in hierarchical organization in both systems result in the maintenance of truant behavior in the child. The child is in a superior position in both systems and protects each system from assuming a superior position vis a vis the other.

When the parents are contacted by the school, already in place on one level of communication is what Bateson termed a complimentary relationship which exists when one individual communicates submissive inferiority and the other dominates. On another level exists a symmetrical relationship of escalating competition for control (Hoffman, 1981). For example, parents in a school conference may respond with deference and verbal commitment to follow through with the school's intervention plan. But privately in the presence of the child the parents are resistant and hostile about the plan, maligning and deprecating the school's authority. Thus the parents give incongruous messages to the child. The overt message is to go to school and succeed. But if the child returns to school, the child is in the position of betraying the parents, shifting the power and placing the school in the dominant power position in the hierarchy between systems. The covert message is, "its them against us." By not going to school the child sides with the parents against the school. In either case, the child loses.

The school gives incongruous messages as well. Overtly, the child receives the message, "listen to your parents," but covertly the school implies that the truant's family is irresponsible, to blame, uncooperative. Thus, the child is placed in a bind. Were the child to attend school all the time he/she shifts the power to the school system and places the family in an inferior position. Should the child not attend school at all the power shifts to the family which feels the school is intolerant, authoritative, distant. The child solves the dilemma of inconsistent messages by inconsistent behavior—(Haley, 1980; Madanes, 1980) attending school at times and not attending at times, thereby disqualifying both systems and ascending to the superior position in both.

A Quest for Peace: Interventions

The act of truancy keeps the two adult systems in a symmetrical relationship in which no participant is to emerge victorious. The child, by choosing truant behavior, is maintaining loyalty to both systems, and is demanding that both of these systems so important to his/her functioning stay involved. Truancy accomplishes equality between the adult systems, a desired goal which needs to be achieved via a less harmful solution.

At this stage in problem formation, the solution does not rest within the three systems, but must occur on a meta level with the aid of an outside person or team of persons capable of conceptualizing problem formation, maintenance and resolution from a systemic perspective. The family therapist must expand his/her scope to identify the system as the child's relevant ecology not from within the family, but within this wider frame. The meta goal is to find a way that the school and the family can share decision making about the life of the child without the child being sacrificed or disloyal to either system. This requires a shift in the interaction between the two adult systems from an emphasis on competition to one of sharing a common goal.

The educational and personal development of the truant child. Positive reframe of each system's involvement must occur from the onset of intervention. Each is involved because of caring concern and good will. Even though each believes that he/she knows what is best for the child with little regards for the other system taken into accord, each in his/her own way is asking the child to choose. The choice, school or family, is a significant one with far reaching ramifications for the child's life. The school and the family, while recognized in their good will, must be convinced to work together for the good of the child.

Aponte (1976) has written most eloquently on intervention strategies with school related problems from an ecological perspective. He suggests that, since the school personnel usually initiate the family—therapist contact, all three systems should be included in therapy from the onset. School officials may react to such a proposal with surprise, but are usually quite willing to participate. It is suggested that the meeting be held at the school, that a representative from each level of the school's hierarchy (i.e. teacher, counselor and principal), both parents (when appropriate), the truant child, and siblings who still live at home be present. The parents and school personnel are represented as resources, and the focus is kept on problem resolution rather than casting blame.

Each system is informally evaluated, and plans are made to intervene where relevant, but the move to single system focus is made under the umbrella of the total system. Table 1 provides a checklist for individual system and meta system analysis.

Restoration of the Boundaries. Often when the family becomes intensely involved in solving problems related to the education of their child, the relationship between parents and school personnel becomes so intense that it spills over into all aspects of the educational process. Notes get sent home with "happy faces" indicating that Judy was in school and was on task in math. When "frowning faces" are sent home or no notes arrive, the parent involved in the systemic struggle is on the phone wanting to know why, who was involved, and what happened next. The amount of contact between family and school becomes exaggerated and dysfunctional. At some point it is important to reestablish boundaries around the school-child system, to disengage the overly involved parent, and to reestablish the responsibility for in-class education with the classroom teacher. The mere fact that stickers are given out and communication is so frequent sets the child apart from other children, and reinforces the impression that normal behavior is the exception. Containment of responsibility for in-class behavior to school personnel is strengthening for all involved. The parents can acknowledge their child's own responsibility for self when not in their presence. Parents can set the mood for the parent-child relationship based on their own experiences and remove themselves from the frustrating position of having to punish or reward behavior that occurs outside of their purview. And by disengaging, they are acknowledging that they trust the school personnel to use their own judgment to educate and control their child's behaviors. Equally the boundary may need to be tightened around the parent—child system.

Implications for School and Mental Health Professionals

A major mistake often made by school personnel (and intervening professionals) when children have problems in school is to act as if the parents do not value schooling. They have literature support suggesting that parents of truants were truant themselves, and that they usually hold jobs with lower status than their education warrants (Nielson & Gerber, 1979). With this attitude the likelihood of successful resolution to the truancy problem is bleak, and puts all involved in a defeatest position from the onset. **Most parents want their children to be successful in school and maintain respect for their parents while doing so.** If successful resolutions are to occur school officials need to hold the basic assumption that a major goal of the family is the child's success in school. The family might be awkward in communicating their value of education, or might seem defensive if the educational establishment defines them as inadequate or their child as deviant, but value education they do. Acknowledgment of this assumption should be made overt to the family and the child.

Families need to be respected as the powerful entities which they are. Any time they are demeaned, repressed, or insulted by the school, the child's education is put in jeopardy. **Acknowledging that the parents and the school are a team, working together to get the child to school and educate him/her while there is the frame that must hold the three systems together.**

Beginnings

Any one approach offering solutions to so pervasive, persistent and multi-systemic a problem as truancy must by its very definition be a limited perspective. In practice all divisions are arbitrary and must be inextricably involved in any solution that results in change.

The problem of truancy does exist and it is not being solved today by traditional approaches. The scope of this paradigm addresses all systems that impinge on the child from a political perspective. It highlights the powerful struggle going on between systems, one that must not be ignored, as a way to resolve truancy and help all systems move on.

Our task is one of restoring power and balance to the adult systems and freeing the child from his/her triangulated role, while simultaneously addressing dysfunctions within single systems that can be metaphors for the inter-system struggle. This is a phenomenal task involving widely differing individuals, systems, and struggles. But the rewards are splendid because the goal is clear and within our grasp. This is, therefore, not a summation, a conclusion, or an end. But a suggestion for how to begin.

Intervention Checklist Focused on Problem Resolution

Child

Authority defying at home __ at school __

Unacceptable behavior
  limited to school setting __
  in both home and school settings __

Stressors external to school __ internal to school __ neither __
  both __
  When present in classroom
  problematic behavior __ well functioning __ withdrawn __

Academic functioning
  not successful __ adequate __ with great success __
  Previous retentions? __ If yes, why __
  History of school success/failure __

Major emotion(s)
  angry __ anxious __ depressed __ shy __ withdrawn __ other __

Role(s) in classroom
  leader __ follower __ isolate __ trouble maker __ other __

History of Antisocial acts? __ Drug use? __

Extracurricular activities __ School Involvement __

Interests __ Strengths __

The Act of Truancy

Truant alone __ with others __

Onset (related to what life events, developmental shifts, developmental tasks)?

Duration of truancy: acute __ chronic __ sporadic __

Academic subject related __ Teacher related __

School atmosphere (e.g., level of violence, staff/children relationships)

How time is spent when truant? Signifies a need for __.

History of illnesses?

The Family

Family structure
  rigid __ chaotic __ supportive __ distant __ uninvolved __

Education held in high __ low __ esteem.

Family models for conflict resolution __.

Family history of truancy __ who __ how handled __?

Family history of educational achievement __

Quality of truant's relationship with mother __ father __ other family members __

How does school absence reflect the relationship? A family metaphor for __.

Support systems of the family? Family's relation to extended family? Family's relationship with larger community?

Are parents in agreement about number of days it is acceptable to miss school? How truancy should be handled? The view of the child's behavior (bad, sick, unavoidable etc.)?

What are parents' fantasies about the child's functioning in adulthood? Are they positive? Are they in agreement?

Who advises the family about how the family should function? Can that person be included in therapy?

How has each parent dealt with truancy in the past? (Consider these to be failed solutions which should not be replicated.)

How would the family make contact with external support systems were the truancy problem to no longer exist?

Peers

Peer phobic at home __ at school __

Names of friends, and nature and quality of relationship

School attendance records of friends

Which friends would support child's success in school?

School

Does one teacher/principal defend __ rescue __ scapegoat __ child?

How have school personnel dealt with truancy in past?

Is there a conflict or difference of opinion among school personnel about how the child/family is viewed, how well the child functions, or how the situation should be handled?

What is the quality of the school's relationship with the child's parents?

What is the degree of respect demonstrated toward child and family by school personnel?

Does any school personnel hope to "reform" the family?

Do they believe that there is a solution for the problem?

What are specific interventions which have been tried by individual personnel? Are any extreme? Are parents and/or other school personnel aware of these interventions? (Consider these to be failed solutions to the problem which should not be replicated.)

Meta System

How is the truancy problem perpetuated? The school does __ the family does __ the child does __ peers do __

Does the family/child/school have any power left without the truancy issue?

How can contact between the family and the school be maintained when the truancy problem is resolved?

Does the family know the school's expectations of the child/family? Does the school know the family's expectations of the child? Are they perceived as reasonable __ or unreasonable?

What are the stereotypes that each system holds about each other system? How do these contribute to the truancy problem?

Which system has the most to lose if the child returns to school?

REFERENCES

Amatu, H. I. (1981). Family motivated truancy. *International Journal of Psychology, 16*(2). 111–117.

Aponte, H. J. (1976). The family-school interview: An ecostructional approach. *Family Process, 15*, 303–311.

Bateson, G. (1972). *Steps to an ecology of mind.* New York: Ballentine Books.

Compher, J. V. (1982). Parent-school-child system: Triadic assessment and intervention. *Social Casework the Journal of Contemporary Social Work, 53*, 415–423.

Eaton, M. J. (1979). A study of some factors associated with early identification of persistent absenteeism. *Educational Review, 31*(3), 233–241.

Emery, R., Weintraub, S., & Neale, J. M. (1982). Effects of marital discord on the school behavior of children of schizophrenic, affectively disordered, and normal parents. *Journal of Abnormal Child Psychology, 10*(2), 215–228.

Galloway, D. (1983). Research note: Truants and other absentee students. *Journal of Child Psychology & Psychiatry & Allied Disciplines, 24*(4), 607–611.

Galloway, D., Ball, T., & Seyd, R. (1981). School attendance following legal or administrative action for unauthorized absence. *Educational Review, 33*(1), 53–65.

Haley, J. (1980). *Leaving home.* New York: McGraw Hill.

Haley, J. (1976). *Problem solving therapy.* San Francisco: Jossey-Bass, Inc.

Hoffman, L. (1981a). *Foundations of family therapy.* New York: Basic Books.

Hoffman, L. (1981b). Therapeutic paradox: Restraint from change: Techniques in family therapy. (Cassette Recording) New York: The Guilford Press.

Kandel, D. B., Raveis, V. H., & Kandel, P. I. (1984). Continuity in discontinuities: Adjustment in young adulthood of former school absentees. *Youth & Society, 15*(3), 325–352.

Keeney, B. P. (1983). *Aesthetics of change.* New York: The Guilford Press.

Little, L. F., & Thompson, R. (1983). Truancy: How parents and teachers contribute. *The School Counselor,* 285–290.

Madanes, C. (1980). Marital therapy when a symptom is presented by a spouse. *International Journal of Family Therapy, 2,* 120–136.

Mandanes, C. The prevention of rehospitalization of adolescents and young adults. *Family Process, 19,* 179–191.

Mazza, J. (1984). Symptom utilization in strategic therapy. *Family Process, 23,* 487–500.

Nielson, A., & Gerber, D. (1979). Psychosocial aspects of truancy in early adolescence. *Adolescense, 54*(14), 313–326.

Ollendick, D. G. (1979). Some characteristics of absentee students in grade four. *Psychological Reports, 44,* 294.

Reid, K. (1983). Differences between the perception of persistent school absentees toward parents and teachers. *Educational Studies, 9*(3), 211–219.

Reynolds, D. (1974). "Some do, some don't." *London Times,* Educational Supplement, 21.

Tittler, B. I., & Cook, V. J. (1981). Relationships among family, school, and clinic: Toward a systems approach. Journal of *Clinical Child Psychology, 10*(3), 184–187.

Tucker, B. Z., & Dyson, E. (1976). The family and the school: Utilizing human resources to promote learning. *Family Process,* 125–143.

Chapter 7

THE MENTALLY RETARDED CHILD

David L. Fenell, James E. Martin, and Dennis E. Mithaug

School systems in the United States, for the most part, have not developed programs to assist students who are mentally retarded into employment opportunities that are commensurate with their abilities (Wehman, Kregel & Barcus, 1985). Schools today assist these students in developing necessary living skills. However, little focus is placed on what will happen to the student who is mentally retarded after he or she leaves the public school system.

Follow-up research on the employment of persons who are mentally retarded is not encouraging. A recent study by the U. S. Commission on Civil Rights (1983) reported that between 50 and 75 percent of all persons who are mentally retarded are not employed. In Colorado, individuals who are mentally retarded fail to make the transition from school to full-time, non-sheltered employment positions and independent living arrangements. Mithaug, Horiuchi and Fanning (1985), in a statewide follow up of former Colorado special education students, reported that two to three years after leaving school 64% of the young adults interviewed continued to live with and depend on their families for support. At the time of the survey, two-thirds of the group were working (including sheltered and non-sheltered positions), but only one-third had full time jobs. About half of those working made less than the state minimum wage. Finally, studies in Vermont (Hasazi, Preskill, Gordon & Collins, 1982) support the finding of unemployment, underemployment and concomitant dependency of the individual who is mentally retarded on his/her family and other external support systems.

The lack of adequate preparation for the transition from school to work of individuals who are mentally retarded has been noted in Public Law 98-199 (Education for Handicapped Children). This law recognizes that "effective programming for youth who are mentally retarded to aid in transition from school to the workplace is lacking. Further, because such programs are lacking, youth who are mentally retarded are likely to become unemployed and dependent on society."

Clearly, the studies mentioned above as well as the initiatives of Public Law 98-199 highlight the problem of transition of students who are mentally retarded from the school to the workplace. For transition and competitive job placement to occur the cooperative efforts of many interacting agencies and organizations are needed. The activities required to prepare a student who is mentally retarded for placement are many and complex requiring coordination and cooperation. The school systems that elect to prepare students who are mentally retarded for transition will need to develop innovative curricula focusing on survival skills in the workplace and providing experiences that relate to competitive employment (Gifford, Rusch, Martin & White, 1984). Potential work sites will need to be contacted to coordinate training and placement opportunities. School or agency personnel will be needed to provide supervision for the student who is mentally retarded while he or she learns the duties associated with the job. Finally, and perhaps most important, families with children who are mentally retarded will need to be educated and supported while their son or daughter is prepared for transition and placed in competitive employment (Brickey & Campbell, 1981; Brickey, Campbell, & Browning, 1985).

While all aspects of transition are essential to its success, this chapter will focus primarily on the important role school personnel play in the education and preparation of the parents of students who are mentally retarded for transition and placement of their son or daughter. Those who seek more detailed information about all aspects of transitions are referred to a comprehensive volume edited by Wehman and Hill (1985).

Interventions

School teachers, special educators, school psychologists, social workers and counselors are concerned with helping each student reach his or her potential. All too often however, students who are mentally retarded have not been able to continue their personal and career development after graduation from school because of lack of opportunities and lack of training programs to prepare them for the few career opportunities that did exist. The more severely mentally retarded students are traditionally prepared to work or function in their home or in sheltered environments. Many special educators believe that even students with severe mental·

retardation have abilities that would permit the placement of these individuals in the competitive work environments (Wehman & Hill, 1985; Rusch & Mithaug, 1980).

Programs supporting transition from school to competitive employment for individuals who are mentally retarded are currently few in number (Wehman & Hill, 1985). However, support for such programs is increasing. The following benefits can be expected from a program designed to facilitate transition:

(1) the person who is mentally retarded can be expected to develop increased levels of self-esteem and confidence as he or she successfully meets job responsibilities.

(2) the family will have decreased responsibility for the care and welfare of the person who is mentally retarded. This will permit a more traditional lifestyle for the family.

(3) the employer will benefit as properly trained workers who are mentally retarded may perform as well as non-mentally retarded workers and in some cases may be more dependable employees (Martin, Rusch, Tines, Brulle & White, 1985).

(4) society benefits by having the person who is mentally retarded as a productive taxpaying member of the workforce rather than as a drain on the financial support systems designed to assist citizens who are mentally retarded.

These benefits of an effective transition program are significant and would seem to clearly indicate the value of such programs. However, many of the parents of students who are mentally retarded are unable or unwilling to be fully supportive of the transition program for a variety of reasons. Wehman and Hill (1985) have stated that it is virtually impossible to place students who are mentally retarded in competitive employment programs without the full cooperation of parents. A study conducted in Virginia by Hill, Seyfarth, Orelove, Wehman & Banks (1985) with the parents and guardians of 291 individuals who are mentally retarded demonstrated that: (a) parents generally did not favor improvement in working conditions (increased wages, responsibilities, etc.), and (b) parents were satisfied with current vocational placements for sons and daughters. These parental attitudes could be based on several factors. First, parents of persons who are mentally retarded may not be aware of the potential their son or daughter poses for successful competitive employment. Second, parents may fear that their son or daughter may be mistreated or harmed in some way if removed from sheltered placement.

Finally, parents may be concerned about the changes that will occur in their own lives as a result of their son or daughter becoming a taxpayer rather than a tax burden. Parents may believe that such a transition will adversely affect the level of financial support received for their child and increase the family's financial responsibility for support of the son or daughter who is mentally retarded.

The discrepancy between the goals and objectives of professionals and parent concerning the placement of persons who are mentally retarded in competitive or supported employment indicates the need for a clearer relationship and dialogue between parents and professionals. If transition and competitive placement are to occur, parent support is critical. Thus, school personnel, especially school counselors, special educators, and school social workers will need to begin dialogue with the family of the student who is mentally retarded clarifying and explaining the advantages of transitional programming and competitive placement for their son or daughter and for the family.

Counseling skills need to be developed by school counselors, special education teachers and other school personnel that will be effective in working with parents. Many counselor preparation programs offer courses specifically designed to assist school personnel in working with family problems (Fenell & Hovestadt, in press). The following specific recommendations will be useful in working with parents toward transition and competitive employment:

Meet With Both Parents. When attempting to communicate with a family it is most beneficial to meet the parental unit. If the family consists of two parents, then both mother and father should attend the initial meetings (Minuchin, 1974; Napier & Whitaker, 1978). Both parents must understand and support the program for it to succeed. If one parent undermines the program, it may block all efforts toward competitive employment of the son or daughter. Working with both parents permits the professional to assess attitudes of each and work with the concerns of both persons. Some school professionals become anxious when dealing with both parents. They may feel outnumbered or intimidated by the strength of the couple. This anxiety will decrease as experience is gained in working with couples. Additionally, communicating with both parents will eliminate confusion and indecision as the professional will be able to speak directly with each parent thus eliminating the frequently problematic technique of sending messages through one parent to the other.

Join With the Parents. Before any attempt is made to present the benefits of transition and competitive employment to the parents the professional must join or establish a trusting relationship with each parent (Minuchin, 1974). This is most easily accomplished by listening carefully to each parent's concerns about the son or daughter and providing support and understanding regarding those concerns. Once the couple believe that the professional understands their concerns, they will be more ready to trust the professional and consider the ideas presented. If the professional is not able to join with the parents in a trusting relationship, further progress will be most difficult (Minuchin, 1974).

Discuss the Abilities and Potential Abilities of the Student Who is Mentally Retarded. This may be a sensitive time in the meeting because parents often have a rigid perception of what their son or daughter can and cannot do. Frequently parents will underestimate the capabilities of son or daughter who is mentally retarded (Zetlin & Turner, 1985). The professional must listen carefully to the parents' assessment of their son or daughter and communicate an awareness that these descriptions are accurate from the parents' perspective. At the same time, the professional must tactfully but clearly describe ways the student's behavior may exceed or differ from that described by the parents. A caution is in order here. If the professional attempts to convince the parents of the son's or daughter's potential, a stand-off may occur. The professional must help the parents expand their concept of the child's abilities without direct confrontation. Often it is useful to present an analogy that the parents can relate to in their own families where their behavior was limited by expectations of their own parents. For instance, the school professional might ask, "Was there ever anything that you knew you were capable of doing successfully that your parents did not believe you could do?" "How did this make you feel?" "What did you want to do?" Another useful way to help the parents expand their awareness is to use the analogy of the glass that is half full or half empty. The professional clearly communicates to the parents that the mentally retarded son or daughter has many limitations. However, all too often it is possible to get stuck looking at only the limitations (glass half-empty). When the family gets stuck looking at limitations they may forget to look at the strengths of the handicapped member (glass half-full).

Once the parents have considered these possibilities the professional may then lead them toward an examination of the strengths of the youth who is mentally retarded. When the parents are able to accurately observe and comment on the strengths of their son or daughter, further consideration of the possibility of transition and competitive employment is possible.

Explain the Transition Program and its Goals and Benefits to the Parents. Once the parents are able to view the strengths of their son or daughter who is mentally retarded, it will be much easier for them to consider the possibility of a transition program leading toward competitive employment. The advantages of the transition program should be explained to the parents in terms of the following benefits: (a) the student who is mentally retarded may develop an enhanced self concept; (b) the parents and family may experience a more traditional lifestyle; (c) the employer will gain an effective employee; and (d) the person who is mentally retarded will contribute to society rather than depend on society for support.

When presented with these advantages, the parents are most likely to express concern in two areas. First, because parents have for many years been heavily involved in the care of their offspring, they may have developed a stable family behavior-pattern centering around the son or daughter who is mentally retarded. To suggest that this stable pattern may change through competitive employment could be a mixed message to the parents. The parents may be pleased that their son or daughter will be more self-sufficient but remain anxious about how the family will function if the child who is mentally retarded is not present as a central focus point. Rarely will the family consciously recognize and identify the above as a concern. However, the professional must be aware that this issue can be a powerful force on the family regardless of whether it operates at a conscious or unconscious level. By being sensitive to this issue and understanding the parents' concern, the professional is more likely to help the parents through this potential impasse.

The second area of potential resistance concerns the economic self-sufficiency of the son or daughter who is mentally retarded. If the son or daughter becomes self-sufficient, government support payments to the family may terminate. Thus, families may regard competitive employment with fair wages as a potential negative factor because it would stop support payments. Again, the professional may be most helpful by listening to parent concerns in this area and assisting parents in realistically assessing the effects of the loss of government support if their son or daughter who is mentally retarded were competitively employed. The professional needs to emphasize to parents that support will continue until the individual is successfully placed and competitively employed. Families who have struggled to work out a system of care for their son or daughter based in part on government support payments will be understandably reluctant to give up this support and change a system that is working for them. The professional and parents, working together, must consider the pros and cons for the person who is mentally retarded and the family of all courses of action. Hopefully, many parents will recognize the benefits of competitive placement and support this process for their son or daughter.

Begin Discussions With Parents as Early as Possible and Keep the Parents Actively Involved in the Program. As mentioned earlier, parental support of the transitional program is the key to success. Professionals should contact parents as early as possible to gain their support. If parents begin thinking about transition and competitive employment when their child is young, it will not come as a shock later. Once parent support is obtained, it is a mistake to believe the work with the parents is finished. Regular meetings with the parents are necessary to apprise them of their son's or daughter's progress and to reassure them of the professional's continuing belief that competitive employment is feasible. Without continuing parent involvement it is possible that support for the transitional program may be withdrawn at times when the family experiences a crisis. The professional, in addition to scheduling regular meetings with the parents, needs to be available for crisis intervention and to talk with the parents at other times when issues and concerns arise.

Implications For School Professionals

For transition programming and placement of individuals who are mentally retarded into competitive or supported employment to be successful, parent involvement and support are critical. In order to gain parental support and involvement, school professionals must demonstrate to parents that transitional programming is in the best interest of both the student who is mentally retarded and the family. This is frequently a difficult task because competitive placement of the son or daughter who is mentally retarded is usually a concept that is foreign to the parent and because of potential loss of government support for the family.

Through the use of the suggestions presented in this chapter, school professionals will be better able to help parents become supportive of transitional programming for their son or daughter who is mentally retarded. However, not all parents will support the program. Professionals are cautioned to spend only an appropriate amount of time working with reluctant parents. It can become counterproductive to spend too much time and effort with reluctant parents. Work with resistant parents becomes especially problematic when time is being taken from working with parents who are supportive of the program. Professionals are more likely to educate reluctant parents through demonstrating a successful transition program with students and parents who are supportive. If the program is successful, reluctant parents will become interested and be more inclined to support transition for their own handicapped son or daughter.

REFERENCES

Brickey, M. P. & Campbell, K. M. (1981). Fast food employment for moderately and mildly retarded adults: The McDonald's project. *Mental Retardation, 19,* 113–116.

Brickey, M. P., Campbell, K. M. & Browning, L. J. (1985). Five year follow-up of sheltered workshop employees in competitive jobs. *Mental Retardation,* 23, (2), 67–73.

Fenell, D. L. & Hovestadt, A. H. (In press). Family therapy as a profession or professional specialty: Implications for training. *Journal of Psychotherapy and the Family.*

Gifford, J. L. Rusch, F. R., Martin, J. E., & White, D. M. (1984). Autonomy and adaptability in work behavior of retarded clients. In N. R. Ellis & Norman W. Bray (Eds.) *International Review of Research in Mental Retardation,* New York: Academic Press.

Hasazi, S., Preskil, H., Gordon, L., Collins, M. (1982). *Factors associated with the employment status of handicapped youth.* Paper presented at American Educational Research Association, New York, N. Y.

Hill, J. W., Seyfarth, J., Orelove, F., Wehman, P., & Banks, P. D. (1985). Parent/guardians attitudes toward the working conditions of their mentally retarded children. In P. Wehman & J. W. Hill (Eds.), *Competitive employment for persons with mental retardation: From research to practice.* Richmond, VA: Virginia Commonwealth University.

Martin, J. E., Rusch, F. R., Tines, J. J., Brulle, A. R., White, D. M. (1985). Work attendance in competitive employment: Comparison between employees who are non-handicapped and those who are mentally retarded. *Mental Retardation,* 23, 142–147.

Minuchin, S. (1984) *Families and family therapy.* Cambridge, MA: Harvard University Press.

Mithaug, D., Horiuchi, C. N. & Fanning, P. N. (1985). A report of the Colorado statewide follow-up survey of special education students. *Exceptional Children, 51,* 397–404.

Napier, A. Y. & Whitaker, C. A. (1978). *The family crucible.* New York: Harper Row.

Rusch, F. & Mithaug, D. (1980) *Vocational training for mentally retarded adults.* Champaign, IL; Research Press.

U.S. Commission on Civil Rights (1983). *Attitudes toward the handicapped.* Washington, DC.

Wehman, P. & Hill, J. W. (1985). *Competitive employment for persons with mental retardation: from research to practice.* Richmond VA: Virginia Commonwealth University.

Wehman, P. & Hill, J. W. (1982) Preparing severely and profoundly handicapped students to enter less restrictive environments. *Journal of Association of Severely Handicapped, 7* (1), 33–39.

Wehman, P., Kregel, J. & Barcus, J. M. (1985). School to work: A vocational transition model for handicapped youth. In P. Wehman and J. W. Hill (Eds.) *Competitive employment for persons with mental retardation: From research to practice.* Richmond, VA: Virginia Commonwealth University.

Wehman, P., Kregel, J. & Seyfarth, J. (1985). What is the employment outlook for young adults with mental retardation after leaving school? In P. Wehman and J. W. Hill (Eds.), *Competitive employment for persons with mental retardation: From research to practice.* Richmond, VA., Virginia Commonwealth University.

Zetlin, A. G. & Turner, J. L. (1985) Transition from adolescence to adulthood: Perspectives of mentally retarded individuals and their families. *American Journal of Mental Deficiency, 84,* (6), 570–579.

Chapter 8

THE CHILD UNDER STRESS

DENNIS M. PELSMA

The subject of stress and the effects of stress on children has been an increasing area of interest for counselors and educators (Chandler, 1983; Dobson, 1980; Elkind, 1981; Postman, 1982; Rutler, 1981). Concerning stress(ors) and the child's ability to cope with stress some basic (thus far untested) assumptions can be made. These assumptions are as follows:

1. Children encounter stress as do adults and that school represents a major source of stress for students.
2. Each child will react to stressors of life (school) in a unique and individual way.
3. A typical pattern of reacting to or coping with stress can be identified.
4. Specific educational and counseling approaches or interventions are more (or less) effective with different coping styles.
5. The goal of counselors and educators is to allow the child an expression of his/her coping style while at the same time encouraging more effective (creative) ways of coping.

The school coping styles model presented in this paper was originally developed by Moore (1982). The model was derived from the research and theoretical formulations found in the area of conceptual systems (Harvey, Hunt, & Schroder, 1961), family systems (Olson, Sprenkle, & Russell, 1979) and learning styles (Rosenberg, 1968). Observations of behavior and/or teacher behavior ratings usually yields a specific pattern of behavior and characteristic way of approaching various learning experiences (stressors) in the classroom.

The family system appears to play a major role in the growth, development and coping of its members. Children learn to adapt and adjust to the world primarily through contact with the family. In describing family functioning, Olson, Sprenkle, and Russell (1979) integrated many of the diverse concepts of family literature in the development of their circumplex model. This circumplex model identifies two dimensions of family interaction: Family **cohesion** and family **adaptability**. Family cohesion represents the emotional separateness vs. connectiveness of family members. Family adaptability represents familial reactions to situational or developmental stress, flexibility vs. amount of structure. Combining these two dimensions provides 16 types of marital and family systems. The concepts related to each of these dimensions are defined elsewhere (Olson, et al., 1979) and the use of the model for clinical diagnosis and assessing treatment outcome has been supported in numerous studies (Fisher, Giblin, & Hoopes, 1982; Fisher & Sprenkle, 1978; Russell, 1979).

Definitions of School Coping Styles are as follows:

1. A COPING STYLE is a child's predictable pattern of behavior when confronted with a stressor.
2. COPING STYLES are similar to learning styles in that they are the "result of our hereditary equipment, our particular past life experiences, and the demands of our present environment." (Kolb, 1984, p. 76)
3. A COPING STYLE emerges as the child tries to solve conflicts in the family, with friends, and at school.

With an understanding of the child's characteristic way of approaching stress, counselors and teachers are able to provide experiences which serve to encourage creative responding.

The model consists of two dimensions. The first dimension represents an orientation to **People** versus an orientation to **Rules**. The second represents a continuum ranging from **Activity** to **Stability**. Although each child can be viewed as having parts of each of these dimensions there evolves over time a particular orientation which emerges and takes dominance over the others. The resulting quadrants identify five distinct individual styles of coping behavior. The four quadrants represent four styles: Power-Dominance, Undisciplined-Impulsive, Anxious-Acceptance and Rigid-Inhibited. The fifth style, Creative-Responsive, is drawn in the central region (circle) for comparison purposes and is designed to correlate with Olson's healthy·family functioning.

Behavioral descriptions of each parent and related student coping style are described by Moore (1982) as follows:

Power-Dominance Style

Parent

A disengaged parent leads to a "power-oriented" child. The parents world is separated and lacks structure. Respect comes from being able to create impact on one's environment. This parent:

1. Encourages independence to the extreme where home can be one of the loneliest places to be.
2. Encourages members to do their own thing, which leads to family members spending their time separately.
3. Speaks their mind without considering how it will affect others.
4. Has difficulty understanding or being aware of what other family members are thinking and feeling.
5. Talks a lot, but nothing much gets done in the family because each member is talking about their own thing and there is little interaction in conversation among members.
6. Gives little to no structure to family; therefore, members seem to be unable to keep track of what their duties are or know how others are going to act; rules are not defined, e.g., each member talks about their own thing.
7. Maintains little physical contact or closeness.
8. Provides little warmth or empathy.
9. Admires and identifies with "winners" and powerful leaders.
10. Rewards blue ribbon achievements, questions reasons for "second place."

Child

The children become individualistic and egocentric because they feel the world is against them and that they have to be "top dogs." They:

1. Manipulate people and things to promote self.
2. Become belligerent if individualism is threatened or when doors to challenge are closed.
3. May become a loner when under pressure.
4. Fear boredom.
5. Treat people as objects.
6. Are competitive—cannot afford to lose.
7. Are poor listeners.
8. Lack patience.
9. Cannot delay gratification.
10. Look for concrete and materialistic rewards.

Observed Behavior

1. Often is described as "bossy" or "pushy."
2. Does what they want rather than meet expectations of others.
3. Ignores implicit rules that govern behavior for their age and sex.
4. Becomes withdrawn under pressure.
5. Expresses emotions in door slamming, angry words, and thrown objects.
6. Lets you know what other authorities have to say.
7. Will usually be straining at the boundaries.
8. Does not do well with routine—does not persevere.
9. Enjoys individual pursuits.
10. Wants to know what the rewards will be.
11. Think the world revolves around them.
12. Are competitive and do not like to lose.
13. Seems to ignore others' feelings.

Undisciplined-Impulsive Style

Parent

An inconsistent or manipulative parent leads to an undisciplined-impulsive coping style. This parent is inconsistent in structure, shows little warmth and has little communication with the child. This parent:

1. Is inconsistent or laissez faire with rewards, punishment and affection.
2. Seems unreliable and unilateral, e.g., "I'll clobber you if you do that."
3. Sees life as a constant battle and makes no effort to hide family discord.
4. May be totally involved one day and withdrawn the next.
5. Shows little warmth for child, leaving feelings of indifference.
6. Makes little effort to communicate or disclose feelings.
7. Has low respect for **child.**
8. Is not dominant in day-to-day child-rearing, especially the father.
9. Either gives total direction or none at all.
10. Can be charming to meet needs.

Child

The children become undisciplined-impulsive because they have not had structure and love while often being manipulated. Therefore, they:

1. Receive maximum authority from parent or are given no guidance and are left on their own.
2. Experience constant conflict with parents.
3. Feel rejected.
4. Talk excessively in functional terms.
5. Use language to defend and attack.
6. Distrust authority and are reluctant to disclose personal feelings.
7. Value friendship but generally indicate that such relationships are difficult to develop, are unstable affairs, and hurt people when they dissolve.
8. Can behave creatively when free of the observation of authority.
9. Make positive statements about the underdog, the loner and minority groups.
10. Show rejection for religion, people, friendship (because of unreliability), government, and more subtly, all freedom restraining devices.

Observed Behavior

1. Negativistic: Says "I won't."
2. Lacks tolerance for tasks they do not enjoy.
3. Tends toward temper tantrums and wild destruction.
4. Asserts independence in a negative manner.
5. Anti-social tendencies (steals, lies, destroys property, bullies, defies, resents discipline).
6. Speaks disrespectfully to teachers.
7. Prone to blame teacher or external circumstances when things don't go well.
8. Makes derogatory remarks about subject being taught.
9. Breaks classroom rules, destructive behavior.
10. Tries to manipulate others.
11. Often interpret efforts to help him as weakness on the other's part.
12. Exploit others.
13. See the world in terms of how useful it is to them (functional).

Acceptance-Anxious Style

Parent

A child-centered parent leads to an acceptance-anxious child. The main goal is to bring the child happiness, but always at the price of "pleasing the parent." Inclined to be over-protective, this parent:

1. Feels the child's happiness is most important and, thus becomes very overprotective.
2. Glosses over conflict saying: "because Mommy or Daddy want you to do this," "If you love Mommy or Daddy . . ."
3. Indicates the child's purpose is to please them (parent).
4. Is reluctant to use physical punishment but exerts control through dependency relationship with potential threat of love withdrawal.
5. Is concerned with social acceptance and social achievement.
6. Is concerned about child getting their feelings hurt.
7. Invests heavily and identifies with children's activities.
8. Stresses manners and friendliness. "I don't want you to do that; it won't be good for you."
9. Cannot afford to be rejected by children.
10. Combines physical contact with sympathy.

Child

The children become acceptance-anxious because they are concerned about living up to expectations and cannot afford to risk failure. Therefore they:

1. Generalize dependency on others.
2. Need constant reinforcement.
3. Will do what you want them to, but not because they want to.
4. Accumulate a large number of friends to safeguard against being thrust upon their own resources in the solution of problems.
5. Believe everyone needs lots of friends.
6. Will voice opinions of the group rather than their own, which may be contrary to the present group.
7. Will refer often to people in general.
8. Have a positive attitude toward situations and ideas which are beneficial for people.
9. Try to create feelings of guilt in others—not doing enough for them.

10. Focus on "reading non-verbal cues" of others—develop an interpersonal sensitivity.

Observed Behavior

1. Often tries "too hard."
2. Wants to show off to impress others.
3. Overly sensitive to criticism or correction.
4. Worries about pleasing others.
5. Frequently seeks adult contact and approval—especially those who are warm.
6. Excessively competitive and jealous.
7. Tries to outdo classmates by producing more in quantity.
8. Outwardly nervous when tests are given.
9. Fearful of failure (failure means rejection).
10. Can tell stories in an interesting way.
11. Prone to do things behind your back.
12. Has ability for abstract thought, but anxiety interferes with functioning.
13. Frequently asks for assistance to get you involved.

Rigid-Inhibited Style

Parent

An authoritarian parent leads to a rigid-inhibited coping style. The parents' word is final and never disputed. This parent:

1. Makes all decisions. The father is most often the dominant parent but mother may invest her total energy in the parenting role.
2. Acts as boss, is highly constrictive and controlling.
3. Sees the world as a win-lose situation.
4. Permits little diversity among family members on moral issues.
5. May stress religion and frequent church attendance.
6. May use explanation sparingly and physical punishment frequently. Often calls child's behavior "bad" but does not explain why. Child becomes a "bad" child.
7. Awards behaviors which conform to parents' standards.
8. Believes all directions should come from parent to child.
9. Becomes anxious if they do not know what the children are doing.
10. Focuses on details of performance and standards.

Child

The children become rigid and inhibited because they feel confused, inadequate and weak. Therefore, they:

1. Have no freedom to grow or operate.
2. Can do everything that everyone else can do but not quite in the same time limit.
3. Are rule followers and to solve a problem they must follow some rule.
4. Insist that most important thing in life is a few good friends.
5. Exhibit a strong need for structure.
6. Adhere to rules, authorities and values which provide strong structure.
7. Reject environmental inputs which are dissonant with their organized modes of interpretation.
8. Have polarized evaluations.
9. Have definite stands on every topic, state them unequivocally and reject those that do not meet their high standards of perfection.
10. Prefer direction from those with high formal status.

Observed Behavior

1. Cannot get a job done unless others are immediately available to help them.
2. Takes a passive role in a conflict situation.
3. Become confused and disoriented easily.
4. Give answers which have nothing to do with the questions being asked.
5. Afraid to assert self or show initiative.
6. Shows signs of nervousness.
7. Generally is unresponsive, hard to get to know.
8. Is upset by a change of routine.
9. Rigidly adheres to rules.
10. Has either repressed or expressed anger in very primitive manners.
11. Approaches life on a concrete level, cannot understand abstract principles.
12. Strives for status and power.

Creative-Responsive Style

Parent

The problem-centered parent leads to a creative-responsive child. There is a clear structure, mutual respect, and no power struggles between child and parents. Parents use initial goal setting by contract. This parent:

1. Promotes communication between parent and child.
2. Realizes conflict and problems are to be encountered (because this is essential to child's development).
3. Allows the outside environment to influence the child's behavior and lets the child actively use their own knowledge.
4. Aids in initial goal setting that gives the child a clear structure within which he or she may function freely, using alternatives of thought and action.
5. Allows diversity of opinions without rancor.
6. Fosters independence while providing a basic sense of security.
7. Treats the child as a person of intrinsic worth.
8. Uses explanations frequently . . . but not excessively.
9. Has faith in the child to solve problems and appreciates their strength to survive adversity.
10. Enjoys the child as a person.

Child

The children become creative because they have confidence to challenge the world and have faith they can survive the consequences. They

1. Function abstractly.
2. Think for themselves.
3. Use available information and experiences to solve problems.
4. Do not fear adult authority, standards, but may believe differently.
5. Are open and sensitive to minimal environmental cues.
6. Welcome friendship but do not feel the strong need to surround oneself with friends.
7. Aware of group needs but do not try to dominate.
8. Can place self on a continuum when making comparisons.
9. Willing to disclose feelings but does not demand sympathy.
10. Does not use emotional behavior to involve others. Becomes excited over "events."

Observed Behavior

1. Completes tasks.
2. Perseveres on tasks even when initially stymied.
3. Finds humor in their own mistakes. Does not take self too seriously.
4. Explores the learning environment on their own.
5. Can demonstrate empathy by describing feelings.
6. Cooperates for the good of a group effort.
7. Plays alone or with group.
8. Can adapt to classroom experiences, e.g., detailed tasks to role playing.

In suggesting interventions Moore (1982) stresses that it is important to be able to view a child's school coping needs from two perspectives. This is done by distinguishing between a child's immediate needs (contemporaneous) and their long term requirements for growth (developmental). The idea is that the child must be able to survive and cope first before growth can take place. A description of each style with examples of suggested strategies for each perspective are found in Table 1.

The goal for using the school coping styles model is to bring each child within the creative-responsive area or as near as possible. Moore (1982) notes that each of the styles represent strengths as well as liabilities as the following describes:

Coping Style	Liabilities	Strengths	Creative Style
Power dominance	"hyperactive" "pushy" "aggressive"	"energetic" "forceful" "assertive"	Autonomy
Undisciplined-impulsive	"clown" "instigator" "deviant"	"playful" "influencing" "inventive"	Ideals
Anxious-acceptance	"pushover" "sympathetic" "pathetic" "boring"	"trusting" "considerate" "sensitive" "practical"	Relationship
Rigid-inhibited	"unflexible" "perfect"	"disciplined" "precise"	Competence

Conceptualizing and intervening with students from this model helps counselors and teachers appreciate both the individual differences between

Table 1

SCHOOL COPING STYLES

(From *School coping styles model* by E. Moore. Atlanta, GA:
copyright 1982 by the Georgia State Department of Education.
Reprinted by permission.)

Style	Contemporaneous Needs	Developmental Needs
Power-Dominance	Require attention to details and routine. Provide pictoral examples or demonstrate. Allow them to be leaders if they attend to structure. Reward perseverance on task by personal attention and concrete rewards. Do *not* explore feelings in competitive situations.	Provide feedback sessions or group work for self disclosure. Reinforce group participation—especially listening to others. Ask them how others feel (empathy). Ask them to compare their feelings with others.
Undisciplined-Impulsive	Provide controls consisting of logical/natural consequences. Explain/warn once, then act in a firm, fair and consistent manner. Do *not* become emotional or get into power struggles. Do *not* expose internal feelings.	Maintain a relationship regardless of the child's behavior. Confront immediately and expose manipulations. Do something together with equal responsibility. Cast in responsible leadership role.
Acceptance-Anxious	Student must complete task or goal before getting personal attention from teacher. Provide feedback in a simple, unemotional manner. Restrict child from "people" contact (peers/teacher) until tasks are completed. Insist that assignments be completed on time.	"Praise the act, not the child"—do *not* personalize accomplishments. Refrain from special favors or using them as assistants. Go to them/make contact when they are involved in tasks alone. Role play anticipated rejection situations they may fear.
Rigid-Inhibited	Provide structure—rules and sequence. Size of step should be small to insure success and also not overwhelm them. Concrete reinforcers work best.	Provide alternatives (choices); ask for generalizations. Ask for feedback; ask "why" and "how." Assign to leadership roles of minimal responsibility. Ask them to label their feelings.

students, as well as the strengths and limitations of each coping style. To encourage creative-responsive coping, educators need to explore new ways that help children develop and promote their strengths rather than liabilities when facing the stress of school.

REFERENCES

Chandler, L. (1983). The stress response scale: An instrument for use in assessing emotional adjustment reactions. *School Psychology Review, 12,* 260–265.

Dobson, C. B. (1980). Sources of sixth form stress. *Journal of Adolescence, 3,* 65–75.

Elkind, D. (1981). *The hurried child.* Reading, MA: Addison-Wesley.

Fisher, B., Giblin, P., & Hoopes, M. (1982). Healthy family functioning: What therapists say and what families want. *Journal of Marital and Family Therapy, 8,* 273–284.

Fisher, B., & Sprenkle, D. (1978). Therapist's perception of healthy family functioning. *International Journal of Family Counseling, 6,* 9–18.

Harvey, O., Hunt, D. & Schroder, H. (1961). *Conceptual systems and personality organization.* New York: Wiley.

Kolb, D. (1984). *Experiential learning: Experience as the source of learning and development.* Englewood Cliffs, NJ: Prentice-Hall.

Moore, E. & Richter, D. (1981). *Personal styles analysis for educators.* Atlanta, GA: Guidance, Counseling and Career Development Unit, Georgia State Department of Education.

Moore, E. (1982). *School coping styles model.* Athens, GA: Guidance, Counseling and Career Development Unit, Georgia Department of Education.

Olson, D., Sprenkle, D., & Russell, C. (1979). Circumplex model of marital and family systems: I. *Family Process, 18,* 3–28.

Rosenberg, M. D. (1968). *Diagnostic teaching.* Seattle: Special Child Publications.

Russell, C. S. (1979). Circumplex model of marital and family systems: III. *Family Process, 18,* 29–45.

Rutler, M. (1981). Stress, coping and development: Some issues and questions. *Journal of Child Psychology and Psychiatry, 22,* 323–356.

Chapter 9

THE UNWED ADOLESCENT MOTHER

Rosemary A. Thompson

Pregnancy among school-age adolescent girls is increasing at an alarming rate. The scenario for the adolescent mother is often bleak, and the resources are often restricted. Moreover, parents, school administrators, counselors and social agencies are frequently uncommitted about the methods and approaches which should be taken to assist young mothers and their children. The dilemma is multi-dimensional involving many psychological, sociological, economic, and cultural issues. There are also many intervening variables (such as poor nutrition and lack of job entry skills) in the lives of the adolescent mother that continue to intensify while potential change agents in the community remain elusive about who will take responsibility for providing services for this growing population.

Adolescent mothers continually exhibit difficulty functioning academically, economically, psychologically, and socially without resource assistance. It becomes more apparent that counselors need to assume a more active role to assist this group. In addition to the enormous stress (both antepartum and postpartum) accompanying the circumstances of birth to a teenager, their offspring may also succumb to inherent risks. Infants of teenage mothers have increased vulnerability to mental retardation and developmental delay as a consequence of complications during pregnancy, labor, prematurity, or low birth weight (Moore, 1978). Other potentially adverse consequences of adolescent pregnancy frequently include recurring pregnancy with negative health repercussions; dropping out of school with no marketable job skills; and early marriages which have a high rate of divorce. Therefore, the adolescent mother often lacks the physical, emotional, economic, educational and social resources that are vital elements in assisting the mother to adequately care for her child.

Single-parent families, welfare dependency, and child abuse have increased among this particularly susceptible group; yet, while legislation, Supreme Court decisions, funding and programs have proliferated, statistics on teenage pregnancy have not decreased. Furthermore, as the training and educational demands of our society become more sophisticated, and the opportunities to meet these demands continually become exhausted, the adolescent mother without necessary job entry skills is invariably handicapped. This further demonstrates this particular population as highly vulnerable where the probability of opportunity, education, employment, and economic stability are diminished. Hence, there are a number of salient questions or concerns regarding this precarious group of adolescents: How do single, adolescent school-age mothers tend to think and feel about themselves? How much control do they exert over their present circumstances and future goals? How do they perceive their chances of success socially, psychologically, and economically?

Lindemann (1974) found that a failure to re-define one's self-concept was an instrumental factor in unwanted pregnancies among adolescent girls. By refusing to admit to themselves that they had become sexually active persons, many girls avoided a decision to use birth control measures and subsequently became pregnant. Lindemann maintained that their self-concepts would allow a spontaneous sexual "happening," but pre-planned, predictable or intentional coitus was too dissonant with self-perceptions to allow realistic and rational evaluations of the probable consequences of their behavior. Therefore, a predominant self-devaluation seems to be a precipitating condition tending to invite greater sexual activity and unwanted pregnancy. Furthermore, there has not been substantial research comparing self-concept with locus of control for adolescent unwed mothers. Hence, low self-esteem and the "it won't happen to me" syndrome seem to merit investigation in order to adequately structure a support group for this particular population.

Therefore, one of the purposes of this preliminary examination of adolescent unwed mothers was to compare the self-esteem of adolescent mothers to a norm or control group. Several studies have extensively examined the self-esteem of adolescents, but none have been found that compared the self-concepts of unwed adolescent mothers to adolescents in general. A second purpose is to provide a blueprint of strategies using a multimodal behavioral approach.

Relevant Studies

Approximately eleven million teenagers fifteen to nineteen years old are estimated to have had sexual intercourse (The Alan Guttmacher Institute, 1976). One in every six teenage females risks pregnancy each year (Kantner & Zelnik, 1973). **Time** magazine recently revealed that "illegitimate births increased so rapidly in the 1970's that 17% of U.S. babies, one out of every six, are now born out of wedlock. In 1979, an estimated 597,000 illegitimate babies were born, up 50% since 1970. Nationwide, nearly a third of the babies born to white teenagers and 83% born to black teens were illegitimate" (**Time,** 1981, p. 68).

The apparent physical difficulties often accompanying early pregnancy have been cited by many (Coates, 1970; Menken, 1975; Menken, 1972; Nortman, 1974; Puffer & Serrano, 1975), as well as the serious psychological problems affecting both the teenager and her infant (Baizermann, et. al., 1971).

The pervasive need for services focusing on personal functioning is intensified if one examines the most profound trend among adolescents in the past decade: a significant increase in both pregnancy (Dryfoos & Heisler, 1978) and the subsequent rearing of children by single, school-age mothers (Ogg, 1976). This trend is becoming a local as well as national concern and is considered by many as an epidemic (Baizerman, et. al., 1971; Braen & Forbush, 1975; Furstenberg, 1969; Klerman, 1975; Piotrow, 1975). Furthermore, Ogg (1976) revealed that the number of one-parent families has been increasing seven times as rapidly as that of traditional two-parent families, with a growing proportion being represented by never-married teenagers. According to Nye (1976) school-age adolescents between 14 and 16 years of age have been the most rapidly increasing age group of single parents. Finally, Moore and Caldwell (1977) estimated that "of all children born out of wedlock, at least 60% end up on welfare" (p. 164). Essentially, there is a vital need for adequate collective services, as well as programs that would enhance self-esteem and self-sufficiency. Providing services within the secondary school setting that would increase the adolescent mother's personal functioning could improve her parenting skills and self-sufficiency skills as well.

Therefore, the literature provides various perspectives concerning the social, psychological, and economic dilemma of the adolescent mother. There are many avenues one can pursue, yet the ramifications are pervasive with many underlying variables that may influence behavior. It becomes the counselor's responsibility to understand this phenomenon and delineate approaches for supportive programs for adolescent mothers. One must find viable means to implement supportive programs to adolescent mothers so they may become self-reliant and develop skills enabling them to lead productive and satisfying lives. Such a program could focus on parenting skills and conflicts, job entry skills, personal management skills, as well as the enhancement of social competency and the ability to develop interpersonal relationships. The scenario for the adolescent mother need not be bleak, nor one of despair and destitution.

Method

A support group was utilized for this particular population of adolescent unwed mothers. Groups are frequently advocated as a mode of treatment and teaching for teenagers because most adolescents turn to their peers for understanding and support, especially if they have similar experiences. New ways of dealing with situations can be learned in action. Finally, group participants can also increase self-esteem and take control over their behavior through their acceptance by the group and through the support they receive in trying out new behaviors.

Subjects

The subjects composing the group were adolescent high school mothers with children ranging from 3 months to two years of age, who also had open service cases at the local department of social services. There were approximately 27 teenage parents (in and out of school); however, the project was designed to work with approximately 15 girls (ages 15–18) who voluntarily chose to attend the group. This team parent group was intended to focus on self-sufficiency skills and to reflect the concern for the quality of life for these young mothers and their children, by cooperating extensively with community agencies. Consequently, the group was named M.O.M.S., an acronym for Mothers and Others Means Success (see chapter appendix).

A control group, used merely for comparison purposes, consisted of a random sampling of nulliparous students from a neighboring high school. The intent was to compare the experimental group (M.O.M.S.) with the published norms of the test instrument and with scores of a control group from the same city.

Instrumentation

The instrument utilized was the Tennessee Self Concept Scale, a self administered test consisting of 100 descriptive statements an individual can use to portray herself. Composed of two forms, a Counseling Form and a Clinical Research Form, the scale yields 30 scores including 20 which have a test-retest reliability in the .80–.90 range. The counseling form was utilized for this particular study.

Another scale utilized to assess motivation and locus of control expectancies was Rotter's (1954) I-E Scale (I = internal; E = external locus of control). Locus of control is a personality construct reflecting one's belief or perception about who controls behavior and life events. This was felt to be an important variable if the girls for this sample were to attain self-sufficiency. The key component is between behavior and its consequences, and the relationship between outcomes and personal effort. The hypothesis explored from this perspective could be: do adolescent mothers feel there is a cause/effect relationship between their behavior and future results or consequences? Essentially, "internals" view themselves as exerting a significant influence over the course of their lives, and "externals" tend to believe events are unrelated to personal effort. Therefore, the researcher attempted to gather data to determine if this sample was more internal or external. High total scores indicate externality and low scores indicate internality.

Procedure

The Tennessee Self Concept Scale (Counseling Form) and the I-E Scale were administered to the sample of adolescent mothers. Since this is a preliminary study only mean scores of the group were compared to the published norms of the Tennessee Self Concept Scale to acquire a profile of the difference of the adolescent mother. The mean of the I-E Scale was also compared to a stratified high school sample.

Results

Initially, the mean scores of the school-age adolescent mothers group were compared to the published norms of the Counseling Form of the Tennessee Self Concept Scale and to TSCS means of a sample of nulliparous adolescents. Essentially, the adolescent mothers projected relatively poor self-esteem, ranking between the 8th and the 48th percentile on 8 out of 9 scales. Results indicate that the adolescent group of unwed mothers scored below the mean of the adolescent nulliparous group, and below the norm group on the TSCS on the following subscales: Total positive-general level of self-esteem; Row 1—self identity; Row 3—behavioral self; Column B—moral-ethical self; Column D—family self; and Column E—social self. Generally, it could be inferred that the adolescent mother in this particular sample seemed to feel less adequate as an individual, had discrepancies between the perception of her own behavior and the way she functions; had less moral worth and feelings of being a "good" person, less than adequate feelings as a family member and poor relationship with peers; and a lower sense of adequacy and worth when compared to an adolescent nulliparous sample and the norm group of the TSCS. T test results also reveal a significant difference (p. < .01) for the behavioral self between adolescent mothers and the norm group of the TSCS.

Another variable which is considered influential in determining reward expectancies and consequent behavior is whether one is inner directed (internal) or outer directed (external). Lamb (1968) examined the relationship between self-concept and locus of control and found that self-concept is a significant predictor of locus of control (high self-esteem is related to internal locus of control). If this is true, then conversely, low self-concept would be a predictor of externality.

The adolescent unwed mothers from this particular sample exhibited high external locus of control in addition to low self-concept. The mean score for the adolescent mothers on the I-E scale was M = 12, which was considerably higher than the national stratified high school sample mean of 8.50, indicating that the adolescent unwed mothers were more external in their locus of control orientations.

Discussion

Responses on the TSCS and the I-E Scale present strong preliminary evidence that adolescent unwed mothers exhibit low self-esteem and high external locus of control. It could be inferred from the self-concept instrument that adolescent mothers project poor self-esteem, feelings of inadequacy and unworthiness, and were more dissatisfied with their family relationships, in addition to feeling that much of what happened to them was generally attributed to chance or fate.

Positive self-perception is central to an adequate personality, enabling the individual to approach life events with a sense of confidence in her ability to handle competently whatever situation may arise. Furthermore, a positive self-perception encourages future growth and an enhancement of one's potential.

Individual and group counseling should be provided to these young people. The many measures of self-concept and maladjusted behavior frequently demonstrate that a large percentage of these girls could be highly vulnerable to distress and disturbance. Essentially, they deviate from the norm of their peer group in terms of the roles and responsibilities they must assume as a single parent. Conflict, instability, low self-esteem, and lack of feelings of control over circumstances inhibit good parenting, especially when this is combined with immaturity and social inadequacy. A program which fosters a support group and focuses on parenting skills, self-esteem, self-sufficiency, and active decision-making about future alternatives is one suggestion for working with the adolescent mother in the school setting. For the adolescent mother, it is important she realize that what she does and what she becomes depend on her own concerted effort.

The ramifications and implications from such a study from a theoretical perspective and in view of the counselor's responsibility are diverse and numerous. Perhaps foremost, the school counselor must utilize community resources to assist this unique population within the school setting.

The present study, however, does not lend itself to any global generalizations about the adolescent mother. It is merely provided as reference point for developing strategies to enhance the personal growth in this particular group. In view of the research, one must account for a number of project weaknesses. First, the sample size must be increased (our sample was 15 girls, 8 were Black, 7 were White). Second, Black subjects, both locally and nationwide, greatly outnumber White subjects, and single mothers considerably outnumber married mothers. This attribute must be considered when viewing any information on self-concept. Yet, there are implications for developing and implementing a support group for this segment of the adolescent population that could provide positive results for the recipients.

Recommendations

Therefore, a recommended model to use with a group of adolescent mothers is a multimodal approach, an application of the BASIC ID. The multimodal approach involves attending to seven modalities initially identified in Lazarus's (1973) Basic ID model. Keat (1978) modified the Basic ID model to address the needs and special concerns of various populations. The multimodal approach could directly focus on the low behavioral self reflected in the data on the TSCS.

As a blueprint of strategies addressing the needs of the counselee's entire behavioral repertoire, this method could be especially effective with adolescent mothers, since they seem to manifest a number of underlying social, emotional, and behavioral problems. Multimodal therapy also enhances the skills of the school counselor who is frequently caught up in a myriad of administrative details because it offers a comprehensive outline for assessing the counselee's needs and for developing treatment plans. It also promotes efficiency of time, while maximizing the personal and emotional benefit to the counselees.

Furthermore, from a group perspective, the multimodal group should be task-orientated and goal-directed with the collective purpose of ameliorating specific problems. In addition, the school counselor should utilize the opportunity to maximize the use of referral sources and adjunct community resources. This approach would also enhance the goals of school counseling by promoting growth and self-actualization in the populations served. The major impetus of this method is educational with an emphasis on targeted goals aimed at helping counselees function more effectively. Finally, another value of such an approach is that it facilitates concrete and measurable improvement which can assist the school counselor in the ever-pressing need toward accountability.

In multimodal behavior therapy, the counselor-counselee interaction focuses on seven modalities: Behavior, Affect, Sensation, Imagery, Cognition, Interpersonal Relationships, and Drugs (which includes diet and related physiological variables). These modalities make up the acronym BASIC ID. The seven modalities are interactive as well as interdependent as they relate to behavioral change. Among the most frequently used group methods are behavioral-rehearsal, and role-playing, positive reinforcement, recording and self-monitoring, feeling identification, bibliotherapy, social skills and assertiveness training. Table 2 provides the multimodal group profile for adolescent mothers.

Conclusions

This study demonstrates the need for continued effort to increase the self-sufficiency and personal success of adolescent unwed mothers. Single parenthood and adequate parenting skills are also issues counselors need to address. From this perspective, the group does not merely consist of adolescent mothers but their offspring as well. This provides the counselor with the opportunity to use a preventive approach to assure the future well-being of the adolescent mother's new responsibility — the rearing and providing for another human being. The most comprehensive and efficient means of providing for this particular population on the secondary level could be a multimodal behavioral group.

APPENDIX
GROUP OBJECTIVES FOR NINE WEEK STRUCTURED SESSIONS FOR M.O.M.S.

The general goal for M.O.M.S. (mothers & others means success) will be to address the specific problems of teenage parenthood in an effort to reduce the incidence of future pregnancy and to increase the educational and employment opportunities for this high risk population.

Sessions will focus on adolescent sexuality, self-esteem, problem-solving skills and concerns held by group members. The developmental and problem solving orientation of the group is intended to foster an informal support group for the recipients.

Objective 1: Offer family planning and adolescent sexual information

- The local family planning project will be utilized to provide a comprehensive workshop with discussion and pertinent literature for group recipients.

Table 1
MULTIMODAL GROUP COUNSELING PROFILE
FOR ADOLESCENT MOTHERS

Modality	Problem Assessment	Potential Intervention
Behavior	Poor academic performance and attendance problems	Self-contracting: recording and self-monitoring
	Negative Self-statements	Positive self-talk
	Discipline of children by yelling or hitting	Teach operant training principles in child management
Affect	Feelings of little self-worth	Increase range of positive reinforcement
	Anger toward significant others	Exercises in anger-expression
	Conflict with others	Behavior-rehearsal Role-reversal
Sensation	Anxiety and depression over present circumstances and future goals	Anxiety-management Training goal rehearsal or coping imagery
Imagery	Unproductive fantasies	Guided imagery
	Image of self as incapable	Goal rehearsal
Cognition	Poor study habits	Study skills training Assertiveness training
	Lack of educational or occupational information	Career counseling; assessment and information
	Sexual misinformation	Sex education; bibliotherapy
	Expectations of failure	Positive self-talk
Interpersonal Relations	Poor relationships with peers	Social skills and assertiveness training
Drugs (Biological Functioning)	Poor dietary habits	Involvement in weight reduction program; nutrition and dietary information

Objective 2: To improve self-esteem

- Throughout the entire group process, the leader will address the members' strengths, rather than weaknesses.
- Positive reinforcement from other members will be encouraged.
- Helping to solve the problems of other group members will assist in fostering self-esteem, along with structured strategies.

Objective 3: Employ the services of community agencies for resources.

- Utilize the services of the local social service department, childcare association and parenting groups.

Objective 4: To improve problem solving skills.

- The leader will guide the group through problem-solving processes by simulating, motivating, and involving the members in discussion around topics selected by the group.
- The members will be given repeated rehearsals in reality-like situations, and role-playing which will be rewarded by success. The focus will center around gaining control of life situations; to enhance the person's sense that she has the power to make things happen, and that by this action something has been affected by her choices and decisions.

Objective 5: To develop a continuing informal support network among the participants.

- The group leader will facilitate trust, openness, and cohesiveness within the group environment. The leader will offer support, understanding, motivation, challenge, approval and recognition to group members.

Objective 6: To address specific areas of concern held by individual group members.

- The major goal of this group, as a family life education model is to help the individual cope with areas that they are currently finding insurmountable (such as childcare, or parental conflicts). Efforts will be made to start where the group members are functioning and to employ viable methods to address their concerns.

- To facilitate discussion of parenting skills, copies of such resources as "Winning Ways to Talk With Young Children" will be obtained from V.P.I. extension office.
- To educate mothers on activities that entertain small children, and how to make inexpensive educational toys, a local resource person from the community day care unit will be invited to make presentations to the group.
- To facilitate discussion of numerous other areas of special concern the following resources will be utilized: local library, public health department, mental health center, local childcare association, and the local department of social services.

Objective 7: To employ the services of resource agencies within the city to strengthen recipients' self-sufficiency skills as parents and prospective employees

- To educate mothers in child development and discipline, a resource person from a local federal project will present vital information to group members.
- To provide young mothers with a modified parenting program focusing on such issues as responsibility, consistency and encouragement, a resource person from the local court services diversion unit will present a series of structured experiences.
- The Virginia Employment Commission will be utilized to provide a workshop on necessary job entry skills, interviewing and job application procedures.

REFERENCES

Baizermann, M., Sheehan, C., Ellison, D., and Schlesinger, E. (1971). Pregnant adolescents: A review of literature with abstracts 1960–1970. *Sharing Supplement, Consortium on Early Childbearing*, 31.

Black and white, Unwed all over. *Time*, (November 9, 1981), p. 67.

Braen, B. B. and Forbush, J. B. (1975). School-age parenthood: A national review. *Journal of School Health*, 45, 256–262.

Coates, J. B. (1970). Obstetrics in the very young adolescent. *American Journal of Obstetrics and Gynecology*, 108, 68–72.

Dryfoos, J. and Heisler, T. (1978). Contraceptives services for adolescents: An overview. *Family Planning Perspectives*, 10, 223–229.

Fitts, W. (1975). Tennessee self-concept scale manual. Counselor Recordings and Tests, Nashville, Tennessee.

Franklin, R. D. (1963). Youth's expectancies about internal versus external control of reinforcement. Unpublished Doctoral Dissertation, Purdue University.

Furstenburg, F. J. (1969). Birth control knowledge among unmarried pregnant adolescents: A preliminary report. *Journal of Marriage and Family, 31,* 34–42.

Kantner, J. F. and Zelnik, M. (1973). Contraception and pregnancy: Experiences of young unmarried women in the U. S. *Family Planning Perspectives, 5,* 21–36.

Keat, D. B. (1978). Multimodal evolution. *Elementary School Guidance and Counseling, 13,* 12–15.

Klerman, L. V. (1975). Adolescent pregnancy: The Need for New Policies and New Programs. *Journal of School Health, 45,* 263–267.

Lamb, K. W. (1968). Self-concept and dogmatism variables in the prediction of internal external reward expectancies. Unpublished Thesis, Butler University.

Lazarus, A. A. (1973). Multimodal behavior therapy: Treating the basic id. *Journal of Nervous and Mental Disease, 56,* 404–411.

Lindemann, C. (1974). *Birth control and unmarried young women.* New York: Springer.

Menken, J. (1972). Teenage childbearing: Its medical aspects and implications for U.S. population. In C. Westcoff and R. Park (Eds.). Demographic and Social Aspects of Population Growth. Washington, DC: U.S. Government Printing Office.

Menken, J. (1975). The health and demographic consequences of adolescent pregnancy and childbearing. Paper presented at the conference on research on the consequences of adolescent childbearing. Center for Population Research, N.I.H., Bethesda, Md.

Moore, K. (1978). Teenage childbirth and welfare dependency. *Family Planning Perspectives, 10,* (4), 233–235.

Moore K. and Caldwell, S. (1977). The effect of government policies on out-of-wedlock sex and pregnancy. *Family Planning Perspectives, 9,* (47), 164–169.

Nortman, D. (1974). Parental age as a factor in pregnancy outcome and child development. *Reports on Population and Family Planning, 16,* 1–52.

Nye, F. I. (1976). School-age parenthood: Consequences for babies, mothers, fathers, grandparents and others. Pullman, WA.: Washington State University, Cooperative Extension Service.

Ogg, E. (1976). Unmarried teenagers and their children. public affairs pamphlet, 537. N.Y.: Public Affairs Press.

Piotrow, P. Y. (1975). Mothers too Soon. Draper world population fund, *1,* 3–6.

Puffer, R. R. and Serrano, C. V. (1975). Teenager pregnancies: High risk for infants. Draper World Population Fund, *1,* 16–17.

Rotter, J. B. (1954). *Social learning theory and clinical psychology.* Englewood Cliffs, NJ: Prentice-Hall.

The Alan Guttmacher Institute. (1976). 11 million teenagers. N.Y.: The Alan Guttmacher Institute.

PART II "NON-TRADITIONAL" FAMILIES

CHARACTERISTICS OF HEALTHY FAMILIES
FAMILIES IN TRANSITION
CHILDREN AND DIVORCE
SINGLE PARENT FAMILIES
STEPFAMILIES
DUAL CAREER FAMILIES

Chapter 10

CHARACTERISTICS OF HEALTHY FAMILIES

ROBERT G. GREEN

It has only been in recent years that school children's classroom behavior has been explained as a function of the levels of health and stress in their family systems (Worden, 1981). Notwithstanding the repeated observations of experienced teachers and educational counselors that healthy school children tend to inhabit healthy family systems, behavioral and social science explanations of school children's achievement and social behavior have historically been guided by **individually focused** theories of human behavior (Green & Kolevzon, 1984). Since these theories and the therapeutic interventions associated with them linked school related problems to processes residing within the child, little was known about the dynamics of either healthy or dysfunctional families. Consequently, children with school related behavioral problems were often understood to be anxious, depressed, immature, passive-aggressive, etc.

In recent years, however, two related processes have served to extend the explanation of children's school related problems to the family unit. The first process, the dramatic increase in the number of school children from single parent and disrupted families, has intensified interest in the dynamics of family interaction (Bundy & Gumaer, 1984). Indeed, the experience with these children has spurred many teachers and counselors to search for more knowledge about the dynamics of healthy family functioning.

The purpose of this chapter, therefore, is to develop a profile of healthy family functioning by examining the literature of the fields of family studies and family therapy. Three areas of family functioning will be examined. The first section examines the characteristics of families as a whole and identifies salient factors which distinguish healthy families from less functional units. Since the counselor and teacher cannot always observe whole families, however, the remaining two sections examine the properties of subsystems of healthy families. Accordingly, the second section profiles the characteristics of individual family members while the final section examines the functioning of marital and parent-child relationships in healthy families.

CHARACTERISTICS OF FAMILY UNITS

Family therapy practice models tell us little directly about the properties of whole family systems. Because their interventions tend to target change in either family subsystems or in the characteristics of individual family members (Green & Kolevzon, 1985), these practice models will be of use to us more directly in the second and third sections of this chapter. Information about the group properties of healthy families, however, can be readily obtained from the rapidly growing number of family assessment models (Barnhill, 1979; Epstein, Bishop & Baldwin, 1982; Kantor & Lehr, 1975; Lewis, Beavers, Gossett & Phillips, 1976; Olson, Russell, & Sprenkle, 1979; Reiss, 1981).

Two of these assessment models, the Beavers-Timberlawn (Lewis, et al., 1976) and the Circumplex (Olson, et al., 1979) have gained particular prominence. Although both models were developed in the late seventies, already both have been used extensively in the testing and evaluation of clinical practice (Beavers & Voeller, 1983; Olson, Russell, & Sprenkle, 1983) and as conceptual frameworks to organize long range research projects on healthy families (Lewis & Looney, 1983; Olson, McCubbin, Barnes, Larsen, Muxen & Wilson, 1983).

Collectively, these two models emphasize the same three core constructs. Both suggest healthy families differ from less functional units with regard to the closeness of family relationships, the responsiveness of family members to change, and the nature of the communication processes they employ. However, the models reflect different assumptions about family health and tend to emphasize different indicators of these three core constructs.

The Beavers-Timberlawn Model

This model refers to family health as competence, the dimensions of which are assumed to exist on an infinite linear continuum (Lewis, et al., 1976). Consequently, similarities between severely dysfunctional and healthy families are emphasized. Healthy families are viewed as possessing more (or less) of the same qualities possessed by less functional families, thereby emphasizing the potential for growth and change.

Five major dimensions contribute to overall family competence. The first dimension, **family structure**, is determined by aspects of family power, the nature of the parental coalitions and the closeness of the family members. Power in healthy families is usually shared by the parents and determined by situations and interactions. This pattern is in rather sharp contrast to the chaotically leaderless or one-parent-dominant patterns found in less healthy units. Similarly, the predominance of a strong parental coalition in healthy families contrasts to the absent or ineffective parental coalitions among dysfunctional families. Indeed, in these poorly functioning families a strong parent-child coalition often predominates. Finally, the closeness of family members in healthy families is accompanied by distinct relationship boundaries. In less healthy family units, relationship patterns may be either characterized by distance or by an inappropriate closeness without recognition of relationship boundaries.

The second major dimension of the Beavers-Timberlawn Model, **mythology**, suggests that healthy families are more likely to have realistic beliefs (congruent mythology) about their group functioning than are less healthy units. Because this dimension of the Beavers-Timberlawn Model is often difficult to assess and may require more than one observation of the family unit, it is less useful to school personnel than the third dimension, the family's ability to solve problems through the use of **goal directed negotiation**. Since stages and situations of the child's school career constantly require family input and decision-making, this diagnostic indicator can be readily observed by the teacher and counselor.

The fourth major dimension of the Beavers-Timberlawn Model, the **autonomy** of family members, obviously refers more to characteristics of individual family members than to a property of the family group. As such it will be discussed in more detail in the next section. However, the Beavers-Timberlawn Model suggests that the members of more competent or healthy families are also more autonomous people. This autonomy is usually quite observable by school professionals. It is often evidenced by the clarity with which the family members communicate their thoughts and feelings, the degree to which they take responsibility for their actions, whether or not they tend to speak for one another and make "mind reading" statements, and the degree to which they are open and receptive to the thoughts of other family members.

The final dimension of the Beavers-Timberlawn Model, **family affect**, can be observed by the teacher or counselor in response to a wide range of family-child-school transactions. More healthy families are likely to express a wide range of feelings. They are usually warm, affectionate, humorous and optimistic—contrasting sharply with the varying patterns of hostility, depression, cynicism and/or pessimism found in less competent family units.

In addition to these five major dimensions of family competence, a more recent development of the Beavers-Timberlawn Model suggests that there are also stylistic differences which distinguish healthy families from less functional units (Kelsey-Smith & Beavers, 1981). Unlike the competence dimension, however, family style is viewed as existing on a curvilinear-centripetal-centrifugal continuum. Centripetal families seek their needs within the family and are less trustful of the outside world. On the other hand, centrifugal families expect gratification from beyond the family. Indeed, members in centrifugal family units trust activities and relationships outside the family unit more than those within it (Beavers, 1982). Neither style is more correlated with family pathology than the other, however. Rather, most experienced counselors and teachers will have observed that children with school related problems tend to come from families where one end or the other of the centripetal-centrifugal is rigidly adhered to by family members. More healthy families, on the other hand, are flexible enough to vary their "inward-outward" relationship tendencies to meet the needs of new situations and developmental stages.

The Circumplex Model

Like the Beavers-Timberlawn Model, the Circumplex Model of family health also addresses the central constructs of family change, closeness and communication (Olson et al., 1983). However, the Circumplex Model embodies different assumptions about optimal family functioning. While the Beavers-Timberlawn Model portrays family life as existing on an infinite linear continuum of competence and thereby emphasizes growth, the Circumplex Model emphasizes family adjustment and change through the use of curvilinear assumptions about the distribution of family characteristics. Indeed, the Circumplex Model defines healthy family functioning as a balance between either too much or too little **cohesion** and **adaptability**, the two major dimensions of family life.

Cohesion is defined as the closeness or emotional bonding that family members have toward one another (Olson et al., 1979). Following the curvilinear assumptions, less healthy families may depart from optimal functioning in one of two ways. Families with little or no cohesion are viewed as disengaged. Their autonomy from the family is very high and like the Beavers-Timberlawn centripetal families, they tend to meet their needs outside of the family unit. At the opposite extreme of the disengaged families are the enmeshed families. These families are characterized by an intense over-identification with the family unit. Family members in these enmeshed families have only limited autonomy. In fact, a child's natural striving for independence may be viewed as a threat to the family's "togetherness." Between these extreme types of cohesion we find the two types of balanced families: the separated and the connected.

In addition to an overall judgment about the type of emotional bonding that characterizes a family unit, teachers and counselors can develop a family profile through four more specific indicators of cohesion: family boundaries, supportiveness, time with friends, and recreation. Balanced (healthy) and extreme (enmeshed and disengaged) descriptions of family characteristics are associated with each of these indicators.

The other major dimension of the Circumplex Model, **adaptability**, refers to the family's ability to change in response to situational and developmental stress (Olson et. al, 1979). As in the case of cohesion, healthy families are more likely to be balanced than extreme on this dimension. Families balanced on this dimension may be either structured or flexible. They differ from both the "rigid" families who resist change almost entirely and the "chaotic" families who are constantly changing or responding to change. The Circumplex Model employs four indicators of adaptability: leadership, control, discipline, and family rules and roles.

The Circumplex Model forms a typology of family types by placing the two major dimensions of family health at right angles to one another. The grid that results from the intersection of the four levels of cohesion (disengaged-separated-connected-enmeshed) with the four levels of adaptability (rigid-structured-flexible-chaotic) identifies 16 family types with the more healthy types occupying the four center cells. However, the model recognizes that the family life cycle as well as the family's cultural context may require differential amounts of both cohesion and adaptability at different stages for different families. Consequently, the model is a dynamic rather than a static one. Families are expected to move across and up and down the grid. Indeed, the third major dimension of the Circumplex Model, **family communication** can either facilitate or impede this movement.

CHARACTERISTICS OF FAMILY MEMBERS

A general systems paradigm with the attendant therapeutic goal of establishing more harmonious and healthy patterns of family relationships organizes the field of family therapy. Consequently, the family therapy literature is rich with descriptions of healthy dyadic and triadic patterns of family interaction. In addition, at least two family therapy models, Murray Bowen's Bowenian Model (Bowen, 1978) and Virginia Satir's Communication Model (Satir, 1967) specify the attributes of individuals in healthy family systems.

Satir describes **maturity** as the most distinguishable characteristic of individuals in healthy families. Mature family members have a sense of being in charge of themselves. They are able to make choices and decisions based on accurate perceptions of themselves, of others, and of the contexts in which they find themselves. They openly acknowledge their life choices and decisions and accept responsibility for the results of those decisions. The counselor and teacher can recognize mature parents and children from healthy families by two primary attributes: self-awareness or consciousness, the process of being in touch with one's own emotional and physiological responsiveness; and self-esteem, the degree to which family members evaluate themselves positively and accept themselves as individuals. Adults and children with low levels of self-esteem are often anxious and uncertain; their ideas about themselves are dependent upon the evaluations of external audiences.

In contrast to Satir's emphasis on affective awareness, Murray Bowen emphasizes a cognitive approach to understanding healthy family functioning. The most basic concept in his approach, the **differentiation of self**, is the key to distinguishing members of healthy families. This concept emerged from Bowen's observation of two major counterbalancing forces in human nature: a force that propels individuals toward separateness or individuality and its opposite, a force toward togetherness and fusion with others. Bowen (1978) suggested that man is ideally a rational creature; he also described the manner in which choices between the two poles become blurred when the boundaries between two distinct biological systems, the emotional and the intellectual, are not maintained. Family members for whom these boundaries are relatively indistinct are viewed as undifferentiated, whereas those for whom the emotional and intellectual systems are distinct are viewed as differentiated.

Bowen (1966) portrayed all individuals as existing on a hypothetical scale of self-differentiation. At the bottom of the scale are members of disturbed families whose emotional fusion is so intense that they cannot distinguish fact from feeling. These family members devote most of their energy to relationships with others. Their efforts to gain the love and approval they seek predominate and thus prohibit awareness of basic life tasks and goals. Moving up this hypothetical scale toward less fusion and consequently greater degrees of differentiation, one finds Bowen's depiction of the individual characteristics of healthy family systems. Although these people are capable of and demonstrate empathy in their relationships with others, individual boundaries remain rather distinct. Although they are warm interpersonally, logical reasoning rather than emotion rules their lives, and they act on the basis of beliefs, principles, and convictions.

Obviously, the individual characteristics identified by Satir and Bowen are not mutually exclusive. Indeed, Satir's emphasis on emotional maturity and Bowen's almost complimentary emphasis on cognitive maturity together describe optimal characteristics for successful marriages and successful parent-child relationships. The next section describes the healthy characteristics of these two essential family dyads.

CHARACTERISTICS OF MARITAL AND PARENT-CHILD RELATIONSHIPS

The nature of the **communication** processes between the spouses and between parents and children distinguish these dyads in healthy families from those found in disturbed family units. Indeed, this intra dyadic communication is probably the most frequent target problem for which family therapy is prescribed.

Satir (1967) has developed a five-fold typology of communication patterns which are easily identified among school children and their families. In healthy families, congruent or "leveling" patterns of communication predominate. Family members feel free to say what they feel and think in undisguised ways without fear of retribution, retaliation, or rejection by other family members. In sharp contrast are the four dysfunctional modes of communication, in which certain feelings are eliminated. In the "blaming" mode the blamer eliminates feelings about the other person; conversely, in the "placating" mode the placater eliminates feelings about self. In the "super-reasonable" mode feelings about the subject being discussed are eliminated, and in the final "dysfunctional" mode the "distracter" causes communication to be focused on the irrelevant (Jones, 1980).

Satir (1967, 1972) also emphasizes another characteristic of healthy marriages and of healthy parent-child relationships. This characteristic concerns the relationship **rules** or the guidelines utilized to regulate behavior within and across these dyadic subsystems of the family. In healthy families these guidelines are flexible, appropriate to given situations, and subject to change, whereas in dysfunctional families rules are rigid, nonnegotiable, and permanent. Healthy families also have an awareness of the origin, rationale, and use of family rules; dysfunctional families, however, are stymied by rules yet often abide by rules of which they are not aware. Thus, intervention with the families of children with school related problems may involve the initiation of a process whereby family members gain insight into who makes the rules, how they were made, what they do, and the consequences when they are broken.

The Bowenian approach to family therapy is also instructive in understanding the role of third parties in relationships between spouses, between parents and children, as well as between teachers and their pupils. Bowen (1978) explained healthy dyadic relationships with the **triangle,** a "three-person emotional configuration" (p. 76). He advised that the dyad is capable of stability only when relationship issues are calm and anxiety is low. Indeed, three-person-systems are normal, natural and expected, the building blocks of human relationship systems. During periods of relative calm the triangle consists of a comfortable dyad and a less comfortable third party who is an outsider. The goal is to preserve the relationship by guarding against the discomfort arising when one of the two forms a more comfortable relationship with the third party. On the other hand, the outsider seeks formation of a "togetherness" with one of the members of the dyad. Obviously, the most typical triangle in the family is also the one school professionals see most frequently—the mother-father-child, wherein stress in the marital relationship is alleviated through the couple's joint focus on aspects of a child's behavior. However, triangles may also explain a variety of other family interactions including marital infidelity as well as sibling conflict and rivalry.

It is not the process of triangulation, however, that differentiates healthy family subsystems from less functional ones. Rather, the differentiating factors are the nature, circumstances, and extent of the triangulation. In healthy families triangulation is not the primary problem solving process, and in such families triangles may be freely discussed. Family members are often aware of the process and may adapt to or prevent relationship consequences of triangulation. Most important, because triangles thrive on anxiety and lower levels of differention and self-esteem, they are not used as often or as consistently in healthy families as in more distressed units.

The **emotional process of the nuclear family** is another Bowenian concept used to explain the healthy functioning of marital and parent-child relationships. It describes four mechanisms employed by spouses to deal with the consequences of poor self differentiation. As with intrapsychic defense mechanisms, some families may employ all four, whereas others may use these mechanisms in combination. All mechanisms, however, are used in response to anxiety and as such may be viewed as functional; they are increasingly used by all families when the anxiety is high and levels of differentiation are low (Bowen, 1978).

Emotional divorce, the first of the four mechanisms, is the most universal. It is a type of withdrawal from the marital relationship that occurs when the marital partners experience more closeness in the relationship than they can cope with comfortably. Manifestations of emotional divorce vary: they may include avoidance of certain types of conversations (particularly those that are emotionally charged), not speaking for extended periods of time, or physical avoidance of one another.

Like emotional divorce, marital conflict, the second mechanism, is often the result of the marital partners' closeness. Unlike emotional divorce, however, marital conflict usually erupts when couples have some ambivalence about this closeness (Bowen, 1978). Rather than avoiding closeness by creating distance, however, these couples use conflict to regulate it.

With the third mechanism, dysfunction of one spouse, the self of the less dominant spouse becomes absorbed by the more dominant spouse, who assumes inappropriate degrees of responsibility for the couple. The resultant dysfunction in the less dominant spouse may include emotional, physical, and behavioral problems.

The final mechanism, projection of symptoms on a child, is the most readily observable by school personnel. This concept demonstrates how the impairment of certain children develops in family systems and how that impairment may be controlled. Although elaboration of the etiology of psychological impairment is beyond the scope of this chapter, Bowen's theory suggests that psychologically impaired children are both results of and contributors to impaired family systems.

Three final family therapy concepts describing the functioning of marital and parent-child relationships are suggested by Salvadore Minuchin's Structural (1974) and Jay Haley's Strategic (1976) approaches to family therapy. Unlike the models of Satir and Bowen, the structural-strategic models give little emphasis to individual characteristics of family members. Rather, therapeutic change and consequently family health is achieved exclusively by characteristics of and relationships between the family unit and its dyadic and triadic subsystems.

Boundaries, are intra-family rules that define both the participants in family subsystems and how they are expected to participate. These boundaries are essential to family life because they enable the family to carry out its function by protecting the separateness or differentiation of both the individuals and the marital and parent-child relationships they comprise.

The "who" function of family boundaries is less important than the "how" function. For example, in the absence of a father or mother in a family, a parental subsystem that includes a grandparent or an older (parental) child can certainly perform well. On the other hand, the specific rules governing the nature of subsystem participation and most important, the clarity of these rules, determine how well the family functions. Minuchin (1974) conceptualized family dysfunction as bipolar, placing families characterized by diffuse or blurred boundaries at one end of a continuum. Like the Circumplex Model's description of these families, they are seen as being overly close with poor differentiation. The excess sense of belonging they possess interferes with autonomy, problem-solving, and skill development—all problems familiar to experienced teachers and counselors. At the other end of Minuchin's continuum are the disengaged subsystems and families. The rigid boundaries characteristic of these families impede communication and provide autonomy to family members at the expense of the proper functioning of their relationship systems.

Although Haley (1976) and Minuchin (1974) emphasized that cultural norms, individual preferences, and family life cycle demands may make enmeshment and disengagement functional, like the Circumplex Model the structural-strategic approaches to family therapy locate family health between these poles. Thus, healthier or more functional families are those in which individuals and subsystems are able to find a balance between being overly connected and being overly separate.

Like Satir and Bowen, Haley and Minuchin also emphasized the primacy of strong and satisfying marriages in healthy family systems. Consistent with their attention to the organization and structure of family relationships, however, the structural-strategic theorists stressed the synchronization of the marital dyad with the other family subsystems (Haley, 1976, 1980; Minuchin & Fishman, 1981). The second structural-strategic concept, the family **hierarchy** perhaps best explains the nature of this synchronicity.

The models of Haley and Minuchin demonstrate that healthy families are characterized by open, clearly defined rules for governing the power and status differentials among family members and among the subsystems in the family. In the intact family this power is shared between the marital pair as suggested by the Beavers-Timberlawn Model. However, a variety of arrangements in single parent families may be healthy. As with family boundaries, the critical factors are that the hierarchy is well defined and the rules governing its operation are understood by all family members.

Both Haley and Minuchin have contended that symptoms, including school related problems, occur in children when the hierarchical arrangement is confused (Haley, 1976, 1980; Minuchin, 1974; Minuchin & Fishman, 1981). Thus, the goals of family therapy always include clarification of the family hierarchy. Haley, however, stressed an understanding of power and influence, whereas Minuchin emphasized the establishment of boundaries to protect the marital dyad from the needs and demands of other family members. Indeed, healthy families are characterized by rules that provide space for the marital partners to experience intimacy as well as to discharge their parenting function.

The final concept of the structural-strategic approaches discussed here, **flexibility**, has been implied throughout the present discussion of healthy families. However, its importance as a diagnostic indicator for understanding the family's relationship with the school community and as an interventive goal for marital and parent-child relationships underscores the need for its formal inclusion in this profile. In general, this concept refers to two related areas of family life: life cycle or situational transitions and problem solving behavior. During life cycle and situational transitions the healthy family recognizes the need for and is capable of adaptation and accommodation in response to change. When a child is born, when the same child begins and completes school, or when one member of the family becomes seriously ill, the healthy family reorganizes its rules, boundaries, and interactive processes to accommodate. Less healthy families become stuck within particular life cycle phases or with particular adaptive (maladaptive) modes. Similarly, in terms of problem solving behavior, less functional families may compulsively apply inappropriate and ineffective strategies that do not lead to problem resolution. These families either have limited repertoires of problem solving behavior or are reluctant to attempt new methods to solve problems.

SUMMARY AND CONCLUSION

The rapidly growing interdisciplinary fields of family studies and family therapy have made tremendous strides in recent years toward the identification of characteristics of healthy families. This chapter has attempted to synthesize the resulting knowledge for use by professionals specifically concerned with the impacts of family experiences on school age children. Since family oriented school professionals cannot always observe and indeed involve the entire family unit in all of their interventions, the profile of whole family relationship characteristics developed was supplemented by a description of the personal attributes of members of healthy families and a summary of the functioning of the marital and parent-child dyads in healthy family systems.

While the extent of the available number of recent theories about the interaction of children and their families has been welcomed enthusiastically by educational and human service practitioners, this chapter must necessarily end with a note of caution. Indeed, the rapid development and dissemination of family theories and concepts in recent years has exceeded the speed at which they have been empirically validated. Consequently, teachers and practitioners who have become convinced of the efficacy of a family oriented view of therapeutic intervention with school children are now struggling to make choices within this broad array of available theory.

Fortunately, many family oriented practitioners and researchers are actively developing empirical profiles of and comparisons between existing theories. This work is the most evident among the assessment models. Indeed, empirical studies have validated both the Beavers-Timberlawn and the Circumplex models of family health (Lewis et al., 1976; Olson, 1985). In addition, instruments measuring both of these models of family health have been subject to continual testing and refinement to improve their utility (Green, Kolevzon & Vosler, 1985; Olson, 1985).

Similarly, some recent research has compared the views of practitioners oriented to each of the family therapy models discussed in this chapter (Green and Kolevzon, 1982; Kolevzon & Green, 1985). However, with the exception of Minuchin's Structural Model, the developers and exemplars of these models of family therapy have not been active in the operationalization and testing of their theories and concepts. Indeed, along with studies comparing the relative efficacy of different family therapy models with different types of family problems, this type of process research is perhaps the most urgently needed by professionals providing educational and mental health services to children and their families.

REFERENCES

Barnhill, L. (1979). Healthy family systems. *Family Coordinator, 28,* 94–100.

Beavers, W. R. (1982). Healthy, midrange and severely dysfunctional families. In F. Walsh (Ed.). *Normal family processes.* New York: Guilford Press.

Beavers, W. R. & Voeller, N. Family models: Comparing and contrasting the Olson circumplex model with the Beavers systems model. *Family Process, 22,* 85–98.

Bowen, M. (1978). *Family therapy in clinical practice.* New York: Aronson.

Bundy, M. & Gumaer, J. (1984). Families in transition. *Elementary School Guidance and Counseling, 19,* 4–8.

Epstein, N. B., Bishop, D., & Baldwin, L. (1982). McMaster model of family functioning: A view of the normal family. In F. Walsh. (Ed.). *Normal family processes.* New York: Guilford Press.

Green, R. & Kolevzon, M. (1982). Three approaches to family therapy: A study of convergence and divergence. *Journal of Marital and Family Therapy, 9,* 39–50.

Green, R. & Kolevzon, M. (1984). Characteristics of healthy families. *Elementary School Guidance and Counseling, 19,* 9–18.

Green, R. & Kolevzon, M. (1985). The correlates of healthy family functioning: The role of consensus and conflict in the practice of family therapy. *Journal of Marital and Family Therapy.*

Green, R., Kolevzon, M. & Vosler, N. (1985). The Beavers-Timberlawn model of family competence and the circumplex model of family adaptability: Separate! But, equal?. *Family Process.*

Haley, J. (1974). *Problem-solving therapy.* San Francisco: Jossey-Bass.

Haley, J. (1980). *Leaving home.* New York: McGraw-Hill.

Jones, S. (1980). *Family therapy: A comparison of approaches.* Bowie, MD: Brady Co.

Kantor, D. and Lehr, W. (1975). *Inside the family.* San Francisco: Jossey-Bass.

Kelsey-Smith, M. & Beavers, W. R. (1981). Family assessment: Centripetal and centrifugal family systems. *American Journal of Family Therapy, 9,* 3–12.

Kolevzon, M. and Green, R. (1985). *Family therapy models: Convergence and divergence.* New York: Springer.

Lewis, J., Beavers, W., Gossett, J., & Phillips, V. (1976). *No single thread: Psychological health in family systems.* New York: Brunner/Mazel.

Lewis, J. & Looney, J. (1983). *The long struggle: Well functioning working-class black families.* New York: Brunner/Mazel.

Minuchin, S. (1974). *Families and family therapy.* Cambridge, MA: Harvard University Press.

Minuchin, S. & Fishman, H. (1981). *Families and family therapy.* Cambridge, MA: Harvard University Press.

Olson, D. (1985). Circumplex model and family functioning: VII. In C. N. Ramsey (Ed.). *The science of family medicine.* New York: Guilford Press.

Olson, D., McCubbin, H., Barnes, H., Larsen, A., Muxen, M., & Wilson, M. (1983). *Families: what makes them work?* New York: Sage.

Olson, D., Sprenkle, D., & Russell, C. (1979). Circumplex model of marital and family systems: I. Cohesion and adaptability dimensions, family types, and clinical applications. *Family Process, 18,* 3–15.

Olson, D., Sprenkle, D., & Russell, C. (1983). Circumplex model of marital and family systems: Theoretical update. *Family Process, 22,* 69–83.

Reiss, D. (1981). *The family's construction of reality.* Cambridge, Mass.: Harvard University Press.

Satir, V. (1967). *Conjoint family therapy.* Palo Alto: Science and Behavior Books.

Satir, V. (1972). *Peoplemaking.* Palo Alto, CA: Science and Behavior Books.

Worden, M. (1981). Classroom behavior as a function of the family system. *School Counselor, 28,* 178–188.

Chapter 11

FAMILIES IN TRANSITION

MICHAEL L. BUNDY AND JAMES GUNMAER

The family has a time-honored importance when evaluating the health and happiness of adults and children. The family unit, no matter how it is defined, provides for the sustenance and growth of its members. If the unit is healthy, persons within it thrive. However, if the unit is dysfunctional, its members suffer and their development is impaired. Conversely, the amount of injury to the family is usually proportional to the dysfunction of any individual within the family system.

What is family? The traditional American family that was popularized by television shows such as the "Walton's" and "Little House on the Prairie" in the 60's and 70's include a strong, hard-working husband who was the "breadwinner" and a warm caring mother who was the "home-maker." These "ideal" families were blessed with several children including both sexes. One of the reasons that these shows became popular and were continued for years is that they provided American viewers with sources for identification in the characterizations. However, television in the 80's, like the family of the 80's, has undergone marked changes. Today viewers tune into the problems of: "Different Strokes," (White widowed father with a White daughter and two adopted Black children), and "One Day at a Time," (White divorced mother with two daughters from her former marriage).

The changes in family television programming are representative of the many changes in family structure, dynamics, and values that have occurred during the last two and a half decades. For example, in the past family was defined as a husband and wife with children living together. Today, in the 80's family might be better defined as at least two persons (one adult and one child) living together. Macklin (1980) reports that U.S. Census figures for the 70's indicated that only a slight majority of households represented traditional families. She attributes these changes

139

to the steady increase in single-parent or dual-career nuclear families, as well as the increase of individuals residing alone or in homes such as communes with non-related persons. Glick (1984b) has substantiated that these changes have continued into the 80's but predicts that the changes will continue at a much reduced rate for the last half of the decade.

What has happened to encourage family change? Macklin (1980), in her review of the last decade, suggested that the increase in pluralistic family forms has resulted from a decline in dependency on "familism" and a growing independence for individuals who have gained more power and control for their lives, especially women. "Probably the most significant change has been the continued evolutionary movement toward individual freedom of choice" (Macklin, 1980, p. 185). Individuals have become more self-aware, autonomous, open, and willing to explore non-traditional alternatives to family as it was previously defined. These alternatives include: remaining unmarried and alone or co-habiting without marriage, single parenting either after divorce or without marriage, divorce and remarriage, convenience marriage such as career marriage or open marriage, gay coupling, and communal living. Traditional values have indeed changed and will continue to change as non-traditional family arrangements are explored. With the growing public awareness of life options comes the individual's understanding of and willingness to make different choices throughout life. There is no question but that the U.S. family is in a period of transition.

CURRENT TRENDS IN FAMILY STRUCTURE

During the past twenty-five years, when two-parent families declined, single-parent families increased sharply. From 1960 to 1983, the percentage of children under 18 living with two parents decreased (88% to 73%), as did the percentage of those living with both natural parents (73% to 62%). Two causal factors are the upsurge in one-parent families and the decline in the birth rate. One of the more profound changes has been the rapid increase in single-parent or one-parent families. In 1960 the percentage of children under 18 years of age who lived in one-parent families was less than 9%, and, 23 years later the percentage of children in one-parent families skyrocketed to 22%. This trend toward single parent status has resulted largely from increasing marital ruptures and growing numbers of never married mothers who are opting to retain child custody.

We see significant shifts in causal factors of single-parent families during the period from 1960 to 1983 with a projection to 1990. In 1960, one of the largest groups of single parents was widowed; today the largest group is divorced. During these years the percentage of children living in single-parent families as a result of divorce increased by 18%, whereas those living with a widowed mother or father declined by 18%. The percentage of children living in separated families remained relatively constant. In these 23 years the percentage of children living in families where a parent is absent, e.g., temporarily away due to military service, dual careers, hospitalization, and incarceration, dropped by 15% and the percentage of children living with a single parent who never married rose by 20%. A combination of the 1983 data for divorce and separation produces a sum of 64% which reflects a significant number of children who are living with one parent due to marital strife.

Glick (1984a) found that the upturn in single-parent families accelerated most during the 70's, a time when the increase in divorce and the birth of children to unwed mothers were the greatest. Arthur J. Morton of the U.S. Bureau of the Census estimated in 1983 that 59% of all children born in 1983 were likely to live for a period of time in single-parent families before they turn 18 years old (Glick, in press). Of those children likely to live with only one parent, almost two-thirds will be with divorced parents (Bumpass, 1984; Glick, 1984a). Generally speaking, 60% of all children today are likely to spend some time with one parent and that parent will most likely be a divorced parent.

The number of children under 18 years of age living in a single-parent family with the father as custodian has increased since 1960. Glick (1984a) found that during the period between 1960 and 1983 the percentage of single-parent fathers rose from about 1% to 2%. In contrast, the percentage of all children younger than 18 living in single-parent families with a custodial mother sharply increased from 8% to 20% during the same period. Although more fathers seem to be seeking and obtaining custody of their children, the percentage of custodial fathers of all one-parent families has decreased from 11% in 1969 to 9% in 1983. While data on remarriage among divorced mothers and fathers with child custody are not available, Glick (1984b) notes the remarriage rate among divorced men is higher than that of divorced women. Thus, single-parent fathers are more likely to move into a step-family relationship than single-parent mothers with child custody.

A comparison of families in 1983 with children under 18 by race in the

United States revealed a considerable difference between Blacks and Whites (U.S. Bureau of the Census, 1984). More than half of the Black families with children (58%) were maintained by a single parent, while 1 of every 6 White families (17%) was a one-parent family. The largest factor contributing to one-parent Black families was never married parents who made up 52% of the total group. By contrast, the percentage of White never married parents was 11%. However, over half of White one-parent families (56%) were due to divorce as compared with about 1 of every 4 Black one-parent families with children (26%).

Glick (1984a) estimates that the children of the man or woman in an unmarried couple total about 5% of all children who live with only one parent. Approximately three-fourths of the children living with unmarried couples in 1983 were the sons or daughters of the woman. According to unpublished census data, twice as many were the men's children as were the children born to the cohabiting couple (Glick, in press). Estimates are that less than 2% of young children born today may live with cohabiting parents at some time before age 18. It is reasonable to assume that many unmarried couples might move their family structure to become married and perhaps form a step-family.

Most one-parent families of divorce are in a transition from the two-natural parent family structure to the step-family structure composed of one natural parent and a step-parent. A recent estimate by Glick (1984a) found that the proportion of step-parent families increased from about 9% in 1960 to 11% in 1983. Precise figures of children living in a step-family are difficult to obtain since the Census Bureau does not compile data on this specific family structure.

This review of trends in family structure between 1960 and 1983 reveals the drastic shifts from the traditional family structure to the one-parent family or step-family composition. Will this transition continue? If so, will it maintain its current rate?

FAMILY STRUCTURE: A PROJECTION

Paul Glick, former Senior Demographer at the U.S. Bureau of the Census, provides some projections of family composition and factors which cause structural change to one-parent families. These projections indicate that the shift from the traditional, two-natural parent family to other family structures will continue to about 1990. The proportion of children living with two natural parents will continue to shrink; the projected percentage by 1990 is expected to drop to 59%.

The percentage of children under 18 living in one-parent families will continue to rise to the degree that by 1990 over one quarter of all children (26%) will be in a single-parent home. The two factors contributing most to this increase continue to be divorced and never married parents. The divorce rate is expected to maintain its upward momentum and reach a position where almost half of all one-parent families (46%) will be caused by marital rupture. The proportion of children living with a never married parent is projected to reach one-quarter of all children in single-parent families.

It is interesting to note that the rate of structural shift in the American family is expected to slow somewhat for the remainder of this decade. Glick (1984b) expects that as the population base of post-war "baby boomers" moves through the critical age group of first marriage, there will be a moderate rate of change in the composition of households.

FAMILIES AND THE LABOR FORCE

As mentioned previously, the traditional view of the family has the father providing economic security for the family, and mother specializing in housework and providing child care. However, this notion has become less and less accurate as more wives and mothers have entered the labor force since World War II. Their numbers have increased to the point that by 1984 over 53% of all families had at least two household members in the labor force (Hayghe, 1984). In 1983, for the first time, half of all mothers with children under age 6 were in the labor force (Kamerman, 1983). In contrast, the proportion of husbands in the labor force declined (Johnson & Waldman, 1983). The labor force participation rate of all married women with spouse present rose from 30.5% to 52.8% during that period of time. Over 25% more married women with children between 6 and 17 years of age were working in 1984 than in 1960. Less than 1 in 5 married women with children under 6 years old were participating in the labor force in 1960; however, by 1984 over half of these mothers were working (51.8%).

As the number of one-parent families has increased, it is reasonable to assume that more women who maintain families are entering the labor market. The term "women who maintain families" is defined as a never-married, divorced, widowed, or separated woman with no husband present and who is responsible for her family (U.S. Bureau of Labor Statistics, 1983, p. 3).

Over half of all women who maintain families are also participating in the labor force. Between 1970 and 1984, the proportion of single-parent women who work increased from 52.9% to 60.9%. During this 14 year period, the labor force participation rate of one-parent mothers, with children ages 6 to 17, rose to a point that over 3 out of every 4 such women were employed. The female single-parents with children under 6 years of age increased their rate of involvement in the labor market from 46.9% to 55.3%, well over half.

The American family seems to be changing residences less often than two generations ago. According to the U.S. Census Bureau (1984), the annual mobility rate has declined steadily for the past 23 years. In 1960, 1 in every 5 persons in the United States moved within a years time; compared with about 16% in 1983. This represents about a 4% decline in the mobility rate of Americans 1 year old and over.

It is interesting to note that families with school-age children are less likely to move than those with younger children (U.S. Census Bureau, 1984). Households whose children were all under 6 years of age had a 30% mobility rate in 1983. By comparison, families with children between 6 to 17 years of age tended to change residences between 1982 and 1983 at a 12% rate. The mobility rate becomes greater (about 18%) for 18 year olds and up as young people leave their parent's home to establish their own households or move in with friends, marry for the first time, go away to college, or join the military.

IMPACT OF TRANSITIONAL FAMILY ON CHILDHOOD BEHAVIOR

As the number of American families which experience disruption increases, it has become important for counselors and other mental health professionals to examine in what ways children are effected. How does family transition impact parent and child relationships? How are school behavior and academic performance of children influenced by family changes? How does distress from family changes impact child development?

Family Relationships

The leading cause of family transition from a traditional, two-parent family to a one-parent family is divorce. Data from numerous studies show that stress from divorce produces a serious decrease in functioning and in mental health. To investigate the degree to which divorce impacts family members over time, two longitudinal studies are presented.

Hetherington, Cox, and Cox (1981, 1982) followed several families for a number of years and documented their observations of interactions between divorcing parents and their children. During the first year following divorce, the study recorded a deterioration of parent-child relationships. Fathers tended to withdraw from involvement in discipline, rule enforcement, and management of day-to-day routines of children. Mothers usually became more authoritarian, that is, they increased their number of direct commands and prohibitions and decreased their responsiveness and affection-giving. Children, especially boys, became less cooperative and more aggressive. However, two years after the divorce, there was evidence that family members attempted to regain an equilibrium in their relationships. Fathers enforced more consistent expectations and reasoning and children became more compliant and cooperative.

The restoration process noted by the researchers occurred at different rates among the various families. It seems that the rate depended upon such factors as the development of new intimate relationships by one or both parents, the mothers' employment, and the economic stability of her household.

Wallerstein and Kelly (1981) reported similar results in their long-term study of 60 families that experienced divorce. An initial effect of marital rupture which they observed was diminished parental care for children. The radical changes in the family unit caused parents to focus their attention upon their own troubles and less upon the needs of their children. Consequently, the lack of ability of parents to sustain interaction and communication with their children intensified the anguish of their offspring.

The reaction of children to divorce differed between boys and girls and across developmental levels. Their responses included separation phobias, anxiety reactions, ego regressions, sleep disturbances, anger, depression, and acute mourning reactions. However, 18 months after the divorce, an improvement in parental care was noted by the researchers. For example, some mothers became more comfortable with setting limits for their youngsters. Thus, the symptomatic responses and regressions in development by the children seemed to disappear. However, Wallerstein (1983) later acknowledged that for many children and adolescents the divorce experience continued to shadow them over the years. In a 10 year follow-up, the researchers noted that the initial responses had abated but that the effects of divorce were "incorporated within the character, the attitudes, the relationships, the self-concept, the expectations, and the world view of the child" (p. 233).

School Performance and Children of Divorce

The effects of divorce and one-parent childrearing on school performance was studied by Hetherington, Featherman, and Camara (1981) in a comprehensive review of the literature. One of their findings revealed that among children from single-parent families, boys are more likely than girls to be adversely effected in cognitive functioning and social behavior. Aside from sex differences, they found that children from single-parent families are not different from children in two-parent homes in terms of their intellectual ability or academic aptitude. However, when a comparison was made of the two groups based upon school performance, a difference was noted. Children from single-parent families tended to receive lower grades and to be rated by their teachers as less motivated. Furthermore, these youngsters are "absent from school more frequently, are more disruptive in the classroom, and may have less effective study styles in their school work" (p. 87).

The researchers implied that perhaps conditions within single-parent families result in the inability of children to concentrate and to exercise effective study habits. However, counselors are advised that not all children of divorce display difficulties or diminution in school performance. Consequently, caution should be exercised in interpreting student behavior in order to avoid a self-fulfilling prophecy. Studies have shown that teacher expectations of students significantly influence their achievement.

Self-Care and Children

While some researchers have investigated how children are effected by divorce or by living in a single-parent home, others have studied the impact of self-care upon children. As more families become dependent upon two wage-earners and more single-parents enter the work force, an increasing number of youngsters below 14 years of age are without direct adult supervision during some portion of the working day. Studies have reported that children who are in self-care for regular periods of time tend to report high levels of worry and fear (Long & Long, 1984, Zill, 1983). The National Survey of Children conducted by Temple University in 1976 found that children who are routinely left in self-care arrangements are more fearful than those who receive adult supervision (Strother, 1984). Also, from interviews with "latchkey" children, Long and Long (1984) discovered that children who spend regular amounts of time alone at home often experienced loneliness and boredom. After reviewing several studies, Strother (1984) concluded that children in self-care situations tend to have lower academic achievement than children whose parents were not employed full-time and could spend more time with them. Moreover, there is a clear indication that school grades drop when children are given the regular responsibility for care of younger siblings (Smith, 1984). However, there is some evidence suggesting that children who are regularly left unsupervised in the suburbs fare better than those in the city (Galambos & Garbarino, 1983). Garbarino (1980) also hypothesized that the neighborhood of "latchkey" children has an influence upon their level of fear and their school performance.

Parent-child communication is often encumbered by self-care arrangements. Long and Long (1984) found that some children will persuade their parents to allow them to stay home alone in order to appear mature and responsible to both peers and parents. However, when they develop difficulties or begin to worry, they are reluctant to talk with their parents about those problems. Children may withhold sharing their worries with parents when they think parents will make other child-care arrangements or when they wish to protect their parents from further worries.

Distress and Child Development

Within families in transition, children are often expected to behave at levels beyond their development. The struggle to meet increased demands and responsibilities that are too great for their age generates considerable amount of additional stress for children today. Elkind (1981) has argued that hurrying children through their childhood without the opportunity to enjoy developmental milestones will increase their likelihood of experiencing depression and personality problems during adolescence or later in life. With the family system weakened by transitional situations, routines are upset and effective communication is many times lacking. Children are frequently set adrift during a tumultuous period when in many cases they are in need of support and encouragement to face typical developmental tasks. Consequently, the problems arising during the transition of the family increase their stress load and tend to impede their healthy development.

IMPLICATIONS FOR COUNSELORS

As research continues to show the ways in which children are effected by family changes, it becomes increasingly clear that many youngsters and their parents need help in understanding and coping with family transition. Drawing from our experiences as a school counselor and a mental health professional in private practice, the authors would like to share some general ideas within the context of the three primary helping roles: counseling, consulting, and coordinating.

Counseling Children from Families in Transition. While not all children from disrupted families need direct long-term counseling, we think that all should be seen at least one time by a counselor in order to assess their needs and to determine how best to meet those needs. During this initial interview, the counselor should ask children for their view about what is happening in the family to obtain their understanding of it. Then the counselor should try to appraise childrens' reactions to this family situation and their level of anxiety associated with it.

If ongoing counseling is required, the counselor needs to develop a support group so the child realizes that other children are involved in a similar experience and it is not an unusual one. We recommend four goals for such groups. One group goal is to provide children with the sense that they are not alone. A major problem for children of disrupted families is insecurity and loneliness. Group counseling can provide the necessary conditions of support. The second goal of the group is to provide pleasure. To develop and grow, children need to believe that life has enjoyment and is not always ugly. The group can be structured to provide pleasurable experiences as well as facing painful realities. A third purpose of these groups is to be with an empathic adult. Children whose families are rupturing need to feel that an adult really understands what is going on. A fourth goal is to deal with some of the day-to-day issues which children must face. There should be discussion of visits, of things to do when they get worried or angry, and of things to do that will help them feel better. It is useful for a child to say, "I can do...when I get angry at my mom." There should also be talk about what they cannot do. They cannot fix the divorce situation.

In order to help counselors assess how a child of divorce is coping, Judith Wallerstein (1983) has conceptualized six psychological tasks which the child must master in addition to typical developmental tasks. The six tasks are interrelated and hierarchical, that is, mastery of each is based upon successful accomplishment of the task before it. The first two must be resolved during the first year of separation; Task I is Acknowledging the Reality of the Marital Rupture, and Task II is Disengaging From Parent Conflict and Distress and Resuming Customary Pursuits. Successful mastery of tasks 3 through 5 may take several years; Task III is Resolution of Loss, Task IV is Resolving Anger and Self-Blame, and Task V is Accepting the Permanence of the Divorce. The last task becomes salient during adolescence; Task VI is Achieving Realistic Hope Regarding Relationships.

As the trend in familial changes continues, children need to develop skills in adjusting to change as a typical process. Dr. Wallerstein recognized this need for school counselors to help prepare children to cope with change in a recent interview with one of the authors. A developmental guidance curriculum which helps understand that change is a natural process and helps them face unexpected events would be meaningful to children today.

Consultation Services for Children and Families in Transition. Counselors must assist teachers and administrators in becoming aware of and understanding the needs of children when their families are disrupted by change. When the family unit is in transition, the school is often the only place where children can obtain emotional support, security, and a sense of belonging. School is where children can find routine and consistency, predictable adult behavior, work expectations, and social contacts for support. However, children react differently, depending upon their stage of development, unique circumstances, and resilience. Therefore, the classroom and school functions need to be sensitive to such differences by avoiding labels and by providing services where needed. Through the consultative role, counselors can offer inservice activities to help teachers enhance the learning environment for children experiencing family transitions. Counselors need to facilitate teacher-parent communication in order to improve the relationship between schools and disrupted families. Workshops for parents are needed to help them develop effective parent-child relationships.

In consulting with teachers regarding children of divorce, counselors need to encourage them to be strong teachers and not therapists. To accomplish this, the counselor might say, "This child is having a crisis at home, but one of the strong things about this child is that he/she seems attached to you. Is there some way you can give the child a little extra recognition, a little extra time? Also, you might give him/her some extra work in a major interest."

Parents, also, need counselor assistance in developing an awareness and understanding of child needs during the family's transition. Most divorcing parents are too involved with their own emotional state and in coping with economic and social changes to be sensitive to their children and their needs. Consequently, the counselor can establish parent-group meetings to address common problems such as improving parent-child relationships, establishing self-care arrangements for children, and understanding typical child development.

Coordination Services and the Family in Transition. Identification and referral of children and families who need extensive counseling in order to resolve difficult issues is an important function of counselors. For parents who are most distressed or in need of long-term work, the counselor can help them find a support group or a counselor in private practice. Parents whose childrens' behavior indicates severe and chronic emotional problems should be encouraged to seek therapy for them.

Additionally, counselors can refer single parents to various community groups that will provide adult supervision and attention to children in need. For example, the Big Brothers/Big Sisters organization provides such services. Counselors may find that their community has an emergency telephone number for children to call when they are home alone or in need. If so, they should help the students to become aware of the number and how to use it.

As the make-up of the American family continues to evolve and family transitions become more the norm, the role of counselors will become increasingly important. So that families can continue to provide their time-honored purpose, we must assist families through their transition. Our message should be that the content of relationships is more important than context of the family structure.

REFERENCES

Bumpass, L. L. (1984). Children and marital disruption: A replication and update. *Demography*, 21(1), 71–82.

Elkind, D. (1981). *The hurried child*. Reading, MA: Addison Wesley.

Galambos, N. L., & Garbarino, J. (1983). Identifying the missing links in the study of latchkey children. *Children Today*, 40, 2–4.

Garbarino, J. (1980). Latchkey children: Getting the short end of the stick. *Vital Issues*, 30(3), 14–16.

Glick, P. C. (1984a). American household structure in transition. *Family Planning Perspectives*, 16(5), 205–211.

Glick, P. C. (1984b). Marriage, divorce, and living arrangements. *Journal of Family Issues*, 5(1), 7–26.

Glick, P. C. (In Press). The role of divorce in the changing family structure. In C. A. Wolchik and P. Karody (Eds.), *Children of divorce: Perspectives on adjustment*. New York: Gardner Press.

Hayghe, H. (1984). Working mothers reach record numbers in 1984. *Monthly Labor Review*, 107(12), 31–34.

Hetherington, E. M., Cox, M., & Cox, R. (1981). The aftermath of divorce. In E. M. Hetherington and R. D. Parke (Eds.), *Contemporary reading in child psychology, 2nd edition*. New York: McGraw Hill.

Hetherington, E. M., Cox, M., & Cox, R. (1982). Effects of divorce on parents and children. In M. Lamb (Ed.), Nontraditional families. Hillsdale, NJ: Lawrence Erlbaum.

Hetherington, E. M., Featherman, D. L., & Camara, K. A. (1981). *Intellectual functioning and achievement of children in one-parent households*. Unpublished manuscript written for the National Institute of Education.

Johnson, B. L., & Waldman, E. (1983). Most women who maintain families receive poor labor market returns. *Monthly Labor Review*, 102(12), 30–33.

Kamerman, S. B. (1983). Child-care services: A national picture. *Monthly Labor Review*, 106(12), 35–39.

Long, T., & Long, L. (1984). *The handbook for latchkey children and their parents*. New York: The Berkley Publishing Co.

Macklin, E. D. (1980). Nontraditional family forms: A decade of research. *Journal of Marriage and the Family*, 42, 175–192.

Smith, T. E. (1984). School grades and responsibility for younger siblings: An empirical study of the "teaching function." *American Sociological Review*, 49, 248–260.

Strother, D. B. (1984). Latchkey children: The fastest-growing special interest group in the schools. *Phi Delta Kappan*, 66(4), 290–293.

U. S. Bureau of the Census (1984). *Current population reports*, 20 (388), *Household and family characteristics:* MARCH 1983. Washington, DC: U. S. Government Printing Office.

U. S. Bureau of the Census (1984). *Current population reports*, 20 (393), *Geographical mobility:* March 1982 to March 1983. Washington, DC: U. S. Government Printing Office.

U. S. Bureau of Labor Statistics (1983). *Handbook of labor statistics* (Bulletin 2175). Washington, DC: U. S. Government Printing Office.

U. S. Bureau of Labor Statistics (1984). Marital and family patterns of workers: An update (Bulletin 2175). Washington, DC: U. S. Government Printing Office.

Waldman, E. (1983). Labor force statistics from a family perspective. *Monthly Labor Review,* 106(12), 16–20.

Wallerstein, J. S. (1983). Children of divorce: The psychological tasks of the child. *American Journal of Orthopsychiatry,* 53(2), 230–243.

Wallerstein, J. S., & Kelly, J. B. (1981). *Surviving the breakup: How children and parents cope with divorce.* New York: Basic Books.

Chapter 12

CHILDREN AND DIVORCE

Ruth K. Goldman

Annually, over one million youngsters are involved in marital dissolution. It is estimated that 11 million children from single-parent families attend school. According to Glick & Norton (1978) approximately one out of every five students in a classroom in the United States lives in a single family. Fifty percent of all divorces involve children (Norton, 1979). Two-thirds of American women who divorce are under 30, and the majority of children are under age seven at the time of the parents divorce or separation (Beal, 1980).

Depending upon socioeconomic status, an estimated 30 to 80 percent of any given school population in the United States lives with only one biological parent. If present trends continue, according to statistics from the Bureau of the Census, the estimate is that of children born in 1983, 45 percent will experience the divorce of their parents and 35 percent will experience the remarriage of their parents, while 20 percent will experience the redivorce of the remarried family before the age of eighteen (Norton, 1983). According to Leahey (1984), the widespread occurence of divorce is not limited to the United States; it is increasing in all social classes and in many parts of the world. For example, in Britain 10% of families have one parent; in France about 6% are single-parent families and similar data emerge from other parts of Europe and Canada.

Coddington's (1972) research makes clear that divorce and marital separation are second only to the death of a parent as stressful events for youngsters. Rapid and multiple changes are introduced which require adaptation on the part of all family members. Typically, anxiety increases at this time and, with it, the need for the youngster to experience a stable environment at the very time when the parents' capacity to provide nurturance is temporarily undermined (Wallerstein & Kelly, 1980). Given the magnitude of the changes, the family is usually unable to sustain intimacy and provide the requisite support, frequently leading to even

153

greater depression and anxiety for the child. For some families, this transitory failure resolves itself within two or three years of the separation; for others, a long-lasting family disequilibrium results. Hunter and Schuman (1980) refer to this latter group as the "chronically reconstituting family."

Reviewing the world-wide trend with regard to the statistics of separation and divorce, it becomes evident that the daily operation of the schools will be greatly effected. Unlike other stressful events, such as a death in the family, the news of a divorce does not herald support from the community. Not uncommonly, members of the divorcing family may be excluded from the social/familial network which would normally provide a source of support in other types of crises. Kalter and Plunket's research (1983) indicates that a substantial number of youngsters from both intact and disrupted families believe that children cause the divorce of their parents. Within the school setting, youngsters from intact homes often fear that their parents, too, will separate. This phenomenon of contagion in relation to divorce is frequently reported in the literature (Wallerstein & Kelly, 1980).

Schools are faced with extensive problems in being able to offer support to families of divorce. Opinion has been divided as to whether it is appropriate for schools to intervene in family-related crises (Drake; Goldman, 1981). Despite this division of opinion regarding the wisdom of offering school-based intervention programs, it is clear that the school **can** offer children a source of nurturance and continuity as well as a place where age-appropriate developmental tasks can be pursued by them. The research literature makes apparent (Peterson, Leigh, & Day, 1984; Stolberg & Cullen, 1983) that an individual's capacity to cope with the stress of familial change is partially dependent on the quality of support and guidance which is available from extra-familial organizations. The school is the **single** most important formal institution providing such support outside the home (Drake, 1983; Kelly & Wallerstein, 1979).

YOUNGSTERS AT RISK

Four major studies will provide the basis for a discussion of children at risk. The pioneering, and most comprehensive of the studies conducted over ten years by Wallerstein and Kelly, while limited in some design respects (60 families with 131 children from Northern California) continues to yield the richest source of clinical and conceptual material (Wallerstein & Kelly, 1980; Wallerstein, 1983; Wallerstein, 1984). Hetherington, Cox, and Cox (1978) conducted a more limited two-year study of 48 pre-school children and their families. According to them, within two years of divorce the majority of debilitating factors which encumber children have subsided and equilibrium is in the process of being restored. Though their research design included a control group matched for age, sex, birth order and numerous parent variables, it too, lacks racial, class and geographic representativeness.

More recently Kurdek and Berg (1983) and Kurdek, Blisk and Siesky (1981) have been following 74 families from an Ohio chapter of Parents without Partners in an attempt to assess and contrast childrens' and parents' post-divorce adjustment. As in the previously cited studies, sample selection and restriction and a variety of methodological problems continue to be present.

Guidubaldi, Cleminshaw, Perry, and Mcloughlin (1983) and Guidubaldi (1984) have attempted to resolve a number of the design limitations of past studies through employing a randomly selected national sample of elementary school youngsters, controlled for age, sex, race, I.Q., family income and geographic location. Currently, the authors have two- and three-year followups of two subsamples from the original group of 699 first-, third-, and fifth-graders.

Long Term Effects of Divorce

Disturbances in social and emotional development in girls have largely disappeared after two years according to Wallerstein & Kelly (1980). Although boys show marked improvement in adjustment in the two years following divorce, many still continue to have problems (Hetherington, Cox & Cox, 1979; Wallerstein & Kelly, 1980). In contrast to girls from divorced families and children from nuclear families, they have a higher rate of behavioral problems both at home and at school (Guidubaldi, 1984). This is true with friends and teachers alike.

Problems in parent/child relations continue to be found more frequently between divorced children and mothers, (especially between mothers and sons), in contrast to mothers and children in nuclear families. On the other hand, if we compare children in single-parent families with those in conflict-laden families, the former group functions more adequately. If this comparison is made in the first year following the divorce, this is not the case. It appears that as the escape from conflict increases, so does a child's adjustment.

Taking a look at the five-year study conducted by Wallerstein and Kelly, results based on 131 youngsters from 60 families are roughly the following: 34% were resilient—doing well; 29% were adjusting reasonably well; and 37% were depressed and wistfully looking back to the pre-divorce family. The longer term adjustment of the child appears to be more related to cumulative responses to stress (Rutter, 1979)—the single situational crisis, while painful, does not usually result in long-term problems by itself; continued, stressful experiences, such as a downward economic spiral and the many following consequences of chronic exposure to discord and loss of personal and social support are what cause long-term, psychological problems.

INTERVENTIONS

A review of the divorce literature on school-based interventions with families, reveals that with few exceptions, only the youngsters themselves are included in the various counseling approaches. The work of Stolberg and Cullen (1983), Stolberg and Garrison (1985), and that of Goldman and King (in press) appear to be the exception to the rule. However, only Goldman and King's program includes both parents in the intervention.

The most comprehensive ongoing clinical and research work with divorcing families originated in the ten-year project developed by Wallerstein and Kelly (1980). This approach to divorcing families has been expanded by Wallerstein and now exists in the form of a new five-year program, with multimodal interventions and a number of community outreach services. The school-based prevention program described later in this chapter by the author, is one of several models developed under the auspices of Wallerstein's Center for the Family in Transition.

Individual Interventions by Age

Since the original work of Wallerstein & Kelly continues to be the richest continuing source of clinical information on family interventions, the techniques developed by them for individual work with parents and children will serve as the primary reference in this section. In their article on brief interventions (1977) they describe the divorce-specific assessment developed to guide their work with youngsters of different age groups (a technique particularly useful to school psychologists). They evaluated the following factors: (a) each child's overall developmental achievements; (b) each child's unique responses to and experience with the divorce; (c) the support systems available to each child. In particular, they were concerned with how the child understood the meaning of the divorce. Drake (1981) has encouraged utilization of this divorce-specific assessment in intervention strategies with students in schools.

Wallerstein and Kelly (1980) suggest that interventions with pre-schoolers, who do not have a history of emotional difficulties, should focus primarily on the parents. The central intent should be to help parents communicate more effectively with their pre-schoolers and understand better the causes of the child's distress. Frequently, preventive interventions involve stabilizing aspects of both the caretaking situation and visits with the non-custodial parent.

Interventions for young elementary school children need to take cognizance of the child's realistic understanding of the basis for the divorce. Just as children of this age generally have difficulty in talking about issues which involve strong feelings, they have considerable trouble in talking about their parents' divorce. Kelly and Wallerstein (1977) found it necessary to develop an indirect technique for discussing the multiple and complex feelings which arose from the marital disruption. For example, the therapist would recount what such an experience was like for other youngsters of the same age, while specifically utilizing familial information unique to this child's situation in order to help the child express the painful feelings. In this way, they conveyed empathy and made clear the universality of the feeling without threatening the child's defensive stance of silence. Typically, this method promoted engagement on the part of youngsters who clearly did not want to participate in the counseling, but allowed them to do so with considerable respect for their privacy and without being overly intrusive. Kelly & Wallerstein (1977) refer to this method as the "divorce monologue."

Adolescents frequently turn to counselors for their support and assistance since they are able to understand their own conflicts and discuss them (Kelly & Wallerstein, 1977; Goldman, King & Lamden, 1980). Counselors are often perceived as empathic advocates who could help make sense of many issues in which split loyalty offered no opportunity for discussion with either parent. Brief interventions proved helpful with them when the problems were primarily divorce-related and concerned a variety of more external or environmental considerations. Frequently, for example, concern over a parent's welfare could be first addressed with a counselor and then taken up with the parent.

School-Based Group Interventions

Beginning with the work of Cantor (1977; 1979), time-limited counseling groups have been used to help students whose parents were recently separated or divorced and who showed signs of behavioral disruptions. Typically, these groups are offered to older elementary-school students of both sexes. Content centers on a child's confusion concerning the reasons for the divorce, loyalty conflicts, visitation issues, problems with step-parents and siblings, etc. Children report that sharing reactions to typical divorce-related issues offers them support and comfort. Group members uniformly indicate, when postgroup interviews are held, that the groups were of help to them. For a more extensive review of early efforts at using group models with children of divorce, see Drake (1981).

To give one example, Cantor (1977) began her school-based program by asking third grade through sixth grade teachers to submit the names of all students whose parents had been recently separated or divorced and who showed signs of behavioral disruption in the classroom. After parental permission had been obtained, students were invited to participate in the group. Mutual feelings which centered on having engaged in eavesdropping, spying, and carrying messages between parents were shared and discussed with one another. The capacity to unburden oneself through reporting such conduct and exploring the intensity of the feelings around this behavior was described by the participants as being of particular value. One boy wrote a play illustrating this range of feelings which was subsequently performed for the parents of participating students, (Cantor, 1979).

Four recent reports of successful school-based group intervention programs are described by Kalter, Pickar and Lesowitz (1984); Stolberg and Cullen (1983); Stolberg and Garrison (1985); and Pedro-Carroll and Cowen (in press). Kalter et al. (1984) have developed a highly structured, eight-week group which utilizes what they characterize as a "displacement format" in order to deal with youngsters' anxieties and cognitive confusions.

Two leaders ran all the groups and began the eight-week session by explaining the purpose, duration, and length of the group meetings. They were first given the four rules of the group:

1. only one group member could talk at a time;
2. each child's feelings would be respected;
3. anyone who did not feel like talking could listen instead and not take a turn;
4. everything that was said in the group was private.

The first group meeting began with the leaders suggesting a group story in which the parents of two children (a boy and a girl) were thinking of divorce. Each group member was given a turn to contribute to the development of the story and the material was summarized by the leaders at the end. Sessions two through six began with the group leaders initiating a post-divorce situation. The skits were intermittently interrupted for members to discuss troublesome feelings and reactions which were aroused.

In the seventh session, the leaders proposed the idea of a divorce newspaper in which all students took turns at being reporters, interviewing one another on topics central to the divorce experience. In the eighth session, a copy of the paper was given to each participant along with a group polaroid photograph. Additionally, a farewell party with refreshments concluded the final meeting.

These investigators confirm that the children's need for some form of help in coping with the family changes brought on by divorce extend well beyond the first year or two after the parental filing for divorce. They note that the majority of themes introduced by the participating children were related to adjustment difficulties in the **post-divorce and remarried** family (author's emphasis). Outcome data from these groups has yet to be compiled, however preliminary analysis reveals that they were viewed favorably by nearly all participants and their parents.

Stolberg and Cullen (1983) and Stolberg and Garrison (1985) discuss groups which are part of a multi-modal prevention program designed to facilitate post-divorce adjustment of mothers and children. Their 12-session childrens' groups were structured to include weekly meetings of one hour each with small groups of students aged 7–13. Participants were from families who were within 33 months of the parental separation. Relaxation, impulse and anger control techniques and communication skills were taught through methods that included modeling and role playing. Outcome data show that the child participants attained better self-concepts at the end of 12 sessions. At the five month follow-up, child participants were also found to have improved social skills.

Pedro-Carroll and Cowen (in press) describe children's school groups in which they used a variation of Stolberg and Cullen's (1983) strategies for teaching effective coping skills to children in the post-divorce family. Their ten week groups included students from fourth to sixth grade, with widely varying amounts of time from the parental divorce. They placed more emphasis on the supportive and expressive aspects of group content than on concrete application of coping skills. The participants reported an increased sense of mastery as well as a decreased sense of isolation and confusion. Positive effects of the group intervention were seen both clinically and statistically.

Illustratively, the groups had the following format over a ten-week period. The first three sessions were focused on an affective component in which the leaders helped the students become acquainted with one another and shared common experiences related to divorce. The next three sessions revolved around cognitive skill-building. The students were given "homework" which consisted of writing down specific divorce-related problems, which were then enacted in the sessions. A key component was the distinction between problems which were beyond the children's control and those within it. Emphasis was placed on understanding this distinction and attempting to deal effectively with problems which fell into the latter group. Sessions seven through nine dealt with the expression and control of anger related to Wallerstein's (1983) mastery tasks in regard to divorce. After identifying experiences which precipitated anger, group members discussed appropriate and inappropriate ways of expressing anger, including the consequences which followed from their actions. The last session was designed to evaluate the group and find ways for the youngsters to maintain friendships and other sources of support which would continue the process begun during the group sessions.

A Comprehensive Model of Prevention

While writers have described efforts at treating children of divorce in groups, little has been written which conceptualizes the activity group as **part** of an overall preventive approach to children as members of schools and communities (Drake & Shellenberger, 1981). Nor have writers sufficiently demonstrated how such group interventions address either the child's particular family situation or the stage of resolution a child has reached regarding the family crisis. Direct work in group settings with children, accompanied by indirect services such as consultation to faculty, is recommended as a way of meeting the needs of these youngsters.

Through the School Services Program of the Center for the Family in Transition, the author has designed a school-based intervention which incorporates activity groups for children of divorced families along with ongoing teacher training and consultation, combined with parent involvement. Through collaboration with administrators and faculty, the group interventions become pivotal in helping to create system changes for families in transition at both the school and the family level.

In formulating school-based interventions for children with familial disruptions, the following must be considered: (1) a youngster's capacity to cope with stress is dependent on his or her sex, age, developmental level, temperament, and problem-solving skills; (2) a youngster may simultaneously lose the support of extra-familial figures and be particularly needy of nurturance from empathic adults with whom they spend time; (3) a youngster may be experiencing a **chronic** and highly stressful **series of events** lasting in some cases for the entirety of a youngster's school years; (4) a youngster may be experiencing a set of indirectly related transitions such as loss of home, change in neighborhood or school, etc., increasing the stress of the actual familial disruption.

Group Format

The primary thrust of this model has been time-limited, activity/discussion groups led on the school site. The goals of the groups have been several: (a) to lessen feelings of isolation and shame; (b) to provide a protected environment in which children could develop effective coping skills in response to the family change; (c) to help emphasize the supportive aspects of the school environment.

Currently, the staff of the Center have worked with over 90 students in fourteen groups from five different schools. Nine of the fourteen groups were attended by latency-aged children and five by young adolescents.

Considerable attention was given to differentiating long-standing psychopathology from largely reactive responses to the familial change. Individual interviews were conducted by the group leader with each child participant, lasting between one and two hours. Non-intrusive measures were emphasized along with the divorce-specific assessment technique (Kelly & Wallerstein, 1977) to gain the necessary information for structuring group interventions.

Referral to the groups was primarily made by classroom teachers and principals. The participants fell into two general categories: (1) those undergoing a recent family change, e.g., divorce, separation or remarriage; (2) those with long-standing, school related difficulties for whom a family change was not a recent event.

The groups met once a week for 50–75 minutes over a six to twelve week period. Variation in duration and number of group sessions was dictated by the vagaries of the school calendar. The staff preference became a one-hour, weekly meeting, over a ten-week period.

It appeared that group members who had experienced a recent (within two years) familial change benefited most from the group. They were able to use the group to lessen confusion, increase coping skills, and gain emotional support. Children who were referred to groups because of long-standing difficulties and who had no recent family change, appeared to benefit least from the brief group intervention.

Examples of Group Activities

First Meeting: **Drawings of Good and Bad Changes:** During the first session, the idea of change was introduced and discussed. Each child was asked to draw a picture of a good change, and another picture of a bad change and then present the drawings to the group.

> One child drew a picture of his parents getting remarried. The ceremony was being performed by the Pope, illustrating the grandiose defense involved in his reconciliation fantasy.

Second Meeting: **Feeling Charades:** As a vehicle for introducing feeling states, a charade game was played. A child was given a card with a feeling written on it, such as happy, sad, angry, jealous, surprised, excited, etc. The child would then enact this feeling until it was guessed by the group.

Fourth Meeting: **Family Wish Drawings:** Each child was asked to draw a picture of something that they wished would change in their family over the next year. The major aim of this exercise was to introduce and discuss the reconciliation fantasy.

Fifth Meeting: **KKID Radio Broadcast:** The format of a mock radio broadcast provided a medium in which children and group leaders could ask and answer questions that concern children of separation and divorce. The interviewers and interviewees would alternate positions, asking questions such as, "What can children do when their parents fight?" and "Are children responsible for the divorce?" At one point in this activity, a distressed child called and asked the children what advice they could give about her parents' recent divorce.

Ninth Meeting: **Coping Skills Diplomas:** During the last group session, each child was given a piece of paper, rolled up like a diploma, on which was written a coping skill, such as, "When your parents are fighting, you can always call a friend, go out on your bicycle or read a book."

Journals: Each child was given a small book at the beginning of the group in which they could write about their concerns and feelings between sessions, thus adding a sense of continuity to the weekly activities. A Polaroid picture was taken of each child and glued onto the cover of his or her journal. Group Polaroid photos were also added to the journals, thus giving the children a concrete memory of the group experience from several perspectives. During follow-up interviews, several youngsters mentioned the journals and said that once in a while they would take them out, look at the pictures they drew, and remember what they had discussed.

Clearly, those children who discussed specific concerns or misunderstandings about their family situations were helped by the group itself. For example:

> One boy stated in a group session that he believed his parents decided to get a divorce because they were fighting over him. The leaders conveyed the idea that his parents may have been fighting about him because they both wanted him, but that the decision to divorce did not have anything to do with him. He then went home and asked his mother about the fighting. She confirmed that the original fights did not have anything to do with him, and the later ones were over their equal desire to have custody of him. This boy became very interested in divorce and brought a book about divorce to school which he shared with his class in a discussion facilitated by his classroom teacher.

The follow-up interventions (one month after termination of the groups) had their own benefits, since more was known about the children at this point. For example, sometimes it was possible to make recommendations which improved visitation patterns, and in several instances referrals were made for longer-term treatment.

In those schools where the Center staff has worked on-site for a period of years, a follow-up procedure has been employed with the students, their parents, and faculty participants. These interviews take place approximately nine-ten months after the initial group intervention. The extent of the follow-up varies with information provided either by faculty or through our own observations regarding youngsters at risk. Depending upon the students' post-divorce adjustment, a variety of interventions are initiated, ranging from special class placement and referrals for psychological treatment to consultation and collaboration with parents and/or faculty and administration.

Parent Participation

Initial contact with the custodial parent was made by a school administrator or pupil personnel employee and almost without exception consent was given for the child's participation in a group. Following this a letter detailing group goals and logistics was sent along with a written consent form. The custodial parent then met with the group leader either, (a) in an individual pre-group interview; (b) a one-time evening meeting for parents of all participating children with individual post-group interviews; or (c) a series of four evening group meetings designed to parallel the children's group. The choice of format was evolved during the five years' of our work in the schools and is based on availability of clinical time and perceived needs of the parents and school.

All parents were requested to complete a questionnaire on their child which asked for the following information: school history, previous psychotherapy, description of current custody arrangements, and their view of the child's strengths and weaknesses. Parents were told that the information would be kept confidential and not become part of the child's school record. Included in the questionnaire was a request to contact the child's non-custodial parent. Since research (Wallerstein & Kelly, 1980; Kurdek & Berg, 1983) clearly indicates that children who have continued, stable contact with both parents generally fare better in the post-divorce family, inclusion of the non-custodial parent seemed critical. When both parents still resided in the same geographic area, permission to contact the non-custodial parent was readily given.

Parent **group** meetings were less specifically child-focused than **individual** consultations with parents. Group participants used the meetings primarily to relieve guilty feelings over pursuing their own needs for development in roles other than that of parent. Individual interventions tended to be more focused on problem areas within the post-divorce and the remarried family, and related more specifically to the child group members. However, both types of interventions tended to cover these focal points: rearrangement of visitation patterns; differentiation of child and parent roles; amelioration of loyalty conflicts experienced by children; and education in expectable reactions to divorce, remarriage, and normal child development. Our own experience suggests that parents of younger children and those who were recently divorced (within one year of the intervention) were more interested in a series of group meetings than were parents of older students and those who had experienced a family change years before.

Teacher Participation

Consistent involvement of school faculty is an important facet of creating successful prevention models for the school system. While direct work with families must be carried out by a person with appropriate professional training, it is the teacher who will have the greatest cumulative effect on the largest number of students over time and therefore must be a central collaborator in this process. Of major importance, as well, are administrators who make policy determinations regarding how the needs of single-parent and remarried families will be incorporated in their schools.

Our intervention has thus included a strong emphasis on consultation to teachers regarding the child participants in the groups. After discussing their referral suggestions with them, each classroom teacher involved in a child participant's education, was asked to fill out two written evaluations at the beginning and end of the group. These evaluations helped teachers to focus their attention on students in a behavior-specific way. During the course of the group, the leader was available for weekly consultations with the teachers of participating youngsters. In many instances such consultations took the form of a five-minute check-in. In some cases, conjoint conferences among teachers, parents, and students were facilitated by the group leader in an effort to enhance communication about a student's school progress.

The following serves as an illustration of how our collaborative efforts with teachers led to a better understanding of a child's school performance, increased empathy for the youngster, and the possibility of reaching the student educationally through the use of alternative strategies.

A frustrated teacher complained of the immature quality of one girl's illustration for an essay, using it as an example of the generally poor quality of the student's work. The clinician was able to reframe the "immaturity" in this particular illustration of a house and a bunny. rabbit in a sunny field by talking about this 12-year-old's need for mothering and comfort which were triggered by the assigned topic, "Those were the Good Ole' Days." When seen in light of a longing for a predivorce family, this child's "immature" work was less frustrating to this teacher.

IMPLICATIONS FOR SCHOOL AND MENTAL HEALTH PROFESSIONALS

Because the school has the capacity to play such a unique role with regard to the learning problems associated with the stressors of separation and divorce, school and mental health professionals also have the opportunity to engage in a wide range of preventive interventions for youngsters faced with this stress. Together, school and mental health personnel may well provide the single most comprehensive continuing array of resources available for children during the crisis of divorce. Given the prevalence of divorce world-wide and indicators that the incidence rate is rising, school personnel are uniquely positioned to effect the learning and behavioral adjustment of children experiencing the process of divorce or separation.

In particular, working from the base of the school, mental health staff have the opportunity to initiate interventions programatically which can be maintained over long periods of time, share information with relevant school personnel, and follow-up individual students. Further, parents can and should be enlisted in a wide variety of interventions in order to broaden and sustain the impact of the help provided. At present, most school-based counseling models neither provide follow-up on youngsters after a group has ended, nor do these programs typically involve parents.

Our experience at the Center for the Family in Transition makes clear that the process of including parents increases the effectiveness of the intervention. Through the involvement of both parents and children it becomes possible to clarify misunderstandings on the part of all family members. The process of parallel counseling for both youngsters and parents affords all participants opportunities to reassess and alter ineffective behavioral patterns which have evolved in response to the divorce crisis.

With regard to the limitations of working on the school site, problems include: confidentiality, logistics of scheduling, interruption of a student's class, etc. Our staff has learned to sensitize teachers and other school personnel to the issues of privacy and to accept limitations on what information can be appropriately shared with them in regard to students. Understandably, parents in particular have doubts about revealing personal problems which may be communicated more broadly than they had intended. While mental health professionals are knowledgeable about the boundaries of confidentiality, frequently other participants in counseling groups may not be, and so potential violation of privacy is a continuing source of concern.

Given the primary responsibility of the school, which is the education of its students, programs such as those described in this chapter necessarily have lower priority, an issue for all mental health professionals working with schools. Sometimes this takes the form of difficulty in scheduling, short notice for a room change, or an unexpected test which will cause the cancelation of a group meeting without prior notice. This same set of problems applies to the teacher's availability to meet with pupil personnel staff in order to share information or help select appropriate members for counselling.

Working effectively in a school setting is slow, requiring ongoing and frequent contact with teachers and administrators. There is a temptation to join the school staff in "putting out fires" or only working with the most chronic, high profile youngsters, typically those who are most disruptive, and ignoring the more recent, less severely distressed students, who may be better candidates for change through short-term counseling groups.

Mental health professionals report frustration over the limitations of establishing a counseling model within an educational institution. The context is different from that of a mental health center. School psychology personnel need to take this difference into account and use it to their advantage rather than dwell on its limitations. For example, our experience makes clear that school-based interventions reach a clientele that would not ordinarily enlist or seek the aid of an outside agency and thereby forego help with their problems.

I would like to thank Mariam King for her many contributions to both the ideas, programs, and clinical material presented in this chapter and to thank Andrew Lamden for permission to report material from his group work in the schools.

REFERENCES

Beal, E. (1980). Separation, divorce and single-parent families. E. Carter & M. McGoldrick, (Eds.) In *The Family Life Cycle.* New York: Gardner Press.

Cantor, D. W. (1977). School-based groups for children of divorce. *Journal of Divorce, 2,* 357–361.

Cantor, D. W. (1979). Divorce: a view from the children. *Journal of Divorce, 1,* 183–187.

Coddington, R. D. (1972). The significance of life events as etiologic factors in the diseases of children—II. A study of a normal population. *Journal of Psychometric Research, 16,* 205–213.

Drake, E. A. (1981). Helping children cope with divorce: the role of the school. I. R. Stuart & L. E. Abt, (Eds.). In *Children of separation and divorce: management and treatment.* New York: Van Nostrand-Reinhold.

Drake, E. A. & Shellenberger, S. (1981). Children of separation and divorce: a review of school programs and implications for the psychologist. *School Psychology Review, 10,* 54–61.

Glick, P. & Norton, A. (1978). Marrying, divorcing, and living together in the U.S. today. *Population Bulletin, 32,* 3–38.

Goldman, R. K. (1981). *Teachers look at children of divorce in the classroom.* Available from the Center for the Family in Transition, 5725 Paradise Drive, Bldg. A, Suite 300, Corte Madera, California 94925.

Goldman, R. K., King, M. J., & Lamden, A. (1983). School-based interventions with children of divorce. Paper presented at the meeting of the American Orthopsychiatric Association, Boston.

Goldman, R. K. & King, M. J. (in press). Counseling children of divorce. *School Psychology Review.*

Guidubaldi, J., Perry, J. D., Cleminshaw, H. K. & Mcloughlin, C. S. (1983). The impact of parental divorce on children; report of a nationwide NASP study. *School Psychology Review, 12,* 300–323.

Guidubaldi, J. (1984). *Differences in children's divorce adjustment across grade level and gender: A report from the NASP-Kent State nationwide project.* Kent, Ohio: Kent State University.

Hetherington, E. M., Cox, M., & Cox, R. (1978). Play and social interaction in children following divorce. *Journal of Social Issues, 35,* 26–49.

Hunter, J. E., & Schuman, N. (1980). Chronic reconstitution as a family style. *Social Work, 26,* 446–451.

Kalter, N., & Rembar, J. (1981). The significance of a child's age at the time of parental divorce. *American Journal of Orthopsychiatry, 51,* 85–100.

Kalter, N., & Plunkett, J. W. (1984). Children's perceptions of the causes and consequences of divorce. *Journal of the American Academy of Child Psychiatry, 23,* 326–334.

Kalter, N., Pickar, J. & Lesowitz, M. (1984). School-based developmental facilitation groups for children of divorce: a preventative intervention. *American Journal of Orthopsychiatry, 54,* 613–123.

Kelly, J. B., & Wallerstein, J. S. (1977). Brief interventions with children in divorcing families. *American Journal of Orthopsychiatry, 47,* 23–26.

Kelly, J. B., & Wallerstein, J. S. (1979). Children of divorce. *The National Elementary Principal,* October, 52–58.

Kurdek, L. A., Blisk, D. & Siesky, A. E. (1981). Correlates of childrens' long-term adjustment to their parent's divorce. *Developmental Psychology. 17,* 565–579.

Kurdek, L. A., & Berg, B. (1983). Correlates of children's adjustment to their parent's divorce. L. Kurdek (Ed.). In *Children and Divorce: New Directions for Child Development Series 19,* 47–60.

Leahy, M. (1984). Findings from research on divorce: implications for professionals' skill development. *American Journal of Orthopsychiatry, 54* 298–315.

Norton, A. J. (1979). A Portrait of the one-parent family. *The National Elementary Principal,* October, 32–39.

Pedro-Carroll, J. L. & Cowen, E. L. (in press). The children of divorce intervention project: An investigation of the efficacy of a school-based prevention program. *Journal of Counseling Psychology.*

Peterson, G. W., Leigh, G. K., & Day, R. D. (1984). Family stress theory and the impact of divorce on children. *Journal of Divorce, 7,* 1–20.

Rutter, M. (1979). Maternal deprivation, 1972–1978: new findings, new concepts, new approaches *Child Development, 50,* 283–305.

Stolberg, A. L. & Cullen, P. M. (1983). Preventive interventions for families of divorce: The divorce adjustment project. L. Kurdek (Ed.) In *Children and Divorce: New Directions for Child Development Series 19,* 71–82.

Stolberg, A. L. & Garrison, K. M. (1985). Evaluating a primary prevention program for children of divorce: The divorce adjustment project. *American Journal of Community Psychology, 13,* 111–124.

Wallerstein, J. S. & Kelly, J. B. (1980). *Surviving the breakup: How children and parents cope with divorce.* New York: Basic Books.

Wallerstein, J. S. (1983). Children of divorce: The psychological tasks of the child. *American Journal of Orthopsychiatry, 53,* 230–243.

Wallerstein, J. S. (1984). Children of divorce: ten-year follow-up of young children. *American Journal of Orthopsychiatry, 54*(3), 444–458.

Chapter 13

SINGLE PARENT FAMILIES

GARY MILLER

The single parent population in the United States mainly consists of four distinct groups of people. Parents who have separated voluntarily represent 70% of the single parent population; another 14% are widowed; 10% were never married and 6% are people who are only temporarily separated due to military service or hospitalization (Weiss, 1979).

Divorced single parents are the fastest-growing single parent group. According to the United States Bureau of Census (1983) there was an increase in the ratio of divorced people from 1970 when 47 in every 1000 individuals were divorced compared to the 1983 figures which indicated that the ratio expanded to 114 divorced people to every 1000 persons. The peak year for divorces was 1981 when 1,213,000 divorces were registered compared to the 1962 figure of 413,000 (the State, 1985). Most divorces occur within the first seven years of marriage and in 1982 the average length of a marriage was 9.4 years (the State, 1985). The number of divorces declined in 1982 by some 43,000 to a figure of 1,170,000 (the State, 1985). Considering some of these figures, it has been estimated that 11 million school aged children are from divorced families and 50% of the children being born will live in a single parent home by the time they reach age 18 (Garvin, 1984).

The manner in which one becomes a single parent influences the individual in many different ways. When couples separate, one person usually places the blame for the disruption of the marriage on the other parent. When the single parent blames the former spouse, anger and bitterness surface. Hunt and Hunt (in Burden, Howton, Kripke, Simpson & Stultz, 1976) have indicated that the strong emotional impact results in some people becoming depressed and others becoming euphoric. It is not uncommon for the individual to experience swings between these extreme moods. Often, the individual feels dislocated from the social contacts they once had when they were part of a couple.

Single parents who have become single due to the death of a spouse are quite different. These individuals according to Weiss (1979) know that their marital relationship remained intact. They are able to see themselves in the single parent role as extensions of the marital relationship, carrying on the approaches to parenting that they shared with the deceased spouse. Weiss (1979) has indicated that the widow or widower usually has continued support and functions as a representative of the couple prior to the death of their spouse.

Irrespective of how one has become a single parent, the individuals must adjust to the termination of the marriage and work at developing a new life style (Spanier & Casto, 1979). The single parent will have legal issues to confront coupled with dealing with relatives and friends and coping with the emotional impact they are experiencing. Weiss (1976) has stated "Marital separation is an extensively disruptive event, not only ending the continued accessibility of the spouse but also producing fundamental changes in an individual's social role and in his or her relationship with children, kin, and friends" (P. 159).

Unlike the divorced or widowed single parent, the never-married mother is in a unique position. She has not experienced either the termination of a marriage or the death of a spouse and consequently has no former spouse to either blame nor does she have death to blame for her current situation. Unfortunately, she may turn to her child as a source of blame for her situation.

As can be seen, people can become single parents in many ways.

CONCERNS AND ISSUES

One of the principle concerns facing the single parent is finances. LeMaster (1971 in Skolnick & Skolnick) found that 25% of mothers without partners can be found in poverty groups. In addition, 40% of the fathers are delinquent in their support payments. Having less money to maintain a household can place much stress on the single parent. The single parent, usually a woman, is often faced with making financial decisions and confronting household and child care expenses that she previously did not have to face. The pressures for the divorced parent to maintain a standard of living commensurate with the pre-separation standard is often greater than the pressure for other single parents. The widowed single parent has insurance settlements, Social Security and family support to assist her. The never-married mother may not have to worry about sustaining a substantive standard of living and consequently may not feel the same pressures as the single parent who is divorced. Even in situations where financial means are adequate, it is still a concern for single parents as they attempt to provide economic support similar to that of their children's peers. Weiss (1979) has observed that single parents who worked before becoming single usually continued to work and those who did not work before becoming single enter the labor market.

Within the single-parent family a redefinition of the parent-child relationship and the role of parents and their children will emerge. The single parents who are employed will not be able to devote as much time to housework as they may have done before. Consequently, the children may be more involved in daily household chores. The children may also assume some responsibilities in decision-making for the family. Gasser and Taylor (1976) indicated that single-parent fathers experienced role adjustments in the home management area. Those fathers with small children assumed the major responsibilities for child care. The single fathers studied by Gasser and Taylor (1976) had an understanding of their roles, but felt overburdened with their responsibilities. When single parents feel overburdened, there is the possibility that they may begin to rely too heavily on the children and actually seek support and companionship from them, which may deny the children their own opportunities for personal development and growth.

Weiss (1979) has indicated three overload areas that impact on the single parent. As one begins to make decisions regarding household finances, and childrearing, there can be a responsibility overload (Weiss 1979) which can result in added stress and tension. The efforts to balance the many new priorities can produce a task overload.

Weiss (1979) also identified emotional overload which occurs as one strives to give emotionally to one's children and eventually becomes depleted. As single parents and their children work at redefining their roles it would be helpful to discuss how responsibilities, tasks, and emotional demands will be addressed in this new family configuration.

Another avenue for the single parent to address is the manner in which they begin to reestablish social contacts. According to Getty (In Getty and Humphreys, 1981), the least desirable social position for an unmarried woman is that of a single parent.

Both men and women who are single parents need to have a sense of membership through contacts with other individuals. Without meaningful contacts people can begin to feel isolated and removed from society at large.

Another area of social adjustment for the single parent focuses on their feelings of loneliness and their need for sexual intimacy. Pett (1982) found that high-risk single parents tend to feel socially isolated, experiencing depression, hopelessness and a lack of control over their lives. Weiss (1979) examined some of the factors attributing to the single parent's hesitance in establishing an intimate relationship with another adult. Single parents struggle a great deal trying to balance and resolve their feelings of commitments both to their children and new relationships. In addition, they make a concerted effort to protect their children from forming any new attachments. Consequently, the parent limits interaction between the new friend and their children. Berry (1981) concluded that while single fathers strive to maintain a social life, their social activity is restricted somewhat by their parenthood.

Single parents are reserved regarding their sexual activity (Weiss, 1979). Although they may be sexually active they do not want their children to be aware of this aspect of their lives. Parents wish to present themselves as a model to their children and do not want the children to engage in sexual activity until they are sufficiently mature to act in a sexually responsible fashion. In Berry's (1981) study, although they were sexually active, single fathers reported protecting their children from this knowledge and generally did not engage in sexual activity in their homes.

As single parents develop new relationships, there are numerous issues the child must face regarding the new person. According to Arnold and Anderson (in Burden, et.al. 1976), the child may see the new individual as a competitor for the parent's love and affection or as a replacement for the position in the family that the child has attempted to fill due to the absence of the original parent. Some children need help in accepting the death of their dream for a family with both parents present. At times the child may see the new friend as a relief from the abandonment felt from the loss of one parent. Sexual activity between the parent and newcomer may also be misinterpreted by the child.

Hunt and Hunt (in Burden, et al. 1976) have examined the nature of relationships that formerly married people enter. Friendship relationships are seen when feelings are vented and advice and support are provided for each other. Such a relationship usually changes as one of the pair marries. Individuals may also enter casual dating relationships wherein life stories are discussed and reasons for failed marriages are examined. In this relationship people find comfort as they share their experiences. Uncommitted love relationships represent another type of relationship people may experience. The individuals are sexually involved, yet seldom mention love. Both parties may be experiencing an ambivalence, and since it may not be an exclusive relationship, it becomes difficult to keep feelings in order. As they describe committed relationships, Hunt and Hunt (Burden, et al) note three factors. People first begin to date exclusively, yet do not make a love commitment. In the second type, people may make a wrong choice due to age differences, insufficient recovery time between the divorce and the new relationship, or incompatible family compositions. The third type of this relationship is when a couple decides to live together.

It is quite obvious that single parents have many stresses in their lives. Adjusting to a single life-style, parenting alone, and developing positive relationships are but a few of the issues they must face.

HELPING SINGLE PARENTS

The single parent as noted above has many issues to face in the adjustment process. Fortunately, many people have addressed these issues and have developed strategies for helping.

Getty (in Getty & Humphreys 1981) has examined numerous therapeutic considerations for working with single parents in various transitional stages. In the initial stage of adjustment to their new role as a single parent, the counselor must try to develop an understanding and appreciation of the impact the event has had on the person, and learn how the individual is dealing with the stress and emotions being experienced. Whether the person is in individual counseling or group counseling, feelings and emotions should be freely expressed and heard. While some people may need to learn how to manage the stress they are experiencing, others may need to come to terms with their feelings and begin to develop productive ways to develop their new lives.

Getty (in Getty & Humphreys 1981) has suggested some things counselors can do to assist the family unit as it begins to deal with social considerations. The counselor may need to determine what information has been shared with relatives and friends about the break-up of the marriage, and how this information was given and received. Sometimes when people have not openly shared the situation with others, they may see themselves as deviant, consequently further inhibiting their adjustment. The counselor can often function as a support person for the family.

Getty (in Getty & Humphreys, 1981) has also addressed the life cycle stage of the person as they attempt to develop a new single-parent lifestyle. There are age-specific needs for family members that must be addressed in the new single-parent family. There are obvious differences between the 30-year-old mother with two young children and the woman in her mid-50's with young adult children.

Sanders and Thompson (1976) developed a model for parenting that incorporated assertive behaviors for parents. Sanders and Thompson (1976) believe that as parents model assertive behavior they teach their children those dimensions of self-respect and sensitivity to others that are necessary to the establishment of healthy human relationships.

A school-based program has been described by Green (1981). In this model, seven modes are incorporated in the helping process for the single parents. In the first mode people are encouraged to examine how they are taking care of their physical well-being by having proper nutrition, exercise, and sleep. Emotions, the second mode, are considered as people gain awareness of their emotions and learn strategies such as relaxation-training and anxiety-management. Learning, the third mode, focuses on learning the legal information regarding divorce in one's state as well as learning to cope with one's life-style needs in the areas of employment, finances and child care. Personal relationships are also addressed in the multimodal approach. Individuals learn communication skills, ways to spend quality time with their children, and how to develop a supportive network for themselves. Issues about one's image and interests promote both the enhancement of group members' self-esteem and the development of new interests and ways to experience fun in one's life. In the need-to-know mode, people learn rational "self-talk" and develop problem-solving and decision-making skills for themselves. The final mode teaches management of one's family, incorporating positive guidance and discipline approaches within the family.

An interesting aspect of Green's (1981) approach deals with the irrational beliefs parents hold about being divorced. Each parent is encouraged to consider various irrational statements and develop a positive change for each. Some examples of irrational statements include: "I must be a terrible person or I would not be in this situation"; "I made a mistake this time so it means I'm a failure"; "I must be a more perfect parent because I am solely responsible for my children"; and "I must always love my child" (Green, 1981, p. 256).

Strom, Fleming & Daniels (1984) were able to examine fathers and the strengths they have in the single parent role. Their findings suggest that single fathers " . . . were more supportive of creative behavior during childhood, more tolerant of immaturity in their young sons and daughters, more willing to be interrupted by children when necessary, more able to share control with children and foster self-reliance, more respectful of children's strengths and preferences, and more relaxed during play with them" (p. 86).

Baruth and Burggraf (1984) have suggested that parent study groups be developed for the purpose of helping single-parent families. They have developed the following guidelines for individuals starting such study groups:

1. Inform parents about study groups by providing basic information such as the time and place for the group's meeting. Letters sent home with children or public service announcements in local media can be helpful in keeping parents informed.
2. Limit the size of the group from 8 to 12 parents. This size range can foster greater parental communication in the group.
3. Set the time and place for the meetings keeping in mind that evening hours are more suitable for working parents. Each meeting should be two hours long and should be conducted on a weekly basis over a 10 week period.
4. Establish a deadline for when parents can enter the study group. New members should not enter the group after two meetings have been completed.
5. Before one teaches a parent study group, one should participate first as a group member, then co-lead a group with supervision.

Baruth suggests the following guidelines for child rearing that can be of real benefit for single parents (1979):

1. Follow the golden rule and treat your children as you wish to be treated.
2. Develop mutual respect with your children by listening to their ideas and opinions. This can promote self-respect in the

children who in turn will respect others, including their own parents.

3. Incorporate approaches that will motivate the child, resulting in more and better cooperation. One should avoid using force and power over one's children.

4. Respect the individual differences of your children. Rather than try to shape or remold the children, help them change some of their differences that may become something of a handicap in the years ahead.

5. Realize that the behaviors of the children do have a purpose. One way to determine the goal is for the parent to examine his or her own reaction to the behavior. By doing this one can quickly identify the goal and then select an appropriate response.

6. Punishment, rewards and praise are not always reliable as each may generate results that are counterproductive to the child—parent relationships.

7. Use consequences to allow the children to realize what happens to them as a result of their behavior. Rather than becoming involved in a lecture to the children about their behavior, let them learn from the consequences of that behavior.

8. Parents who encourage their children stress what is right, not what is wrong with the children. Encouragement can do much to promote feelings of acceptance, appreciation and respect.

9. Parental attention that demonstrates interest and friendliness is positive for both the parent and the children.

10. Avoid acting on your first impulse when a disruption starts, instead:
    a. Take time to examine what is happening
    b. Weigh the wisest and the least wise things to do in the situation.
    c. Be alert as to what your child anticipates you to do, then do the opposite.
    d. Communicate after your anger has lessened.

11. Take time to train your children in successful living skills that promote a satisfactory life style. This will eliminate spending excessive time and energy to correct the untrained child.

12. Do not dwell on mistakes. Use them to learn and develop better ways to deal with some similar situations in the future.

13. When power struggles emerge, leave the scene of the situation. Don't worry about doing something everytime disruption develops.

14. Attempt to do only what you can manage to do in a situation. Strive to be consistent and firm in your behavior in the situation.

15. When talking with children about misbehaviors, be friendly. Don't talk to punish, talk to work out the problem at hand.

16. Be sensible in what you expect from your children. Try not to overburden the children with too many tasks to complete.

17. Promote self-responsibility in your children by letting the child complete activities presented to him or her.

18. Discourage self-pity in children by teaching them to take what comes their way in life rather than bemoan what they are experiencing.

19. Parents should not become overly dependent on their children as if the children are their sole reason for existing. Rather, promote responsible independence that leads to mutual respect, not unhealthy dependence.

20. Children may have fears, but parents need not overreact to these through sympathy and pity. Try to assure the children and encourage them to do the thing they are fearing. Overcoming a fear can be enhancing to one's self-concept and promote a feeling of success.

21. Bossy parents raise bossy children. To avoid having bossy children one should let children know what is expected without being bossy. A matter-of-fact statement of expectations and patience can be very valuable in getting the desired behavior from the child.

22. Be specific in what you say to your children, and consistent in your expectations of them.

23. Develop regular routines for doing things. Such structure provides for predictability and consequently clarifies expectations within the family unit.

24. Conduct family meetings on a regular basis and allow children to activily participate in the decision-making process for the family. Such meetings can be most productive when people can air their feelings, discuss their needs and feel accepted and appreciated as individuals. Much cooperation and harmony in the family is often generated through family meetings.

25. Families should take time for having fun and playing together. In light hearted moments of free interactions, friendships in the family can develop. Individuals can use recreation for the purpose of re-creating themselves and their relationships.

SUMMARY

The family in the United States has undergone significant shifts in the last decade. The emergence of single-parent families has become acceptable reality as individuals strive to successfully re-work their lives with their children.

Counseling services at both the school level and community level can assist single parents in their own personal adjustments and in their adjustments with their children. This chapter has presented some issues facing single parents along with strategies that may be helpful to the parent.

The author thanks Lynda Ann Neese for her contributions to this chapter.

REFERENCES

Arnold, K. & Anderson, J. (1976). New relationships. In S. Burden, P. Houston, E. Kripke, R. Simpson & W. F. Stultz (Eds.). *Proceedings of the changing family conference V. The single parent family* (pp. 11–16). Iowa City: The University of Iowa.

Aslin, A. (1976). Counseling "single-again" women. *Counseling Psychologist. 6*, 37–41.

Baruth, L. G. (1979). *A single parent's survival guide: How to raise the children.* Dubuque: Kendall/Hunt.

Baruth, L. G. & Burggraf, M. Z. (1983). Helping single parent families. *Counseling And Human Development. 15*(7), 1–15.

Baruth, L. G. & Burggraf, M. Z. (1983). The counselor and single parent families. *Elementary School Guidance and Counseling. 19*, 30–37.

Berry, K. K. (1981). The single male parent. In I. R. Stuart & L. E. Abt (Eds.). *Children of separation and divorce* (pp. 34–52). New York: Van Nostrand Reinhold.

Garvin, J. P. (1984). Children of divorce—A challenge. *Middle School Journal. 16*, 6–7.

Gasser, R. D. & Taylor, C. M. (1976). Role adjustment of single parent fathers with dependent children. *Family Coordinator. 25*, 397–401.

Getty, C. (1981). Considerations for working with single parent families. In Getty & W. Humphreys (Eds.). *Understanding the family stress and change in American family life* (pp. 401–417). New York: Appleton-Century-Crofts.

Green, B. J. (1981). Helping single parent families. *Elementary School Guidance and Counseling. 15*, 249–262.

Henderson, A. (1981). Designing school guidance programs for single-parent families. *School Counselor. 29*, 124–132.

Hunt, M. & Hunt, B. (1976). Patterns and potential for the single parent relationship. In S. Burden, P. Housont, E. Kripke, R. Simpson & W. F. Stultz (Eds.). *Proceedings of the changing family conference V. The single parent family* (pp. 28–29). Iowa City: The University of Iowa.

Jenkins, G. G. (1976). The single-parent family: An overview. In S. Burden, P. Houston, E. Kripke, R. Simpson & W. F. Stultz (Eds.). *Proceedings of the changing family conference V. The single parent family* (pp. 11–16). Iowa City: The University of Iowa.

LeMaster, E. E. (1971). Parents without partners. In A. S. Skolnick & J. H. Skolnick (Eds.). *Family in transition rethinking marriage, sexuality, child rearing, and family organization* (pp. 403–410). Boston: Little, Brown.

Moses, H. S. & Zaccaira, J. S. (1969). Bibliotherapy in an educational context: Rationale and principles. *High School Journal, 52,* 401–411.

Number of divorces stems 20-year rise. (1985, March 7). *The State,* p. 5-A.

Pett, M. G. (1982). Predictors of satisfactory social adjustment of divorced single parents. *Journal of Divorce. 5*(3), 1–17.

Sanders, J. & Thompson K. (1976). Assertive behavior — A model for parenting. In S. Burden, P. Houston, E. Kripke, R. Simpson & W. F. Stultz (eds.). *Proceedings of the changing family conference V. The single parent family* (pp. 92–93). Iowa City: The University of Iowa.

Skolnick, A. & Skolnick, J. (Eds.). (1977). *Family in transition.* Boston: Little, Brown.

Spanier, G. B. & Casto, R. F. (1979). Adjustment to separation and divorce: An analysis of 50 case studies. *Journal of Divorce. 2,* 241–253.

Strom, R., Fleming, G., & Daniels, S. (1984). Parenting strengths of single fathers. *Elementary School Guidance and Counseling. 19,* 77–87.

Tedder, S. L., Libbee, K. M. & Scherman, A. (1981). A community support group for single custodial fathers. *Personnel and Guidance Journal. 60,* 115–119.

U.S. Bureau of the Census (1983). *Marital status and living arrangements:* March, 1982 (Current Population Reports, Series. P. 20 No. 380). Washington, D.C. U.S. Government Printing Office.

Weiss, R. (1976). The emotional impact of marital separation. *Journal of Social Issues. 32,* 135–146.

Weiss, R. (1979). Going it alone. *National Elementary Principal. 59*(1): 14–26.

Chapter 14

STEPFAMILIES

WILLIAM A. POPPEN AND PRISCILLA N. WHITE

During the 1960's and until the latter part of the 1970's, remarriage rates increased in our society from a total of 19% of all marriages annually in 1960 to 29% in 1977 (Albrecht, Barr & Goodman, 1983). The great majority of these remarriages occurred following divorce. Glick (1979) has estimated that by 1990, 15% of all children will be living in a stepfamily. When these figures are viewed within the context of the school setting, Prosen and Farmer (1982) estimated that one in every six children in any school classroom is a stepchild.

These figures support the conclusion that the stepfamily is an increasing family form in our society. Practitioners working with children will be dealing with these types of families and the unique problems and issues which they face.

A number of scholars have attempted to develop descriptions of the different types of stepfamilies based on the former marital and parental status of partners in a remarriage (Katz and Stein, 1983; Schlesinger, 1983). Schlesinger (1983) found the most common types of stepfamilies to be those that involved previously divorced and unmarried partners and those in which both partners entered remarriage following divorce. The term stepfamily as used in this chapter denotes a situation in which one or both partners have been formerly married and have children. For a majority of stepfamilies the former marriage or marriages were terminated by divorce.

INTACT FAMILIES VERSUS STEPFAMILIES

In what ways do stepfamilies differ from intact, nuclear families? Stepfamilies are formed out of a past which has involved the experience of loss and disruption of attachment. Poppen and White (1984) developed a model that illustrated the complex interrelationships of subsystems involved in the various transitions that have been experienced by stepfamilies as they move from intact family to single-parent family to stepfamily.

In addition to this experience of disruption of attachment, stepfamilies are comprised of parent-child relationships which predate the marital relationship. Visher and Visher (1983) stated that this characteristic of stepfamilies may be the most stress-producing aspect of this family form. Stepfamilies do not have a period in which to solidify the marital bond before dealing with the demands of parent-child relationships. These demands, at least initially, are even greater than in nuclear families because of the lack of continuity in parent-child relationships.

Individuals in stepfamilies bring with them past histories which influence their beliefs about how families are supposed to function. The rights, roles, and responsibilities of family members must be redefined. Often, the past experiences of children and adults have shaped differing expectations in these areas.

Perhaps one of the most complex characteristics of the stepfamily is the existence of a biological parent external to the stepfamily. Boss (1983) discussed the issue of family boundaries and emphasized that boundaries in families are determined by **both** the physical and psychological presence or absence of individuals. The other biological parent is not physically present in stepfamilies but psychologically may be a strong force in how the stepfamily functions.

In a majority of stepfamilies not only is there a biological parent elsewhere, but children in the stepfamily are members of two households or what Jacobson (cited in Rubenstein, 1983) referred to as "linked family systems." In her study of linked family systems, Jacobson found considerable variation in the extent to which the conflicts inherent in this situation are handled. Trying to juggle the demands and inconsistencies between households can be frustrating. Unless linked family systems evolve ways of handling conflicts constructively, stresses escalate over time.

Finally, Visher and Visher (1983) discussed the blending of atypical developmental stages in stepfamilies. The tasks and goals of families are influenced by the stages of both individual and family development. Some stepparents have stepchildren close to them in age, children often are widely spaced, and age differences for spouses many times are greater than in intact families.

PARENT-CHILD RELATIONS IN STEPFAMILIES

Our purpose is to focus most directly on issues that impact on parent-child relationships. Carlson (1985) recommended that in working with stepfamilies in the context of school-related problems the most appropriate focus is on the functioning of the parent-child dyad.

Recent research on stepfamilies shows that an often problematic issue for both adults and children is discipline (Lutz, 1983; Messinger, 1976; Visher and Visher, 1979). Discipline of children is a primary source of conflict in all families and given the uncertainty, complexity, and ambivalence surrounding adult-child interactions in stepfamilies, child discipline can become a very emotionally charged arena. Visher and Visher (1979) pointed out that effective discipline is based on mutual trust and caring between children and adults. It takes time to develop trust and caring in relationships. Trying to "force" instant caring and reciprocity or as Visher and Visher (1979) termed it, the "myth of instant love," is counterproductive and produces resentment and hostility instead of genuine caring. Child discipline may be especially problematic for stepfamilies until trusting and caring relationships are established. One of the most crucial elements for effective discipline is for biological parents and the stepparent to agree that the ultimate goal is the best interest of the child. To as great an extent as possible, the limits and disciplinary measures used by adults in the child's life need to be consistent.

The standard of living in stepfamilies is usually lower than was the case in the predivorce family (Wallerstein and Kelly, 1980). Added to this change in standard of living is the reality of trying to integrate the functioning of what had been, until remarriage, two independently functioning economic systems. Fishman (1983) examined the patterns used by stepfamilies in handling financial resources and found "common-pot" families in which resources were pooled and "two-pot" families in which the resources brought by individuals into stepfamilies were safeguarded. She concluded that the "common-pot" family created an atmosphere more conducive to unification of stepfamilies.

In terms of decisions about the management of both time and money in stepfamilies, alternatives need to be evaluated in terms of what is most equitable. Both children and adults can more easily accept decisions if there is a belief that over time there is a fair distribution of costs and benefits in the pattern of decision-making.

Lutz (1983) found that children in stepfamilies reported experiencing the most stress around issues of divided loyalties. Children often experience confusion and guilt in terms of how their affection and allegiance should be expressed. Wallerstein and Kelly (1980), in their longitudinal study of children following divorce, found that most children seem to be able to resolve these conflicts satisfactorily if parents and stepparents were not competing for the child's affection and allegiance. The child needs to be reassured that human beings function throughout life in a multiplicity of loving relationships and that these relationships can co-exist without diminishing one another.

One of the most important concepts for understanding stepfamilies and the stresses they face is the concept of "pile-up." McCubbin and Patterson (1982) defined "pile-up" as the cumulative effects of changes and stresses on families. Stepfamilies are characterized by a complex history of disruptions and discontinuities. Both stamina and resources for coping with change can become depleted, especially if changes are closely timed.

Positive adaptation takes time for stepfamilies, and research has shown that the most stressful period of transition is the first two years following remarriage (Lutz, 1983; Visher and Visher, 1979). The importance of helping families develop positive parent-child relationships is reflected in Issacs's (1982) summary of factors that work against the "process of blending." She stated that the three most common problems for stepfamilies in achieving positive adaptation were: 1) The stepfamily tries to achieve instant integration; 2) The stepparent and the non-custodial parent develop an adversarial relationship; 3) the hierarchy of roles in the family is reversed, with the stepparent being lower on the hierarchy than children.

One element that seems to be basic for positive adaptation of both adults and children in stepfamilies is the nature of the relationship between adults in the linked family system. The more civil and cooperative adults can be in their interactions with one another, the fewer the difficulties experienced in making a positive transition (Wallerstein and Kelly, 1980). When difficulties do occur, it is likely that children may act out in the school setting some of the conflicts they are experiencing.

Interventions

What is so confounding about intervening with either the stepfamily or individual members of the stepfamily is that there usually are two main areas in which they are having difficulty (Robinson, 1982). One area is dealing with the unresolved feelings of loss, separation, and rejection associated with the break up of the previous family unit. The second area is the task of developing new attachments. In effect, members of the stepfamily unit are faced with giving up the old while at the same time trying to accept the new. Trying to accomplish these two tasks simultaneously can be very perplexing.

One of the first steps to be taken by the counselor is to assess the situation in order to determine which interventions may be most appropriate. Carlson (1985) has presented a detailed interview assessment outline which includes the following information:

A. A complete description of the presenting problem, the extent, the duration and consistency in different settings and relationships. How, specifically, is the family affected by the problem?

B. A diagram of the family composition and a developmental history. What is the family history and how resolved, supportive, and stressful is the family structure?

C. A detailing of current family functioning to include how family members describe the stepfamily experience. How does the stepfamily influence the couple's relationship? How do the children get along in the family? Across households? What is the relationship of the family to previous spouses or significant friends and relatives?

D. A listing of factors related to external support and stress. For example, family income, employment, parent's support network, childrens' support network, and social and recreational outlets.

The assessment interview is intended to be completed with the entire stepfamily unit. When this is not possible attempts should be made to talk to as many members as possible. Including both parents and at least one of the children would be considered minimal in order to obtain ideas about different perspectives and existing conflicts.

COUNSELING CHILDREN AND ADOLESCENTS

The primary goal for counseling children in stepfamilies is to help them make the adjustment to the stepfamily arrangement and resolve the feelings of loss that they have about past arrangements. Some children are better candidates for counseling than others. Children ages 9–12 are generally more interested in counseling than younger children. Children above 12 seem somewhat reluctant, with boys generally being more resistant than girls. Children as young as four and those at every age are able to benefit from counseling, both group and individual, as a means of coping with divorce and remarriage situations (American Institutes for Research, 1982).

Remarriage can make things better for younger children but for approximately one in four children, remarriage was not seen as improving their life, especially if the children were age ten or older at the time of remarriage (Wallerstein and Kelly, 1980).

Children and adolescents commonly report three things that block their transition to the remarriage: feeling responsible for what happens in the family, feeling less worthy and feeling helpless about what is happening to them. Jewett (1982) has noted ways to determine what may concern the young client. One method is to **ask directly**. The counselor might say, "So your dad is not going to see you during the week now that your mother has remarried. What would make him do that?" Or: "Other children have told me that when their parent remarried someone with children, they felt less important. Do you think it will be like that for you?" The counselor might also make personal statements such as, "I'm wondering if you are worried that you will not be close to your real parent." "I'm wondering if you think that your stepparent will not like you." "I'm guessing that you think your mother or father no longer loves you, or that the new marriage will break up" (Gardner, 1982).

A second technique is to use a more **indirect method** of asking children to communicate their helplessness, self-blame, or low self-esteem symbolically. The counselor, using this approach, may tell the child about a boy or girl who wakes up afraid and says, "I had a very bad dream." The client is then asked to imagine what the child's dream was about.

In other instances the counselor might use the indirect method by telling a short fictional story and asking the client to label the strong feelings of the main character. The child may suggest what the character could do in order to make things better.

It may be important for the counselor to **convey** some message which encourages the child. Obviously it does little good to tell a child not to worry about the feelings or concerns expressed, but a message of encouragement can be helpful. It is important that the counselor convey a message, not by advising, but by making reference to someone outside the counseling setting. A counselor might say, "I talked to someone last year who was worried that his new stepbrother would get to use all of his toys and wear all of his clothes. It only took him a few weeks to find out that no one would get his stuff." The client is encouraged by the message that other children feel this way yet they end up solving their problems. Another encouraging message the counselor can convey is that there are ways that new marriages can help make children happier. The counselor can ask if the child would like to " . . . talk about that," thereby helping to establish the acceptance of changes.

Once the reality has set in, the child may have a number of questions about remarriage arrangements. Whether the counselor is meeting with children in a small group or individually, some topics and themes (mentioned earlier in this report) will recur. Reviewing these may be essential in order to innoculate the client to the effects of thinking these happenings are unexpected and unique.

The complexities of divorce and remarriage may have the counselor feeling like a spectator without a program at a ballgame. By using a specific procedure for identifying the members of the stepfamily and other significant persons, the counselor also helps the child accept it as an alternative to the intact nuclear family. Whenever children share information about the members of their previous family arrangement(s) and their present stepfamily in counseling groups, they gain a sense of commonality with the other group members. Jewett (1982) suggested that it might be helpful to look at the child's personal history by doing a time line. With older children the time line traces, complete with dates, the child's history from birth to present. With younger children, a piece of string or yarn might serve as the line, much like a clothesline, and drawings or notes might be hung from the line to depict the sequence of the family formation, break-up, remarriage and other key events in the child's life.

Discussions with children about their "stepfamily" usually elicit statements about being left out or feeling helpless. These children develop an inability to ask for the things that they need especially if the needs are for affection or support. Role playing or visualization may be useful in order to help the client learn to say, "I need a hug" or "I'd like to have a story read to me at bedtime."

Many times feelings of helplessness may result in the child attempting to influence what happens to them in the new family structure. Children, through discussion, usually come to see that when they test limits, they may be trying to control their situation. The counselor can ask children to recount scenes of conflict and to make judgments about whether they wanted a hug or a fight. Was what they did a good way to go about getting a hug? If they wanted a fight how did they think it would pay off for them? In effect, by asking the child to make judgments about these behaviors the child begins to see that individual choices affect what will become of the new family.

A good way to improve the child's or adolescent's problem-solving abilities is to use problem-solving techniques within the counseling sessions. One procedure which is very popular with younger children is the brainstorming game. The counselor begins by drawing three or four circles on a page and saying, "We need some ideas to help solve this problem. Let us see if we can get one idea written in each of these circles. Will you start by giving me one plan that might solve this problem?" If the child is stumped the counselor may suggest ideas. First, the counselor must give at least two ideas so that the child must decide between alternatives. Second, the ideas are presented as originating with some-one other than the counselor so that the child will not be afraid of letting the counselor down if the plan is rejected. For example, a counselor might suggest that a client handle his anger by asking him to save his "I'm mad abouts" for the counseling time or by writing down his "It's not fair feelings" on a sheet of paper and bringing them to the next counseling session (Jewett, 1982).

Children do stop worrying about their most dreadful fears as they progress through the grief process. Sometimes clients will cease their attempts to fix things that cannot be changed when a counselor gives or sets a different expectation for them. For example, the counselor might say, "I will be glad when you are ten because two years after a divorce most children do not feel quite so bad about their parents not living together." An especially useful expectation is that of the Phoenix or helping the child understand that "a stepfamily can be a reborn family, reborn from the ashes of the old, dead marriage (p. 44)."

COUNSELING STEPPARENTS AND BIOLOGICAL PARENTS

Schulman (1981) discussed how stepfamilies fall into two major categories: one is father and children versus stepmother and the other is mother and children versus the stepfather. It has been said that three is a crowd. No doubt one reason stepparents report feeling so crowded in the remarried family is because they are the third party of the "we versus you" triangle. Counseling can be useful to the stepparent as a way of identifying existing feelings and deciding how to deal with these feelings. Previous sections have noted the false expectations stepparents can develop about their role as a parent. Counseling can also focus upon helping the stepparent review his/her expectations.

One stepmother recently stated, "I wish that just for a while my husband could be a stepparent. Maybe then he would know what it is like for me." Stepparents feel overburdened, unappreciated, left out, and crowded. How can a counselor help a stepparent deal with this mixture of conflicting feelings?

A bibliotherapy approach can be very useful for either the prospective stepparent, one who is already experiencing difficulty or the biological parent who doesn't understand what it is like to be a stepparent. Rowlands' **Love Me, Love My Kids,** (1983) and Mynatt's **Remarriage Reality** (1984) are two examples of helpful books based upon personal experiences. Rowlands' ideas about telephone communication with a mate's ex-spouse is alone worth the price of the book! Mynatt has presented a "no holds barred" discussion of the many nasty things that can go on in a stepfamily arrangement. Gardner's book about stepfamilies (1982), although written for boys and girls, would be a useful guide for a stepparent to use in responding to problems presented by stepchildren.

The counselor asked the client to "imagine yourself having unexpressed feelings and ideas while you are in the company of the person who is not here." If the client can evoke this image s/he is asked to describe the situation as carefully as possible and to identify what blocks his or her expressions in this situation. Next, the client is asked to visualize expressing feelings and opinions to the person who is not there. The client is encouraged to practice this visualization until it feels comfortable or nearly natural. Subsequently, the counselor plays the role of the absent party. The roles played by the counselor are of a tentative nature and subject to the acceptance of the client. The counselor looks for the client to say, "That is just how he would respond," or "He would never say that." Finally, the client is asked to play both roles, in effect, moving from chair to chair and playing out the scenario. A negative rehearsal can be used to help the client decide what should be avoided.

Family counseling approaches are widely advocated as an appropriate intervention for the stepfamily which is having difficulty (Gardner, 1984). Many experts suggest that ex-spouses or significant non-family members should be included in the counseling.

Touliatos and Lindholm (1980) have determined that children living with a parent and a stepparent were perceived by teachers as having more behavior problems than those in intact families (e.g., negative behavior, verbal and physical agression, etc.). Carlson (1985) has pointed out how teachers should be encouraged in accepting a nuturing role toward the child, providing greater structure in the learning situation and recognizing bias in assigned work.

Groups for parents, either educational groups or self-help (support) groups, can be useful as an adjunct to counseling or as a single intervention for those with "normal" problems. It can be very gratifying to observe parents from a group begin to visit each other in order to provide playmates for their children. Equally pleasing is observing a prospective stepparent describe her plans for the upcoming weekend visit from a child and then report the following week about the successful visitation! The videotape, **Active Parenting**, although used only to augment another program, proved to be acceptable to those stepparents involved. **Systematic Training for Effective Parenting** (Dinkmeyer and McKay, 1976) and a communication skills book for parents by Faber and Mazlish (1980) are also valuable. Whiteleys' film, **Stepparenting** (1980), provokes considerable discussion among groups of stepparents. Discussion groups or counseling groups are proving to be valuable for children of divorce and for stepchildren. Gardner's book, **Counseling Children in Stepfamilies**, would serve as a good resource for a group who were interested in trying to support each other and to learn to cope with the stepfamily arrangement.

Implications

Some cautions need to be mentioned concerning the techniques presented in this chapter. Should members of the stepfamily be counseled individually or as a part of the family unit? Many factors dictate how to proceed. Gardner (1984) made a strong case for family counseling or for at least some level of involvement with the parents. He also pointed out the advantage school counselors and psychologists have in terms of easy access to the child in the school setting. Agency mental health counselors and private therapists have easier access to the family unit and perhaps have more motivated clients because the clients are paying for at least a portion of the cost of counseling. In either case, the child or adolescent is frequently the family member seen as having the problem and consequently is referred for counseling. The child is therefore the point of entry for the counselor. Bowen (1975) suggested that family counseling might occur by counseling one member rather than the entire family. According to Bowen, if one of the more mature members can obtain an even higher level of functioning then the other members will take steps to follow.

Finally, the research and studies completed with stepfamilies and about stepfamilies possess severe limitations. Most of the studies reported are about cooperative stepfamilies. Needed are findings that apply to those family members who are less agreeable and are products of the second or third wave of divorce and stepfamily arrangements. In addition, most samples have been white, middle class families and few studies have been longitudinal in nature. Much remains to be understood about stepfamilies. However, based on available information, practitioners can now formulate effective interventions.

REFERENCES

Albrecht, S. L., Barr, H. N., & Goodman, K. L. (1983). *Divorce and remarriage: problems, adaptations, and adjustments.* Westport, Conn.: Greenwood Press.

American Institutes for Research. (1982). Mourning the divorce: A project in Marin County, California. *International Journal of Family Therapy, 4,* 164–176.

Boss, P. G. (1983) The marital relationship: Boundaries and ambiguities. In H. I. McCubbin and C. Figley (Eds.), *Stress and the family: Coping with normative transitions* (Vol. I, 26–40). New York: Brunner Mazel.

Bowen, M. (1975). Family therapy after twenty years. In S. Arieti, D. X. Freeman, and J. E. Dyrud (eds.), *American Handbook of Psychiatry V: Treatment* (2nd ed.). New York: Basic Books.

Carlson, C. I. (1985). Best practices for working with single-parent and stepfamilies. In A. Thomas and J. Grimes (Eds.), *Best practices in school psychology.* Kent, Ohio: National Association of School Psychologists.

Dinkmeyer, D. C. & McKay, G. D. (1976). *Systematic training for effective parenting.* Circle Pines, MN: American Guidance Service.

Faber, A. & Mazlish, E. (1980). *How to talk so kids will listen and listen so kids will talk.* New York: Avon Books.

Fishman, B. (1983). The economic behavior of stepfamilies. *Family Relations, 32,* 359–366.

Gardner, R. A. (1982). *The boys and girls book about stepfamilies.* New York: Bantam Books.

Gardner, R. A. (1984). Counseling children in stepfamilies. *Elementary School Guidance & Counseling, 19,* 40–49.

Glick, P. C. (1983). Children of divorced parents in perspective. *Journal of Social Issues, 35,* 170–181.

Issacs, M. B. (1983). Facilitating family restructuring and relinkage. In J. Hansen and L. Messinger (Eds.), *Therapy with remarriage families.* Rockville, MD: Aspen Systems Corp.

Jewett, C. L. (1982). *Helping children cope with separation and loss.* Harvard, MA: Harvard Common Press.

Katz, L. & Stein, S. (1983). Treating stepfamilies. In B. Wolman and G. Stricker (Eds.), *Handbook of family and marital therapy.* New York: Plenum.

Lutz, P. (1983). The stepfamily: An adolescent perspective. *Family Relations, 32,* 367–375.

McCubbin, H. I. & Patterson, J. M. (1982). Family adaptation to crisis. In H. I. McCubbin & J. M. Patterson (Eds.), *Family stress, coping, and social supports.* Springfield, IL: Charles C Thomas.

Messinger, L. (1976). Remarriage between divorced people from previous marriages: A proposal for preparation for remarriage. *Journal of Marriage and Family Counseling, 2,* 143–200.

Mynatt, E. S. (1984). *Remarriage reality.* Knoxville, TN: Elm Publications.

Poppen, W. A. & White, P. N. (1984). Transition to the blended family. *Elementary School Guidance & Counseling, 19,* 50–61.

Prosen, S. & Farmer, J. (1982). Understanding stepfamilies: Issues and implications for counseling. *The Personnel & Guidance Journal, 7,* 393–397.

Robinson, M. (1982). Reconstituted families. In A. Bentovim, G. G. Barnes, and A. Cooklin (Eds.), *In family therapy: Complementary frameworks of theory and practice* (Vol. 2, 389–415). London: Academic Press.

Rubenstein, C. (1983). Forging the linked family. *Psychology Today, 4,* 59.

Rowlands, P. (1983). *Love me, love my kids.* New York: Continuum Publishing Company.

Schlesinger, B. (1983). *Remarriage: A review and annotated bibliography.* Chicago: CPL Bibliographics.

Schulman, G. L. (1981). Divorce, single parenthood and stepfamilies: Structural implications of these transactions. *International Journal of Family Therapy, 3,* 87–112.

Touliatos, J. & Lindholm, B. W. (1980). Teachers' perceptions of behavior problems in children from intact, single-parent families. *Psychology in the schools, 17,* 264–269.

Visher, E. & Visher, J. (1979). *Stepfamilies: A guide to working with stepparents and stepchildren.* New York: Brunner Mazel.

Visher, E. & Visher, J. (1983). Stepparenting: Blending families. In H. McCubbin and C. Figley (Eds.), *Stress and the family: Coping with normative transitions* (Vol. I, 133–146). New York: Brunner Mazel.

Wallerstein, J. S. & Kelly, J. B. (1980). *Surviving the break-up: How children and parents cope with divorce.* New York: Basic Books.

Whiteley, J. M. (Producer & Director). (1980). *Stepparenting.* [Film]. American Association for Counseling and Development, 5999 Stevenson Avenue, Alexandria, VA 22304.

Chapter 15

DUAL CAREER FAMILIES

ROBERT REARDON AND BERT BENNETT

O ne of the major changes in the American family system over the past few decades has been the rapid increase in both partners working. Shaevitz and Shaevitz (1979) have described the dual-earner couple phenomenon as the most important social change in the twentieth century. There has been debate over what these families should be named. Both the terms dual-career and dual-worker have been used, but both have received justified criticism. Aldous (1982) has suggested the term dual-earner families. This term clearly addresses the phenomenon of both partners working outside of the home without implying, as the term dual-career does, that both partners have professional jobs. The term dual-earner also avoids the problem of the term dual-worker, in that the non-paid work of homemaking is not discounted. Thus, the term dual-earner will be used throughout this chapter.

About 50 percent of all married women work outside of the home (Hall & Hall, 1979). It appears clear that this phenomenon is hear to stay, and it is thus increasingly important to discover the effects of dual-earner families on the individuals involved.

The research pertaining to the effects of dual-earner families on children, as well as the effects of maternal employment, are presented below. We believe it is important for counselors and other professionals to be informed of the larger body of research information available on this topic. The reader is referred to an article and technical report by Bennett and Reardon (1985a, 1985b) on the dual-earner family, for a more detailed review of this extensive literature.

Historical Overview

Prior to the 1960's the widely held belief was that mothers should not work if they had children school age or younger (Hoffman, 1974). This belief stemmed primarily from the psychoanalytic view that children could only be raised by their mothers (Etaugh, 1974; Hoffman, 1974, 1979; Smith, 1981). Many of these same researchers believed that a working wife would also harm the marital relationship.

By the 1960's this negative view of maternal employment had begun to change. However, like a pendulum, the change shifted to one where most researchers believed that maternal employment had no effect on adjustment (Hoffman, 1974).

By the 1970's researchers were looking at specific variables within maternal employment. The two major reviews of literature done during the 1970's both concluded that even though there were sex, class, age, and daycare quality differences which affected results, maternal employment was not seen as having negative effects on children's adjustment (Etaugh, 1974; Hoffman, 1974).

The Current Research

Studies being performed in the 1980's are beginning to suggest that the issue is not so much whether or not the mother is employed as much as it is how the whole family copes with the additional stresses of both partners working. The current research is briefly reviewed below.

Preschool Age Children

This research appears to clearly show that a child can form strong attachments to both the mother, the father, as well as to substitute caretakers without causing problems in adjustment (Cordes, 1983; Etaugh, 1974, 1980; Hoffman, 1974, 1979; Owen, Easterbrooks, Chase-Lansdale, & Goldberg, 1984; Smith, 1981). However, almost all the researchers in this area agree that the adult caretaker needs to be a stable figure and that the care has to be consistent and of high quality in order for healthy attachments to form. Stith and Davis (1984) found that both working and non-working mothers provided high quality care but that the care provided by substitute caretakers did not have the same high quality.

The preschool studies have found that both positive and negative outcomes are possible. The determining factor is not the employment of both parents, but how the family copes with this situation. The specific positive and negative outcomes will be discussed in the following section on school age children.

School Age Children

The research on school age children is similar to preschool age children. Generally, the literature shows that the mother's working (i.e., being from a dual-earner family) does not have to adversely affect the child (Bennett & Reardon, 1985a; Smith, 1981). Several issues addressed by the research are outlined below.

Time Spent and Sex Role Modeling

The recent evidence indicates that working mothers spend as much direct time with their children as do non-working mothers (Hunt, 1984; Sweeney, 1982). Therefore, the concern over working mothers not being able to spend enough time with their children seems to be unfounded.

As with preschool age children, school age children from dual-earner families have broader and less stereotyped sex role concepts (Jones & McBride, 1980; MacKinnon, Brody, & Stoneman, 1982; Smith, 1981). Montemayor and Clayton (1983) and others have found that if the family is having problems coping with both parents working there is a greater chance of negative outcomes.

Academic Achievement, I.Q., and Career Aspirations

The most recent evidence indicates that maternal employment, in and of itself, has little to do with academic achievement or I.Q. (Farel, 1980; Mann, 1983; Rockwell, 1983; Rosenthal & Hansen, 1981). There is some research to support sex and class differences regarding these variables. Girls appear to perform better than boys, and boys in the middle class seem to suffer when their mothers work. On the other hand lower class boys whose mothers work score better than boys with non-working mothers (Etaugh, 1974; Hoffman, 1974, 1979; Smith, 1981). These studies show that being from a dual-earner family has either no effect on career aspirations or that for girls there is a positive benefit because they tend to have higher career aspirations when their mothers work.

Adequacy of Substitute Care

This is a crucial issue. If the substitute care is not adequate then problems are likely to occur. There has been some concern that when both parents work they provide less supervision thus increasing the chance for delinquency. This has not been supported by the research. However, it is generally accepted that quality supervision is important in psychological adjustment. O'Connell (1983) has studied non-maternal child care and has found it to have no adverse affects on children's adjustment or development. The question of adequate substitute care still remains, and it is perhaps the single most important issue that the parents can control. With quality substitute care the chance of problems decreases, and without it problems are likely to arise.

Psychosocial Adjustment and Perceived Rejection

Most of the recent research indicates that children from dual-earner families are as well socialized as those from single-earner families (Henggeler & Borduin, 1981; Reis & Burton, 1984).

There is evidence to suggest that boys of working mothers show poorer psychosocial adjustment (Etaugh, 1974; Hoffman, 1974, 1979; Smith, 1981). Some of these studies indicate that working mothers who are satisfied with their jobs are better mothers and have more well-adjusted children. There is evidence that being from a dual-earner family can offer benefits, as seen in Asha's (1983) finding that children from dual-earner families are more creative than are the children of single-earner families. Another benefit was noted by Johnson and Johnson (1980). They found that dual-earner families are able to differentiate more easily from their children. By differentiate, Johnson and Johnson refer to the parents as well as the children's ability to separate and be independent in a healthy fashion.

There is no evidence that working mothers deprive their children or that the children feel rejected. The research points to the fact that children of working mothers approve of their mothers working and that the more involved the father, the more accepting are the children (Etaugh, 1974; Hoffman, 1974, 1979; Smith, 1981). Trimberger and MacLean (1982) found that other factors, such as after school supervision and mother's attitude toward her job, significantly effected the child's perceptions of maternal employment.

Effects on the Couple and the Role of the Father

The rapid increase in dual-earner families is generally believed to be a signal of greater equality in relationships. There does appear to be a slight shift toward more equality, but today's dual-earner families are much more traditional than one might expect (Fox & Nickols, 1983; Levitan & Belous, 1981). For example, studies point to the fact that the majority of both child and home care is still the responsibility of the woman (Abdel-Ghany & Nickols, 1983; Maret & Finlay, 1984; Sanik & O'Neill, 1982).

One of the major mediating factors in dual-earner families is the role of the father. The father's support of the mother's working and his involvement in the family is critical in predicting whether or not the dual-earner family experiences major problems. Cordes (1983) and others have found that highly involved nurturing fathers enhance children's sex role development, cognitive growth, and self-esteem. Thus it appears that having a warm, nurturing father present significantly decreases the chance of negative effects and increases the chance for positive benefits on child behavior.

Conclusions and Critique of the Research

The research pertaining to the effects of dual-earner families on children shows that there is no universally predictable effect. Whether the results are positive or negative appear to depend on whether or not conditions are favorable (Bennett & Reardon, 1985a; Crouter, 1983; Dail, 1982; Smith, 1981; Stuckey, McGhee, & Bell, 1982). As has been pointed out previously, this is not a simple question of "are there two parents working." The issue is much more complex than previously thought. There are many mediating factors that are crucial in determining whether the dual-earner lifestyle results in harm or benefits. Some of these factors are: (a) the child's age, sex, and relationship to parents; (b) the family's socioeconomic status; (c) the nature of the mother's work; (d) the family's coping resources; and (e) the role of the father (or mother's partner).

A number of methodological flaws in the dual-earner research have been noted by both Crouter (1982) and Smith (1981). Smith points out several methodological problems some of which are: (a) a lack of standard operational definitions for common terms; (b) an inability to adequately control variables; (c) unclear descriptions of procedures; (d) questionable validity and reliability of instruments; and (e) the use of university sponsored or demonstration project day care which is likely to be of higher quality than the norm, thereby making broad generalizations impossible.

Smith (1981) addresses the issue of the difference between the dual-career couple and the dual worker family. She criticized the literature for promoting the myth that women who work are professionals in exciting careers with romantic lives. In reality this is not true, for the majority (80%) of women are in "pink collar" jobs such as clerical and secretarial work ("The Work Revolution", 1983).

Smith also points out a sex bias inherent in the research which has been termed a motherhood mandate (Russo, 1976). The motherhood mandate is the belief that a woman has to have children and raise them well. She may have education and work as long as she first fills this obligation. Raising her children well means being physically present when they need her. Smith asserts that the studies on maternal employment reflect this bias.

Crouter (1982), in addition to discussing the methodological problems, also points out that the field needs to refocus away from the work status of the parents and move toward an investigation of the strategies employed in coping with being a dual-earner family. It has been this perspective that the reader has seen throughout this chapter. As has been noted earlier, being a dual-earner family means little in and of itself. What we as professionals need to recognize is that there are some specific stresses as well as additional tasks these families must cope with in order to continue functioning in a healthy fashion. In addition, there are also some very positive benefits that can be realized by healthy dual-earner families. Our job becomes one of understanding the dual-earner lifestyle and being able to offer assistance in helping families take advantage of the benefits of being in a dual-earner family.

Implications for Professional Practice. Parents, teachers, and counselors may be called upon to assess the impact of the dual-earner family on the child's adjustment. Parents may seek professional support or advice regarding this topic. While each case must be treated individually, this review has sought to provide general evidence or conclusions from research literature that might help professionals respond to such questions.

Directions from the Literature

Our review indicates that the literature on preschoolers does not support the conclusion that no harm is done by mothers working when the child is of preschool age. Nor does the literature indicate that the child is harmed if the mother works. For school age children the literature shows that girls do better in most areas of adjustment if the mother works. The working mother apparently serves as a positive role model. Boys on the other hand are more likely to be harmed by both parents working. Moderating factors were the mother's job satisfaction, the amount of paternal support, and the quality of the substitute care. Some specific actions that can be taken to enhance the experience of children, especially boys, in dual-earner families are (a) encourage the active participation and support of the father, (b) make an effort to have the mother's job be as satisfying as possible, (c) be aware of the potential problems and offer special attention to the boys in dual-earner families, and (d) work to ensure that substitute and after school care is of high quality.

To summarize the findings as best we can, it appears that if both parents are going to work when the children are young, then part time work is advisable if possible. If the parents have to work full time, then finding a caretaker, who is stable, stimulating, warm, and nurturing, is essential. Once the children are in school the stability and quality of substitute care remains critical. The after school supervision needs to be structured and should offer positive attention, fair limits, and a warm nurturing atmosphere to the child. The father should be active and involved in all aspects of family life. The research clearly indicates that having both parents actively involved with both home and child care increases the possibility for positive outcomes. The work of both parents needs to be validated in a positive manner and both parents should communicate to the children that the other's job is important. If being in a dual-earner family is the reality, then it helps to accept this and to begin to look for the benefits. We are suggesting that the family approach their dual-earner life from a positive attitude and that the entire family pull together to make this lifestyle work in their favor.

Areas of Intervention

There are at least four different ways in which counselors and other helping professionals might intervene to help dual-earner families. These are (a) diagnostic, (b) guidance and counseling, (c) consultation and program development, and (d) referral. Each of these is briefly discussed in the following sections.

Diagnostic

When counseling with children and other family members, counselors must be alert to problems stemming from dual-earner issues. Children of all ages may exhibit behavior problems or adjustment difficulties because of unresolved issues growing out of both parents working outside the home. Younger children of dual-earner couples may be "latch key children," which Robinson (1983) and others have described. Counselors should explore the fears, as well as related problems, which many of these children and adolescents have regarding fire, robbery, assault, being alone, as well as other concerns. Older children and adolescents, especially boys, who are unsupervised by adults after school, are susceptible to negative peer influences, substance abuse, poor time management, and lowered academic performance (Montemayor and Clayton, 1983; Harper, 1983). Counselors working with children and youth in dual-earner families must be increasingly alert to problems such as these. There is evidence that children may not discuss these problems with their parents because the parents are seen as powerless to change the situations.

Guidance and Counseling

Besides identifying and diagnosing problem situations, counselors and other professionals can initiate many positive, preventive steps to help family members of dual-earner families. These may take the form of group based guidance with children and/or families or individual counseling. Several activities that are illustrative of this guidance and counseling function are discussed below.

Group Counseling. Group counseling may be offered for parents or parents and children to increase communication about dual-earner family member roles, expectations, needs, conflicts and so forth. Research suggests that children who know why both parents are working and how parents feel about their new work/family roles adjust better to dual-earner situations. Likewise, parents need to hear clear messages from children and youth about how the dual-earner lifestyle is impacting upon them in order that they might deal proactively with problems.

Group Guidance. Group guidance activities can focus on helping adults and children explore new family roles and lifestyles that are not gender based. This may mean focusing on more androgynous sex role behavior. Support groups for families, offering peer support and networking, can also be very beneficial.

Career and Life Development Groups. Career and life development groups can help late adolescents engage in more realistic planning in preparation for dual-earner and family roles (Hester & Dickerson, 1982). Many observers agree that planning and negotiating skills are essential to success of adults and children in dual-earner families. The **Campus Resource** presently under development by Catalyst (Naimark & Pierce, in press) and **Going Places** (Amatea & Cross, 1980) are notable examples of such programs.

Counseling Interventions. Counseling interventions may be useful when individual attention is needed. This type of intervention may be especially critical for adolescent boys who appear most likely to be negatively impacted by maternal employment.

Stress Reduction Interventions. Since the dual-earner lifestyle has the potential for generating many more stressors with which the family has to cope, it is important that helping professionals be aware of the potential stresses and be familiar with various stress reduction strategies. One major method for reducing stress is to reappraise the event that is perceived to cause the stress. If the dual-earner family is viewed in a positive light, then it stands to reason that the chance for positive outcomes will increase. For example, maternal employment can be viewed by the woman as mitigating the traditional stress of full-time homemaking and, by the man, as decreasing the burden of being family provider. In addition to cognitive methods of stress reduction, there are many means professionals can use to help families better monitor their stress level and then either adapt to or change the situation that is causing distress.

Consultation and Program Development

The tremendous breadth and scope of the dual-earner phenomenon has created large gaps in public policy and knowledge (Zigler & Muenchow, 1983). There is much that we do not know and much we need to prepare for. Counselors and other professionals can be an active force in this regard. For example, school counselors can collect information concerning the special needs and concerns of dual-earner families at their school. These needs assessments can provide useful information for new policies and programs designed to help dual-earner families.

In addition, new after-school programs may be needed and office hours may need to be adjusted so working parents can more easily meet with professional staff. The latter seems to be one of the most critical problems for dual-earner parents.

Finally, counselors may be able to help set up parent networks for childcare information, legal rights issues involving child abuse, job relocation, as well as other problems.

Referral

Counselors and other professionals must view the dual-earner phenomenon in a broad systems view. Many community agencies, including employers, courts, childcare centers, neighborhood associations, mental health centers, recreational programs, private counseling services, and others have a positive role to play in this area. School counselors need to be connected with these outside agencies in order to draw upon their resources and make appropriate referrals.

Conclusion

There is much to be learned about dual-earner families and their impact on children and youth. This chapter has reviewed what we do know about this phenomenon and offered suggestions for improved professional practice. Counselors and other helpers must dedicate themselves to continued study of this social transformation of the family system and to helping family members cope with the resultant stresses as well as opportunities for growth and change.

REFERENCES

Abdel-Ghany, M. & Nickols, S. Y. (1983). Husband/wife differentials in household work time: The case of dual-earner families. *Home Economics Research Journal,* *12*(2), 159–167.

Aldous, J. (Ed.). (1982). *Two-paychecks: Life in dual-earner families.* Beverly Hills: Sage Publications.

Amatea, E. & Cross, E. (1980). Going places: A career guidance program for high school students and their parents. *Vocational Guidance Quarterly, 28*(2), 104–282.

Asha, C. B. (1983). Creativity of children of working mothers. *Psychological Studies, 28*(2), 104–106.

Bennett, B. & Reardon, R. (1985a). Dual-career couples and the psychological adjustment of offspring: A review. *The School Counselor, 32*(4), 287–295.

Bennett, B. & Reardon, R. (1985b). *The dual-earner family's impact on the child and the family system: Review and implications for counseling practice.* Tallahassee, FL: Florida State University, Department of Counseling Psychology and Human Systems.

Cordes, C. (1983, December). Researchers make room for fathers. *APA Monitor,* pp. 1, 9–11.

Crouter, A. C. (1982). The children of working parents. *Children Today, 11*(4), 25–28.

Dail, P. W. (1982). Who will mind the child? A dilemma for many employed parents. *Journal of Home Economics, 74*(1), 22–23.

Etaugh, C. (1974). Effects of maternal employment on children: A review of recent research. *Merrill-Palmer Quarterly, 20*(2), 71–98.

Etaugh, C. (1980). Effects of nonmaternal care on children: Research evidence and popular views. *American Psychologist, 35*(4), 309–319.

Farel, A. M. (1980). Effects of preferred maternal roles, maternal employment, and sociodemographic status on school adjustment and competence. *Child Development, 51,* 1179–1186.

Fox, K. D. & Nickols, S. Y. (1983). The time crunch: Wife's employment and family work. *Journal of Family Issues, 4*(1), 61–82.

Hall, F. S. & Hall, D. T. (1979). *The two-career couple.* Reading, MA.: Addison-Wesley.

Harper, T. (1980, September). Anybody home: What life is like for latch-key kids. *Seventeen,* pp. 136–138, 172.

Henggeler, S. W. & Borduin, C. M. (1981). Satisfied working mothers and their preschool sons. *Journal of Family Issues, 2*(3), 322–335.

Hester, S. B. & Dickerson, K. G. (1982). The emerging dual-career life-style: Are your students prepared for it? *Journal of College Student Personnel, 23*(6), 514–519.

Hoffman, L. W. (1974). Effects of maternal employment on the child: A review of the research. *Developmental Psychology, 10,* 204–228.

Hoffman, L. W. (1979). Maternal employment: 1979. *American Psychologist, 34*(10), 859–865.

Hunt, J. C. & Kiker, B. F. (1984). Parental time devoted to children in two- and one-wage-earner families. *Economics of Education Review, 3*(1), 75–83.

Johnson, C. L. & Johnson, F. A. (1980). Parenthood, marriage and careers: Situational constraints and role strains. In F. Pepitone-Rockwell (Ed.), *Dual-career couples* (pp. 143–161). Beverly Hills, CA.: Sage.

Jones, L. M. & McBride, J. L. (1980). Sex-role stereotyping in children as a function of maternal employment. *The Journal of Social Psychology, 111,* 219–223.

Levitan, S. A. & Belous, R. S. (1981). Working wives and mothers: What happens to family life? *Monthly Labor Review, 104*(9), 26–30.

MacKinnon, C. E., Brody, G. H., & Stoneman, Z. (1982). The effects of divorce and maternal employment on the home environments of preschool children. *Child Development, 53,* 1392–1399.

Mann, J. (1983). Viewpoint. Learning. *Young Children, 38*(5), 12–13.

Maret, E. & Finlay, B. (1984). The distribution of household labor among women in dual-earner families. *Journal of Marriage and the Family, 46*(2), 357–364.

Montemayor, R. & Clayton, M. D. (1983). Maternal employment and adolescent development. *Theory into Practice, 22*(2), 112–118.

Naimark, H. & Pierce, S. (in press). Transferable skills: One link between work and family. *Journal of Career Development.*

O'Connell, J. C. (1983). Children of working mothers: What the research tells us. *Young Children, 38*(2), 63–70.

Owen, M. T., Easterbrooks, M. A., Chase-Lansdale, L., & Goldberg, W. A. (1984). The relation between maternal employment status and the stability of attachments to mother and father. *Child Development, 55,* 1894–1901.

Reis, J. & Burton, R. (1984). Maternal employment and child socialization practices: An instructional test of cross-cultural theory. *Journal of Comparative Family Studies, 15*(1), 1–16.

Robinson, V. M. (1983). 5,000,000 latchkey children. *PTA Today, 8*(7), 13–15.

Rockwell, T. A. (1983). The relationship of maternal employment to academic achievement among high school sophomores and seniors. *Dissertation Abstracts International, 43,* 3159A.

Rosenthal, D. & Hansen, J. (1981). The impact of maternal employment on children's perceptions of parents and personal development. *Sex Roles, 7*(6), 593–598.

Russo, N. F. (1976). The motherhood mandate. *Journal of Social Issues, 32,* 143–154.

Sanik, M. M. & O'Neill, B. (1982). Who does the family work? *Journal of Extension, 20,* 15–20.

Shaevitz, M. H. & Shaevitz, M. H. (1979). *Making it together as a dual-career couple.* Boston: Houghton-Mifflin.

Smith, E. J. (1981). The working mother: A critique of the research. *Journal of Vocational Behavior, 19*(2), 191–211.

Stith, S. M. & Davis, A. J. (1984). Employed mothers and family day-care substitute caregivers: A comparative analysis of infant care. *Child Development, 55,* 1340–1348.

Stuckey, M. F., McGhee, P. E., & Bell, N. J. (1982). Parent-child interaction: The influence of maternal employment. *Developmental Psychology, 18*(4), 635–644.

Sweeney, J. (1982, November 21). Working mothers spend equal time with kids. *The Tallahassee Democrat,* pp. 1G, 7G.

Trimberger, R. & MacLean, M. J. (1982). Maternal employment: The child's perspective. *Journal of Marriage and the Family, 44*(2), 469–475.

The work revolution. (1983, January). *Newsweek,* pp. 29–32.

Zigler, E. & Muenchow, S. (1983). Infant day care and infant-care leaves: A policy vacuum. *American Psychologist, 38,* 91–94.

PART III INTERVENTIONS IN THE SCHOOL

CLASSIFYING AND MANAGING
  SCHOOL BEHAVIOR PROBLEMS
THE IEP AND SCHOOL–PARENT PROBLEM SOLVING
CULTURAL ISSUES IN SCHOOL AND FAMILY
COUNSELING CHILDREN AND FAMILIES IN THE SCHOOLS

Chapter 16

CLASSIFYING AND MANAGING SCHOOL BEHAVIOR PROBLEMS

Johnnie Word Medina

INTRODUCTION

Classification is a logical step in an approach to the understanding, management, and resolution of children's problems. However, the "how and what" of classification are seen by the different people involved in as many different ways. The result for the child can be a confusing approach to treatment. Classification should help practitioners and teachers identify common goals, move toward effective management of school related problems, and find new avenues of intervention with families.

Purpose and Use of Classification

Achenbach (1974) points out that the real purpose of classification is to select people who will gain the most from a particular intervention. For professionals who work with children on a daily basis, classification must serve a practical and direct purpose. The many labels attached to students with problems may confuse rather than clarify issues relevant to daily management. Those who are confronted with children who are having problems do not have time to research whether or not the classification system is reliable, diagnostic labels correct, or etiology clear. The pressing need is to deal with the "here and now."

Management issues are further complicated by the school setting where a child may interact with several different administrators and teachers each day. Kershaw (1984) observes that most school psychologists are trained from an individual psychology mode and may treat children and adolescents apart from their family context. From a family system perspective, problematic behavior on the part of a child would be viewed as a part of a dysfunctional interaction. Even professionals and the school itself can be part of the "dysfunctional system" in which a child is having problems. The fact is that all concerned would greatly benefit from a classification of problems that provides important correlates that "can be applied uniformly by different workers" (Achenbach, 1974, p. 61) and "attributes that are related in important ways" (p. 62) to the goals of treatment and improving communication between parent, child, school, and therapist.

The Diagnostic and Statistical Manual III (DSM III), published by the American Psychiatric Association in 1980, has done much to standardize the classification of behavior. The purpose of **DSM III** is "to provide clear descriptions of diagnostic categories in order to enable clinicians and investigators to diagnose, communicate about, study and treat various mental disorders" (p. 12). Because school psychologists and diagnosticians use the system routinely to label children's problems, the groupings are widely known by school personnel. These groupings are an obvious base for formulating management strategies. Children evidencing certain behaviors and sharing a cluster of characteristics may be similar in etiology, amenability to treatment, management and prognosis (Achenbach, 1974).

One Solution

An ideal classification system should define symptom clusters which can serve as guides to treatment and management. Parents and teachers must necessarily be more concerned with the latter. The goals of therapy are frequently the province of the therapist while teachers and parents who spend the most time with the child may perceive dimly at best what their role is in assisting the child to function. When the goals of management describe the developmental needs of children, then real understanding begins. In the exercise of relating a variety of schema to child development, a common language about children's behavior and needs begins to emerge (Achenbach, 1982).

Medina (1978) has adapted the developmental concepts of Erikson to help teachers identify the critical elements present in the classroom setting which are necessary for psychosocial growth. The emphasis is on designing an environment in which the child's interactions with others are productive for developmental growth, instruction, and classroom management.

Description of problem behaviors furnished by psychological testing, subsequent DSM III classification, and parent and teacher reports are related to the schema provided by Erikson. Categories of behavior which represent the ways children accomplish developmental tasks are identified. These categories suggest specific ways children's needs may be met in the classroom setting. Problem behaviors which result when these needs are **not** met cluster into categories of "acting-in" and "acting-out." Now a simple formula emerges which helps teachers to relate behavior directly to the child's needs and the way these needs can be met in the classroom: **need — supply = demand.**

The reader is referred to the first column of Chart I which lists the developmental tasks set forth by Erikson (1963) along with a one word description of the kinds of behaviors children normally use to accomplish their **need.** Column two lists the possibilities present in the classroom to **supply** these needs. Column three defines acting-in and acting-out behaviors as **demand.** Teachers classify observed or reported behaviors as acting-in or acting-out and relate these to the **need** column. For example the child who sits and refuses to work is acting-in ("no-ing"). The needs implied are autonomy and initiative, and opportunities for the child to make legitimate choices about how he will do his work may supply some of his need. The formula suggests that **demand** behaviors will decrease when the needs are identified and an appropriate, consistent supply made available.

CHART I

NEED	minus	SUPPLY	equals	DEMAND
Trust (Knowing)		Structure		
Autonomy (No-ing)		choices		DEMAND is
Initiative (Trying)		opportunity		defined as inappropriate
Industry (Doing)		tasks		"acting-in" or
Identity (Role-ing)		groups		"acting-out" behaviors
Intimacy (Sharing)		cooperation		
Generativity (Caring)		responsibility		
Ego Integration		evaluation		

Golden (1984) indicates that the functionality of the child's family should be considered carefully in designing school management, especially if parental involvement is to be considered. Golden identifies families as functional or dysfunctional. Functional families can be worked with because they rate high on the criteria Golden defines. These criteria may be stated as questions. 1) Are the needs of the child for security and survival being met? 2) Is the problem behavior of relatively short history? 3) Does the family system provide for healthy individuation and interpersonal involvement? 4) Is parental authority stable and effective? 5) Is the family able to implement agreed upon problem solutions? (Golden, 1984, p. 349). School counselors can assist functional families to implement brief interventions or adapt school management strategies for home use.

Golden points out that dysfunctional families are organized to oppose change, and efforts on the part of the school to involve the family lead to defeat and frustration. He believes these families should be identified and referred for family therapy. Children whose families are dysfunctional will also need more structure within the school setting. It is important that school personnel lower expectations that these families will be able to participate productively in the school treatment plans.

The Medina Management System

In the Medina model the goal is to put the child back on the proper developmental course. Five management systems are suggested which teachers use in a "mixed milieu" approach facilitated by one basic management plan. Recalling the formula, **Need** minus **Supply** equals **Demands**, our emphasis here is on increasing **Supply**. Specific techniques, some commonly used by teachers, are identified and utilized to provide daily opportunities for normal children to work on appropriate age-stage developmental tasks.

Sources of supply are translated into management concepts. For example, **role management concepts** describe four relating roles which help children use adult interactions to accomplish developmental tasks. The roles redefine two traditional roles, those of teacher-authority and teacher-helper, and add two new roles, teacher-leader and teacher-facilitator. The teacher can help Johnny work through autonomy struggles by reserving the authority role for task organization and lesson presentation with the class group. When Johnny gets out of his seat without permission, the teacher shifts into the facilitator role to redirect him to task. A one-to-one approach which facilitates Johnny interacting with the rule-consequence system is used. Personal demand is not used and class rules are stated positively to describe the behavior needed. Johnny can choose how far to push because results of his choice of behavior are predictable and consistent.

The **time and task management concept** helps teachers organize instructional strategies to provide a secure, predictable environment. The teacher provides a careful definition of task objective, describing or even rehearsing the behaviors needed to complete the task successfully. The teacher can lower Mary's anxiety and help her work on basic trust issues by using time lines. When Mary knows she is expected to listen to the teacher for ten minutes, she is able to sit still and give her full attention.

The academic setting suggests the concept of **interaction management.** Teachers plan activities which involve students in interacting with each other in the class group, in small groups, and with partners. The concept of **energy management** helps teachers to organize techniques which help children to practice making choices, label their own feelings, and take responsibility for their own behavior. Jimmy can learn to ask the teacher for a "time away" from other students when he is angry. A teacher-made problem solving worksheet can help Jimmy think through the problem and select a solution from those suggested.

The **feedback management** concept lists ways teachers can give immediate, concrete information to students about their behavior. For example, when Jane learns to use feedback to debrief herself, she can set goals for growth and improvement.

Children of all ages who are experiencing temporary, situational problems are also well served by the basic system; since they are furnished a secure, predictable environment. The remaining systems utilize the framework provided in increasingly structured ways to assist students with more severe developmental problems.

System 1 organizes procedures for managing students exhibiting mild acting-in behaviors (timidity, sensitivity, worrying, anxiety, overcompliance, social withdrawal, sadness). The special goal is to practice skills of independence. When Mary fails to complete assignments because she is too shy to ask for help, the teacher initiates a "target behavior" contract. The teacher and Mary agree that each time Mary is willing to raise her hand and ask for help (the target behavior), she will receive two bonus points which can be cashed in for a special library privilege. The result is positive. Mary learns to ask for help; she completes her work and both Mary and the teacher feel good about her newly acquired behavior.

For some acting-in students a "wants and needs" list made out by student and teacher working together can help. Jimmy only attempts to complete the problems he is sure he can do. He wants more help from the teacher. He and the teacher contract for five minutes of special help each time he is willing to try to answer each problem assigned. Parents of System 1 children are usually able to successfully adapt some of the management strategies for use at home, especially with some assistance from counselor or teacher.

Management System 2 is designed for mild, short term acting-out students. Techniques used establish a clear cause-effect relation between the child's choice of behavior and a predefined consequence. Acting-out behaviors such as testing limits, disobedience, showing off, talking out of turn and arguing point up the need for the student to work on trust and autonomy. Positively stated rules describe the appropriate school behavior and a step process of consequences provides consistency and models of behavior for the System 2 student.

When Johnny pushes in front of someone else in line the teacher reminds Johnny of the class rule which states, "Be respectful and helpful to others". Behavior rehearsal is used. When Johnny is able to model the behavior, the teacher and the class clap for him. If Johnny chooses to push ahead as soon as the teacher looks away, he is placed on the next step. This is usually a short time out.

System 2 students are taught to take the option of moving themselves to a time away when they begin to feel they are having problems. Special rewards are available for students who use the system of moving away, thinking about the problem, and then coming back to handle problems in appropriate ways. Teacher-made problem solving sheets use simply stated questions to help the student to think through the problem, label feelings, and choose one of the suggested ways of problem resolution.

More severe, long term behaviors indicate a need for formal testing with specific developmental needs defined using the DSM III classifications system. These students may need smaller, structured, self-contained classrooms and teachers with special training. System 3 serves students with severe long term, acting-in problems such as severe depression, poor reality testing, and thought disorders. Special techniques help students to deal with what is happening in the classroom. For example, Jeannie says to the teacher, "I can tell you are mad at me." The teacher redirects and clarifies the child's perceptions by asking a question. "Jeannie, will you please ask me if I am angry with you?" The teacher may need to phrase the question and have Jeannie repeat, "Are you mad at me, Mrs. Jones?" Now the teacher answers the question. Teachers clarify perceptions and give these children feedback about what is happening, what it means, and what is expected of them. Students are especially rewarded for recognizing their own feelings.

Maximum, concrete structure and business-like interactions are designed to manage students who have severe, long term acting-out problems. In management System 4, the emphasis is on real, concrete structure. Language, reasoning, and explaining give way to the cause-effect relation of behavior and consequence. When Tommy slams his book on the desk and attempts to get the teacher into an argument about the assignment, she uses the facilitator role to direct him to the consequence (five minute time out). He challenges her. She moves him to the next step (10 minutes time out) explaining only that his choice of behavior has moved him to that step. Basic trust is established more quickly when the environment is reactive, consistent and predictable. Children with severe language learning difficulties, mild retardation and even mild autism, function at higher levels with the clean-cut structure of System 4. Cindy, who is mildly retarded, learns the value of doing a good job sorting colors quickly when she receives the immediate reward of a handful of popcorn and a smile.

CASE INTERVENTIONS

Tessa, An Acting-In Fourteen Year Old

Tessa, an eighth grader, was described by her teacher as being shy, compliant, needing reassurance, failing to complete work or bring needed school supplies. A close look at the family showed no unusual problems but rather a steadily growing conflict between Tessa and her parents in recent months. Parents reported moodiness and angry outbursts when they attempt to help her with school work. Tessa is an only child and perceives her parents as too strict, demanding and critical.

The school psychologist found no serious problem. Tessa seemed to be making unsuccessful attempts to resolve developmental issues.

Management in System 1 was recommended with emphasis on providing an environment with enough structure to lower anxiety and give Tessa daily opportunities to make choices and take responsibility. Tessa was told what she was supposed to do and given two choices about how she would complete the given task. She was asked to fill out a task planning sheet on which she indicated how she would complete the assignment. Teachers were advised to provide assistance only when she asked for it.

Contracting was extended into the home setting. It was important to Tessa that her parents not push her about her homework. She agreed to use the task planning sheet. Tessa's grades and attendance improved quickly, but when her parents failed to recognize success, she stopped completing her work again. In a problem resolution session with the counselor, Tessa and her parents worked on using a "wants and needs" list. "Wants" listed describe what Tessa would like to have happen; "needs" listed describe what she feels she **must** have in order to function well. Tessa agreed to be responsible for using the list to help her parents be supportive of her efforts. The family is learning how to help Tessa gain independence and responsibility at this critical developmental stage.

Charlie, An Acting-Out Ten Year Old

Charlie was referred for psychological testing by the principal after aggressive incidents with teachers and peers, which included scratching, pinching and hitting. Charlie had been disruptive since enrolling in the school two years ago. Teachers were concerned about temper outbursts, disobedience, minor disruptions, violation of minor rules, refusal to work, and conflict with authority figures.

Charlie is the older of two children in a family where both parents work. His younger brother, age four, stays with his grandmother until parents return from work. Charlie stays alone, often until after dark. Neighbors complain of minor thefts and have reported parents for lack of supervision. Parents were uncooperative and, when testing was completed, refused to have a test interpretation. Charlie was diagnosed as Conduct Disorder, socialized, non-aggressive (DSM III, 313.21). Intelligence was in low average range.

Family intervention was begun by the principal who followed up on the neighbor's report of lack of supervision and was able to get a social worker from a community agency assigned to the case. Charlie has been placed in a special resource class.

Charlie's resource teacher recommended System 4 management with added structure and consistency to help Charlie with trust issues. The teacher-facilitator role was seen as especially important. Rules are stated positively. Behavior rehearsal is used. Charlie is rewarded for choosing appropriate behavior with card punches that can be cashed in for special privileges.

A step process of pre-defined consequences begins with a clarification of the rule broken and a redirection to task. The school day is divided into four segments so that Charlie can go through the steps during each segment. On the second and third step, he is "timed out" in the classroom for five minutes. No card punches can be earned in time out. If he escalates to the fourth step during any segment, he loses a special reward. Charlie's behavior is now manageable in the school setting and he is learning socially appropriate behaviors.

No goals for family intervention, other than the participation of parents in the planning of Charlie's management, have been set at this time. Family therapy was recommended.

IMPLICATIONS FOR SCHOOL AND MENTAL HEALTH PROFESSIONALS

A critical process is set in motion when school personnel and practitioners meet together with parents to discuss a child's behavior in the school setting. Parents learn both from hearing professionals discuss behavior in terms of growth and development and from the model of management worked out in the problem solving process.

The team that evolves as a result of this process provides additional role definition for all its members and points up the kinds of intervention needed. All of this requires much communication and teaming, which may be considered a drawback by some. Time is needed for training teachers to use the system. Even with dysfunctional families, effective intervention by school personnel can result in moving families into needed psychotherapy. A way of classifing school behavior can provide the impetus for a cooperative process.

REFERENCES

Achenbach, T. M. (1974). *Developmental psychopathology.* New York: Ronald Press.
Achenbach, T. M. (1982). *Developmental psychopathology.* (2nd ed.). New York: Wiley.
American Psychiatric Association. (1980). *Diagnostic and statistical manual mental disorders.* (3rd ed.). Washington DC: author.

Erikson, E. H. (1963). *Childhood and society.* (2nd ed.). New York: Norton.

Golden, L. B. (1984). Managing maladaptive behavior in ill children through family interventions. *Journal of School Health, 54,* 389–391.

Kershaw, C. J. (1984). Family therapy. In J. G. Cull & L. B. Golden (Eds.). *Psychotherapeutic techniques in school psychology* (pp. 67–81). Springfield, IL: Thomas.

Medina, J. W. (1978). *A diversified milieu system for classroom management, K–12: A guide to classroom management for teachers of regular and special education classes.* Unpublished manuscript.

Chapter 17

THE IEP AND
SCHOOL–PARENT PROBLEM SOLVING

ALLEN J. OTTENS, KATHLEEN MAY, AND AMY OTTENS

The regulations of Public Law 94-142 have provided increased opportunity for parents to be involved in the special education of their children. The impetus for the involvement is the Individual Educational Program (IEP). The IEP is a document that spells out the child's present academic level, long-term educational goals, short-term objectives, types of school services required, and percentage of time mainstreamed. This document is to be cooperatively planned by school officials and parents at the IEP meeting. Once agreed upon, the school is obliged to make an effort to provide the services stipulated in the IEP.

How parents are to be involved at the IEP meeting is clearly delineated in the **Federal Register** (1981):

> The IEP meeting serves as a communication vehicle between parents and school personnel and enables them as equal participants to jointly decide what the child's needs are, what services will be provided to meet those needs, and what the anticipated outcomes will be (p. 5462).

Instead of a one-time meeting, the IEP is often a series of communications—a working relationship—which thereby increases the frequency of school-parent contacts.

Unfortunately, the type of participation described in the **Federal Register** can turn out to be more idealistic than realistic. Instead of equal partnership and joint participation, the school and parents may operate from different motives or presumptions so as to "desynchronize" the relationship. School or parent may enter into contact possessing discrepant agenda so that establishing a collaborative relationship becomes problematic.

School professionals may not welcome parent contact and may try to avoid it. For example, Yoshida et al. (1978), in a survey of Connecticut

221

special educators, uncovered resistance to parental involvement in educational planning and evaluation. Shevin (1983) noted the tendency among school professionals to limit their involvement with parents to the narrowest extent within the letter of the law.

On the other hand, McMillan and Turnbull (1983) pointed out that parents of special education students differ greatly with respect to age, intelligence, energy level, income, social class, and emotional stability. These factors influence the parents' degree of involvement and presumably how tractable they can be to deal with.

Furthermore, when Federal guidelines allow for increased parent participation, it also means that parents will have greater opportunity to present their concerns, problems, needs, and dissatisfactions to the school. If the concerns, needs, and dissatisfactions are dealt with ineffectively, then the school-parent relationship is jeopardized; if these problems are dealt with effectively, then both parties should be able to work more collaboratively.

The importance of this last point for school professionals should not be underestimated. As Owens (1981) pointed out, a major task of schools will be learning to cope productively with the conflict and challenge arising from P. L. 94-142's mandate to include parents in the educational decision-making process.

When the school-parent relationship is not balanced or fully functioning, school, parents, and especially the child, can emerge as losers:

- The school may fail to channel parent interest into a constructive direction, thereby losing potentially valuable parent input.
- With less parent input and involvement, the child's educational program may be less flexible.
- With less parent involvement in the IEP process, the child's placement may be needlessly more restrictive (Lauder et al., 1979).
- The school's anger or frustration with a parent could backlash against the child.
- Lack of parent-school cooperation could result in the child's school gains not being maintained at home.
- Frequently the special education child faces emergencies and/or developmental crises during the school year which could be better resolved with positive parent-school collaboration.

This chapter will present a case study where a school-parent imbalance exists. The situation involves a parent who perceives deficiencies in the school's special education program and who believes that her child's needs are not being met. Additionally, she appears overinvolved on behalf of her child. The case study focuses on how school personnel responded to the parent's concerns in such a fashion that they were appropriately addressed and a positive school-parent relationship was thereby facilitated. Commentary is provided in order to analyze the strategies used to facilitate the relationship and to point out, in hindsight, how school personnel might have responded more effectively. In the chapter's concluding section, general problem-solving techniques, which school professionals can utilize when they encounter parents who present concerns and/or dissatisfactions, are discussed.

INTERVENTIONS: CASE STUDY AND COMMENTARY

July 9. On this date Mrs. W* brought her 6 year old daughter, Melody, to the school for a visit and intake interview. Mrs. W was to meet with the principal, social worker, and assistant principal. Mrs. W's local school district referred her to the school, an approved facility for special education students.

Records indicated that Melody was brain-damaged. Her prenatal history was uneventful until the fifth month when her mother was involved in a severe automobile accident. Mrs. W delivered Melody at 5½ months following fetal distress. At birth Melody suffered from anoxia and jaundice. Melody and her mother, a divorcee who works as a paralegal, reside with Melody's maternal grandmother.

At the intake interview, Melody presented herself as an attractive, well-groomed, and energetic youngster. However, lapses in her speech responses were evident, and she appeared cyanotic. During the interview Melody experienced an apparent tachycardia episode which Mrs. W attributed to a medication readjustment. Melody separated easily from her mother when the psychologist arrived to perform an assessment and observation.

.Later while touring the school with the principal and his assistant, Mrs. W peppered them with numerous questions, such as:

"How many students will be in Melody's classroom?"

"What is the mean social age of the students in the classroom so I'll know if Melody is compatible?"

---

*Names and identifying information have been altered to protect confidentiality.

"Is any extraordinary behavior evident among the other children in the class?"

"The classroom looks awfully small. Are you sure it's not undersize?"

"Is there a teacher's aide for the class?"

"Are occupational and physical therapy services available?"

Her questions seemed to reveal herself as a sophisticated educational consumer and concerned parent. The school personnel fielded each question and supplied forthright answers:

"There will be five other children with Melody."

"The mean social age is 2.8."

"No, we can't think of any extraordinary behavior problems."

"Actually, the room size is well within regulations."

"We don't have a teacher's aide yet, but we expect to hire one soon."

"Yes, P.T. and O.T. services are available."

Within a week after this interview, the school selection committee recommended admitting Melody, and Mrs. W enrolled her.

July 23. By this date an interim IEP for Melody had been proposed and agreed upon by Mrs. W. When she phoned to accept the interim IEP, Mrs. W again inquired about obtaining related services such as O.T., P.T., and speech and language therapy. The assistant principal reassured her that customarily the school performs evaluations to determine the appropriateness of these services within 90 days from the beginning of school.

September 7. Melody was driven to school by her mother. Mrs. W informed the school of her intention to drive Melody herself every day until she can determine the school bus service's reliability.

While Mrs. W was at the school this day, the assistant principal asked her if Melody could participate in the physical education program. Although Mrs. W said Melody could participate in all school activities, she added the caveat: "But just make sure you are careful!"

The assistant principal tried to assure her: "We take every precaution. Don't worry because the staff is well trained and very experienced."

September 20. This date marked the onset of Mrs. W's frequent telephone contacts with the school. She phoned to ask two questions: had an aide been hired for the classroom and when would Melody's special service evaluations commence? The assistant principal promptly returned the call and informed her that aide candidates were being interviewed and that Melody's speech and language evaluations were underway. With respect to the other evaluations, the assistant principal referred Mrs. W to the OT/PT director for current information.

Commentary: In these transactions, school personnel honored Mrs. W's questions with straight answers. This is the recommended procedure at this stage of relationship-building and problem-solving. When school personnel supply answers and non-confidential information, they demonstrate to the parent that he or she is an involved and collaborating partner.

In this regard, the eminent psychologist, Dr. Arnold Lazarus (1971), provided a case vignette of a female patient who grilled him with question after question during the first few minutes of their initial session. The patient had previously consulted five therapists and had been labeled "difficult." Dr. Lazarus gave forthright answers to every question. He remarked that her other therapists had been trained to circumvent this questioning or to comment about her "hostility." Lazarus tendered his replies not because he believed in patients interrogating therapists but to see where the questions would lead and to begin building trust. A parallel can be drawn here with Mrs. W.

Note that school personnel avoided making any unsubstantiated interpretation of the parent's behavior (e.g., "she uses questions as a way of taking control"). Such unfounded and negative interpretations act as a barrier between school and parents. Instead of making pejorative interpretations, it is best to view the situation at its "face value"—a mother who is trying to obtain desired information.

Finally, in hindsight **the school administrators should have inquired** as to what Mrs. W meant by some equivocal terms. For example, how does she define "extraordinary behavior" in the classroom? And what did she mean by warning the staff to "be careful" during physical education class? School personnel should ask for clarification or explanation whenever the parent uses a term which is loaded with idiosyncratic meaning. Do not assume a particular meaning. It is important that both school personnel and parents share the same assumptive world in order to avoid subsequent confusion or frustration.

October 19. Mrs. W telephoned the assistant principal to arrange a visit to Melody's class. During this conversation, Mrs. W expressed displeasure that Melody's OT and PT evaluations were not yet completed. Mrs. W claimed authoritatively that P.L. 94-142 requires such evaluations to be completed within the first 30 days of school.

Later, the assistant principal asked a colleague about the federal requirements and was told that the law does not stipulate a specific time deadline, but rather suggests that the evaluations be done in a timely fashion. The assistant principal decided not to challenge Mrs. W with this information.

October 22. After observing Melody's classroom, Mrs. W paid a critical visit to the school's administrative office. She said that she felt "deceived" because the class still had no aide, and she was "appalled" that two pupils in the class spent "90%" of the time climbing on classroom furniture.

The administrators felt attacked and angered, but through the use of cognitive restructuring techniques, they managed to defuse the anger so as to respectfully address Mrs. W's criticism. They acknowledged that the hiring of an aide had not proceeded as quickly as desired. Furthermore, they explained that one student, Brian, had been recently behaving inappropriately in the class, but that his behavior during the previous school year had been acceptable.

October 29. On this date it was learned that during the preceding week Mrs. W had made phone calls to several higher-level school administrators to inquire about hiring the aide. The principal and assistant were angered, believing that she had gone over their heads. Again, they used cognitive restructuring methods to defuse their anger.

November 8. The assistant principal phoned Mrs. W to inform her that an aide had been hired to begin in two weeks. Mrs. W was not appeased, reiterating her dissatisfaction that the aide had not been in the classroom from the beginning of the school year.

Commentary: The key for school personnel in these interactions was anger control. There would have been little chance of affecting a collaborative relationship if school personnel had responded angrily to Mrs. W's criticism. Instead, the criticism was dealt with in a constructive manner. For example, school administrators evidenced good follow-through: Mrs. W's phone calls were promptly returned and her class observation was ungrudgingly arranged. The school-parent imbalance could have been frozen in place had the school branded her a "troublemaker" and lackadaisically followed up on her calls and requests in order to "teach her a lesson." Also, the assistant principal correctly did not challenge Mrs. W's inaccurate information regarding an OT/PT evaluation deadline. Such a challenge would not have served the purpose of enlightening Mrs. W; rather, it could have been viewed as a piece of one-upmanship, hardly conducive to trust building.

School personnel used cognitive restructuring techniques to defuse their anger. According to cognitive therapy theory, anger is the result of how one chooses to perceive or interpret another's behavior and/or intentions. Defusing anger, therefore, requires one to restructure (i.e., to think differently about) what one tells oneself about another individual.

Several examples illustrate how school personnel used these cognitive restructuring techniques:

Situation	Perception Resulting in Anger	Restructured Perception
Mrs. W inquires about OT/PT evaluations	She's an imposition	Her inquiry shows parental concern
Mrs. W claims a 30 day deadline	She's a pushy know-it-all	She's trying as best as she knows how on behalf of her child
Mrs. W comments critically on classroom practices	Her comments are an intrusion	Her comments are evidence of parental involvement
Mrs. W phones higher-level administrators	This is an aggressive manuever against me	She may resort to this tactic because it's how she thinks she gets service
Mrs. W remains unappeased with news of aide's hiring	She's impossible to please and doesn't understand what we're doing for her	It's her prerogative not to be pleased; after all we didn't make the aide situation clear at the beginning

Thus, with cognitive restructuring techniques, apparent negative behaviors or qualities (she's an imposition) get relabeled into positive ones (she's a concerned parent); condemnation is replaced by understanding, and criticism gets **depersonalized** ("it's an aggressive manuever against me" vs. "it's the way she thinks she gets service").

In hindsight, school personnel failed to do some important probing. It would have been extremely helpful if school personnel had elicited Mrs. W's **expectations** regarding her daughter's educational experiences. What behavior does she expect in a special education classroom? What improvements does she expect that an aide will make on a class? Again, the key word is: **inquire**. By uncovering the parent's expectations, the school may be better able to meet her needs or to correct any misperceptions.[1]

December 3 and 4. Mrs. W made a second classroom observation to determine if positive changes had occurred since the aide's arrival. The classroom teacher reported that while Mrs. W was observing, Brian threw a chair at Melody. On December 4 Mrs. W called the school to say that she desperately feared for Melody's safety. Also, she claimed that Melody's out-of-school behavior was deteriorating, and she attributed this to the "chaotic" classroom environment. She demanded to know how the school planned to control Brian's behavior.

December 5. A conference was convened which included the principal, his assistant, social worker, school psychologist, and teacher. After considerable discussion and information-sharing, the psychologist recommended that it would be appropriate to temporarily place Brian in the school's behavior shaping unit. The assistant principal phoned Mrs. W to inform her of this decision, and she felt "very relieved" by it.

December 12. Mrs. W was sent a copy of the formal IEP document for amending or approval. She was also informed that Melody's OT and PT evaluations were completed.

January 8. Mrs. W made a third observation. Afterwards she met with the assistant principal and said that the class was "shaping up" due to the presence of the aide and Brian's improved behavior.

January 16. Mrs. W returned the IEP with her signature of approval.

February 14. A crisis occurred. During physical education class, Melody became faint. She had become cyanotic and was brought to the school nurse. The assistant principal immediately phoned Mrs. W to report the incident. Mrs. W was grateful for the call. She said that the school need not be unduly alarmed because Melody's medication was again being adjusted and that her color returned after a half hour rest.

Commentary: This sequence of events further illustrates the school personnel's responsiveness. They have demonstrated that they take seriously Mrs. W's requests—arranging additional classroom observations, dealing with the acting-out behavior, and contacting the parent during the emergency.

---

[1] Note that "what" is the preferred interrogative rather than "why." Compare the different parental responses that might be elicited by these two questions: "what contributions do you think an aide can make to the class?" vs. "why do you think an aide is so important?" What-questions usually help the interrogator elicit more specific information.

Commendably, the school exercised caution regarding the disposition of the chair-throwing student. His behavior had become increasingly intractable during the school year, culminating in the aggressive action against Melody. Hence, his temporary placement in a more restrictive classroom environment was deemed appropriate. Such an educational decision could not be made simply to appease a vocal parent.

Apparently as a result of the school's responsiveness, Mrs. W became more cooperative and approving—she signed the IEP document and made a favorable comment about Melody's class. Significantly, she did not catastrophize upon learning of Melody's feeling faint during physical education. We might speculate that her cooperation grew out of knowing that the school is **influenceable**: once she grasped that her requests and criticism were attended to, the need for an adversarial relationship diminished.

At this point with the school demonstrating responsiveness and the parent evidencing increased satisfaction, it is hoped that a more congruent, trusting, and congenial school-parent relationship has been established. Perhaps nothing more was needed than to have her initial concerns and needs ironed out. School personnel should wait to see if this is the case. However, they should also be alert to the possibility that there may be a pattern to the parent's behavior. That is, does the parent feel compelled to adopt an adversarial or aggressive stance to get the school to act? If other dissatisfactions surface, will the parent habitually respond by making additional, perhaps inappropriate, demands?

April 18. The assistant principal sent Mrs. W Melody's interim progress report. This report delineated progress toward each objective specified in the IEP. Progress notes were written by Melody's classroom teacher and special service therapists.

April 24. Various school professionals and administrators each received copies of a very critical letter from Mrs. W. She took umbrage with the fact that the interim speech therapy progress note was written by a student speech therapy intern. Mrs. W said she was upset that a noncertified person was allowed to work with Melody. In part the letter read:

> "Why hadn't I been informed that the school used student trainees? This is like letting a medical student perform delicate surgery . . . I can't see any good coming from this. What worries me is that these students come and go every semester so Melody will never get the continuity of speech therapy that she needs!"

Mrs. W concluded by insisting that Melody receive speech therapy only from the regular staff speech therapist.

School administrators and staff conferred this same day and decided to convene a conference with Mrs. W to discuss her concerns.

May 6. When school personnel and Mrs. W met, three main topics of concern were on the agenda. First, the principal took some time to explain to her the details of the student teacher/intern training program at the school. He described the kinds of supervision these interns receive, and he answered each of Mrs. W's questions. Furthermore, he allowed that the school would have better served Mrs. W had they informed her earlier about the student intern arrangement.

Second, Mrs. W's demand that Melody receive speech therapy only from the staff speech therapist needed to be considered. The school staff had confidence in the speech intern and believed she was working effectively with Melody. Through a **negotiation** process, the school and Mrs. W finally agreed that the intern would provide the speech therapy for Melody but that the staff speech therapist would prepare progress notes for Mrs. W.

The assistant principal broached the third topic. She told Mrs. W that the school was having difficulty knowing how to respond to her criticism and dissatisfactions. She said that school personnel thought they were serving Melody well, but that Mrs. W's dissatisfactions seemed to indicate otherwise. The assistant principal communicated this in an earnest and sincere way, not at all condescending or accusatory. Also, the assistant principal had a hunch, a hypothesis that she wanted to have Mrs. W confirm or reject: "Are you worried that we'll neglect Melody's needs?"

At this juncture, Mrs. W began to sob softly. She apologized for the tone of her letter and said that she was not a hypercritical person. But she felt that unless she made vigorous demands and "shook somebody's tree" that Melody's needs would not get attention. She said she learned that "as the mother of a special ed. child, unless you speak out, all you get is the run-around."

The school administrators expressed understanding. They pointed out that they made honest efforts to be responsive and address her concerns. Moreover, they assured her that they would continue to hear her concerns without her needing to resort to pressure tactics, and that within their capabilities they would attempt to resolve any of her concerns.

Commentary: It became apparent that Mrs. W's criticalness was her way of being assertive. She equated aggressiveness with obtaining results.

She believed she needed to be vocal or risk her daughter getting lost in the shuffle. Viewed from this perspective, her behavior and attitudes are quite understandable.

Her demand that the speech intern cease working with Melody required **negotiation**. The circumstances surrounding this demand differed significantly from her earlier one to remove the aggressive student from class. In that case Brian's behavior warranted a more restrictive, temporary placement. But Melody's intern was performing satisfactorily; splitting them could not be justified. Hence, administrators needed to negotiate an acceptable alternative with Mrs. W.

Note how skillfully the assistant principal broached the topic of Mrs. W's criticalness and dissatisfaction. Instead of projecting the problem onto the parent (the parent is "difficult" or unreasonable"), the administrator chose to "own" it. In other words, the assistant principal suggested that the problem resided within administration and staff: **they** were not sure how to proceed. This is a very effective technique, because it prevents the parent from feeling defensive.

It was crucial that the third agenda item got covered. The heretofore unaddressed (covert) but very evident issues of Mrs. W's anger and dissatisfaction needed eventually to be commented upon (made overt). Once these issues had been made explicit between parent and school, future contacts could be more readily facilitated. Thus, if Mrs. W should call feeling angry or exasperated, the school administrator might constructively **inquire**: is she feeling the need to "shake someone's tree"? Does she doubt that the school would take her concerns seriously? Does she figure she must be aggressive to get action? Such a comment might help the parent to relax and therefore make it easier for parent and school to collaboratively problem-solve.

IMPLICATIONS

The case study depicts a series of school-parent encounters that required effective problem-solving. The case study has relevance for school personnel who are impacted by P.L. 94-142 which mandates parent involvement in special education. When schools must elicit parent involvement, it is likely that some parents will present concerns, criticisms, perceived needs, and dissatisfactions. If the school avoids or otherwise ineffectively deals with parents' concerns, the school may risk losing the parents' involvement, input, and collaboration. When these concerns are addressed in a problem-solving manner, school professionals are more likely to establish a relationship where the parent can function as an "equal participant." In this section we shall highlight the case study's basic techniques for performing effective problem-solving.

1. **Answer Parents' Questions and Provide Adequate Nonconfidential Information.** Information is essential for helping parents make decisions and may allay some parents' fears or concerns. Providing information is always an important problem-solving tactic, perhaps even more so in the early stages of school-parent relationship-building. Of course, the variety of questions is virtually unlimited, but if you were the special educator, school social worker, or administrator, how would you provide forthright answers to these queries:

> "What do I need to do to initiate the due process procedure?"
>
> "Will my child get speech therapy, and how will I know if it's helping?"
>
> "They've been working with my son for four years now to get him to recognize numbers. Do you think it's worthwhile to have that as a goal again this year?"
>
> "Why doesn't the school purchase the XYZ reading series? I've heard it's very good."
>
> "Why doesn't the school have a model kitchen for teaching domestic skills?"

Remember, too, to be alert for attitudes on your part that would discourage information flow (e.g., "with parents, the less they know, the better"; "if I keep answering questions, they'll bug me more," etc.).

2. **Make Explicit Parents' Expectations.** This recommendation goes hand-in-hand with number one above. For example, a parent may ask a question—"Why isn't Johnny in a regular math class?"—that requires certain information. However, the school professional should also inquire about possible parental expectations: What kind of math performance does the parent expect from Johnny? What placement procedures and decisions does the parent expect from the school?

3. **Have Parents Define Any "Loaded," Idiosyncratic, or Ambiguous Terms.** Effective problem-solving cannot occur if school professionals assume unintended meaning. If, for example, a parent asks: "Will you restrain my child if he acts temperamental?" inquire as to what the parent means by the loaded word "restrain." Is the parent talking about physical (encumbering clothing), chemical (tranquilizing medication), or spatial

(time-out room) restraints? Also, ask the parent to explain his or her meaning of the ambiguous term "act temperamental." Once the terms are made clear, the school professional can next inquire about parent **expectations**: what behaviors does the parent expect will result in the child being restrained? How does the parent expect school personnel to respond if the child physically aggresses against a staff person or another child?

Bear in mind that this technique can strengthen the school-parent relationship: parents are more likely to feel listened to when they see school professionals working to clarify and to understand.

4. **Evidence Responsible Follow-Through.** Resolving a parent's concern or dissatisfaction sometimes takes nothing more than old-fashioned legwork. But this is crucial for establishing the school's credibility. Follow through on promises to obtain information for parents. Return phone calls without undue delay. Schedule parent conferences promptly. Get paperwork done on time.

5. **Avoid Negative Labeling.** If parents express concerns or dissatisfactions or make requests, avoid attaching pejorative labels to them. Once parents get labeled as being "unreasonable," "demanding," "impractical," and so forth, school professionals will find it harder to properly serve them. Also, by all means avoid amateur psychologizing (e.g., "I'm dealing with a classic passive-aggressive parent").

6. **Avoid Responses That Will Put Parents on the Defensive.** Sometimes when parents present with a concern, school professionals respond in such a way to place the parents in a defensive posture which discourages collaborative problem-solving. For example:

Parent Concern	School Response #1	School Response #2
"Why doesn't the school purchase the XYZ reading series? I've read good reports about it."	"What do you want that series for? Don't you know that you'd be buying out-dated material?"	"We had that option, but the more we looked into it, the more we saw it was outdated."
		+
		"By the way, what benefits do you see with XYZ?"

The choice of pronoun ("you") imparts an accusatory ring to Response #1. In effect, the parents are squelched, and the matter is settled to the school's satisfaction. This response leads to **one-sided** rather than mutual problem-solving.

In Response #2, the choice of a first person pronoun ("we") has the opposite effect: here the school "owns" responsibility for the choice instead of belittling the parents. This response was followed by a question to elicit the parents' expectations regarding XYZ. Once school professionals have obtained the parents' expectations and opinions, they can better involve the parents in the problem-solving process and/or provide them with confirming or disconfirming information.

7. **Defuse Anger Through Cognitive Restructuring Techniques.** If you become angry, exasperated, or impatient when parents express a problem or dissatisfaction, ask yourself whether you first attached any negative label to the parents' behavior (see #5). If you did, it could have precipitated the angry emotion you feel, an emotion that hinders an effective school-parent relationship. Try substituting a more positive interpretation of the parents' behavior. It is almost always possible to do such a "cognitive flip-flop" because virtually every behavior can be viewed from two perspectives. Thus:

The "imposing" parent who wants to schedule a class observation	becomes	An "involved" parent who cares about her child's education
The "trouble-making" parent who initiates due process procedures	becomes	A "resourceful" parent who takes advantage of the legal machinery
The "impractical" parent who wants her child dismissed before the legal end of the school day	becomes	An "uninformed" parent who isn't knowledgable about school regulations

Sometimes school professionals experience anger when they **personalize** parents' criticism. Instead of viewing the criticism as a personal attack, defuse it by depersonalizing the thrust of the criticism—understand it in terms of what it says about the person who is being critical:

Criticism	**Personalized Meanings**	**Depersonalized Meanings**
"My child's teacher isn't fit to be in a classroom"	"I've got to defend against this remark"	"This may be the parent's way of getting the problem attended to"

| "If you criticize, I respond in kind" | "She's not so much angry at me but exasperated about what to do" |
| | "She may be right. I'll hear her out" |

8. **Use Negotiation and Compromise to Resolve Parent Concerns or to Address Parent Requests.** Sometimes parents use the IEP process to seek an **ideal** array of services for their child when the best the school can do is provide an **adequate** amount. When the parents' request seems impractical, perhaps a compromise can be worked out. For instance, parents may request speech therapy twice per week for their child, but the school's speech evaluations suggest therapy only once per week. A compromise might involve allowing an outside evaluator to determine the child's needs, with parent and school abiding by this evaluation.

When negotiating, make sure that the compromise is acceptable to both parties. Also, thoroughly ascertain the parents' expectations regarding the services before entering into negotiation.

9. **If Necessary, Tactfully Make Explicit the Parents' Covert Agenda.** Sometimes after extensive observation and experience, school professionals develop a hunch that, for whatever reason, the concern which parents are raising is actually subordinate to some larger issue. Uncovering the core issue is essential for effective problem-solving. Again, it may be useful for school professionals to check out their hunch provided they use a tactful, nonaccusatory approach that minimizes parent defensiveness. One useful method couches the inquiry in the form of a vague hypothesis following the words, "I'm wondering if . . .

. . . you believe that his slow development is something your son will outgrow"

. . . you think your daughter ought to be in a regular classroom"

. . . you aren't satisfied with the information we've been providing you"

With this method, the school professional "owns" responsibility for the doubt, thereby permitting the parent to more easily agree or disagree with the hypothesis.

REFERENCES

Federal Register (1981, January 19), Washington, DC: U.S. Government Printing House.

Lauder, C. E., Kantor, H., Myers, G., & Resnick, J. (1979). Educational placement of children with spina bifida. *Exceptional Children, 45*, 432–437.

Lazarus, A. A. (1971). Behavior therapy and beyond. New York: McGraw-Hill.

McMillan, D. L. & Turnbull, A. P. (1983). Parent involvement with special education: Respecting individual preferences. *Education and Training of the Mentally Retarded, 18,* 5–9.

Owens, R. G. (1981). Organizational behavior in education (2nd edition). Englewood Cliffs, NJ: Prentice-Hall.

Shevin, M. (1983). Meaningful parental involvement in long-range educational planning for disabled children. *Education and Training of the Mentally Retarded, 18,* 17–21.

Yoshida, R. K., Fenton, K. S., Kaufman, M. J., & Maxwell, J. P. (1978). Parental involvement in the special education pupil planning process: The school's perspective. *Exceptional Children, 44,* 531–534.

Chapter 18

CULTURAL ISSUES IN SCHOOL AND FAMILY

Donald R. Atkinson

Culture has been defined as "the configuration of learned behavior and results of behavior whose components and elements are shared and transmitted by the members of a particular society" (Linton, 1945, p. 32). Although cultures can vary within ethnic groups, ethnic groups typically serve as the "society" for sharing and transmitting learned behaviors and their products. In the United States there are numerous ethnic groups including, to name but a few: Irish, Greeks, Italians, Blacks, Cubans, Russians, Mexicans, Vietnamese, and American Indians.

Some ethnic groups, after three or four generations in this country, assimilate into mainstream U.S. culture to the point that the ethnic culture is lost and inter-ethnic marriages obscure ethnic differences. For other ethnic groups, particularly those that are racially as well as culturally distinct, complete assimilation has not been possible or, in many instances, desired. Some ethnic groups, because of their skin color or physical characteristics, have been denied full assimilation into U.S. culture. Also, some ethnic groups have made deliberate attempts to remain culturally distinct, preferring cultural pluralism to cultural assimilation. Furthermore, since 1975 the United States has been in a period of heavy immigration, perhaps the heaviest of any time in our history. The combination of ethnic groups who are disfranchised, those that have intentionally remained culturally different, and those that are recent immigrants creates a cultural diversity in the United States that cannot be ignored by educators.

The purpose of this chapter is to help school personnel respond to the cultural diversity in their schools. The first section examines areas of potential conflict between the school and ethnic minority cultures. The second section discusses stress that ethnic minorities experience that may contribute to school-related problems. The third section describes how counselors and other school personnel can help reduce the potential

237

for conflict between the school and the culture as well as help ethnic groups deal with the stress they encounter as minorities.

AREAS OF POTENTIAL CONFLICT

Most ethnic minority parents have the same goal for their children as the school has. Within the general goal of educating children to be successful in later life, however, differences may arise that lead to antagonism between the school and home. The school and home may have differing expectations about the kind of education and training to which a child should aspire. Educators are frequently criticized by Black parents, for example, for underestimating the academic talents of Black children and for channeling them into vocational education tracks rather than college preparatory courses (Hines & Boyd-Franklin, 1982).

The school and ethnic minority parents may have differing views about the parents' role in educating the child. The school sometimes misinterprets parental shyness or insecurity or conflicting work schedule as evidence of lack of interest and makes only perfunctory attempts to involve the parents in their child's education. School officials, for example, may give up on trying to involve a Latino mother after she misses a parent-teacher conference without realizing that she must take time off from work, arrange child care for her family, and travel by bus in order to keep the appointment. Although minority parents may lack the English language fluency or academic skills to tutor their child, they can provide incentives and motivation for their child to achieve—an important contribution that is often lost when the school assumes a lack of interest on the part of the parents.

The school and the home may also have differing expectations about the role each should play in promoting cultural values. Intentionally or not, it is generally acknowledged that U. S. public schools provide a "hidden curriculum" that includes promoting middle class values, traditional sex roles, and conformity to rules. Some ethnic parents may support this "hidden curriculum" since they hope to have their children assimilate fully into the U. S. culture. Others may resent the conflict it creates with traditional ethnic values and may prefer that the school teach only academic content. Asian American parents, for example, may resent pressures placed on their child to share family problems in a family health class since they view public knowledge of such information as shameful.

Counselors need to be sensitive to these areas of potential conflict between the school and ethnic parents that may be the result of differing cultural values. Efforts should be made to accommodate the cultural values of the family whenever possible and every effort should be made to involve the parents in their children's education.

SOURCES OF STRESS EXPERIENCED BY ETHNIC MINORITIES

Each ethnic group in the United States has its own unique cultural components that make it different from any other group. By virtue of being ethnic minorities in the United States, however, they all share some experiences in common. To some extent, the sources of stress discussed in this section are common to all ethnic minorities in the United States. Some of these sources of stress are related directly to immigration (or in the case of American Indians, emigration). For some ethnic groups their migration occurred several generations ago; for others, it is a new or continuing phenomenon. Whenever it occurred, migration is likely to have created a source of stress for the ethnic family that has ripple effects for several generations after the actual migration. Other sources of stress are related to discrimination, a phenomenon that affects some minority groups long after their ancestral migration.

Migration

The United States is currently in a period of heavy immigration. The recent immigrants have come primarily from South East Asia, Mexico, Cuba, and Haiti with a scattering from almost every country in the world. For some of the recent immigrants, the move has involved physical hardship and threat of danger. Often there is considerable sacrifice and loss of property.

The migration from one country to another puts tremendous pressures on the family. Sometimes school-related problems will develop in direct response to these pressures as children attempt to escape stress or seek security through involvement with peer groups. Listed below are some of the specific sources of stress experienced by immigrants and their offsprings.

Separation from Extended Family. Many new immigrants come from agrarian-based, third-world countries where extended families provide support in times of stress. Among Vietnamese families, for example, the eldest family member often serves as "adviser" to younger members of the family (Atkinson, Ponterotto, & Sanchez, 1984). Immigration disrupts the extended family support system, just when it is needed most. Landau (1982) makes this point in her discussion of families in cultural transition:

> An individual, or a small nuclear unit moving away from a close traditional extended family into a new culture where nuclear independence is expected, is likely to feel severely threatened. There is a sudden lack of extended family support at a time when it is most needed. (p. 554)

Separation from the extended family can also create a source of stress when the immigrant family is expected to provide fiscal support for those relatives left behind. Mexican-American families, for example, often pool their resources so that money can be sent to relatives living in Mexico. This obligation may strain the resources of the family members living in the United States.

Loss of Self-Esteem. Recent immigrants often must take jobs far beneath their education and training in order to survive when they first arrive in the United States. For someone who has worked as a nurse or businessperson or mechanic to have to accept a job requiring no training, sometimes at below minimum wages, means a severe loss of self-esteem. White collar Cuban immigrants, for example, have sometimes been forced to accept jobs as custodians and street vendors. When one or both parents experience this loss of self-esteem it can have severe repercussions on the entire family.

Cultural Conflict. Cultural conflict refers to the conflict between the values of the original culture and the values of mainstream culture in the United States. Cultural conflict is a source of stress that begins soon after the initial immigration and continues long afterward, creating the greatest stress in generations that appear to be fully acculturated. First generation (immigrating) minorities often maintain their original culture in spite of pressures to adopt the new culture's values. Second generation minorities frequently adopt U. S. cultural values despite the presence of traditional values in their parents' home. Third and fourth generation minorities attempting to reestablish ties with their ancestral culture often experience the greatest cultural conflict. The term "marginal person" has been used to describe the individual caught between their ethnic culture and mainstream U. S. culture.

Generational Conflict. Generational conflict can occur in any family in the U. S. but is particularly stressful in an ethnic family where parents and children are assimilating at different rates. Children who move to this country at an early age assimilate the language and customs much more rapidly than do their parents (and sometimes against their parents' will). Some of the newly learned customs are repugnant to the older generation; some of the old customs are anathema to the younger generation.

Landau (1982) suggests that when family members are adjusting to new cultural values at different rates the family system can become severely distressed and that "recognition of transitional conflict is the key to helping families in cultural transition" (p. 556). While each individual member of the family may be aware that the source of family tension is related to differences between new and old cultural values, they may not realize that generational conflict is an almost inevitable part of migration. Schools unknowingly contribute to conflict between parent and child by asking children to act as interpreters for their parents at teacher-parent meetings. This can have the effect of undermining the indigeneous hierarchy of authority.

Language Differences. Language differences can be a source of stress for ethnic minorities, both for those who are recent immigrants and those who have lost the ability to speak their native tongue (research by Smith, 1957, and Smith and Kasdon, 1961, documented that having one or both parents who speak a native tongue can impair the acquisition of English). Feelings of insecurity about their ability to communicate in English may result in non-participation in class discussions by minority students and a reluctance to interact with school officials by their parents. School officials may interpret silence as sullen, uncooperative, and dullard behavior.

In addition to insecurity about their use of English, cultural factors can affect the communication patterns of ethnic minorities and lead to misinterpretation by school officials. D. W. Sue and D. Sue (1977) point out that "there are . . . complex rules regarding when to speak or yield to another person" (pp. 426–427). In some cultures silence serves as a sign of respect, in others it serves to emphasize a point of discussion. In some cultures indirectness may be misinterpreted by fully assimilated Americans who value directness and the importance of "getting to the point" (D. W. Sue & D. Sue, 1977).

Differences in communication at the nonverbal level may also lead to misinterpretation. D. W. Sue and D. Sue (1977) point out that "different cultures dictate different distances in personal space" (p. 426) and that as a result professionals often misinterpret minority behavior as too intimate or pushy. They also suggest that eye contact varies culturally. Blacks, for example, tend to maintain eye contact when talking but not necessarily while listening, the reverse of White behavior. For Mexican Americans and Japanese direct eye contact is often avoided as a sign of respect.

Identity Crisis. For many ethnic minority people an identity crisis occurs when they attempt to move up the socioeconomic ladder. Upward social mobility in this country has typically meant a loss of ethnic identity. An identity crisis, then, is not so much a conflict between two cultures as it is a conflict between the ethnic culture and the desire to be upwardly mobile in the United States.

Discrimination

Regardless of whether they just immigrated or were indigeneous to this country, ethnic minorities continue to experience discrimination as long as their physical features, customs, or language distinguish them from "White" Americans. Although physical forms of discrimination are on the decline, more subtle forms of discrimination continue unchecked. Blacks and Hispanics still represent a disproportionate share of those living below the poverty level and are still underrepresented in institutions of higher education. Even Asian Americans, often referred to as the model minority, who are qualified for management positions by virtue of their education and experience, continue to be passed over for these positions (Yu, 1985).

OVERCOMING CONFLICT AND REDUCING STRESS

Counselors and other school personnel can help overcome potential conflict between the school and ethnic minority parents by involving the parents in the educational process. In setting up a parent-counselor (or teacher) conference it may be necessary to arrange for a translator, preferably not a younger member of the family. Telephone contact may be problematic if the parents are limited English speaking. Many Vietnamese parents, for example, have taken English reading and writing courses in their home country but experience a great deal of difficulty understanding an English speaker on the telephone. Mexican

American parents, on the other hand, may have a good speaking knowledge of English but no formal training in reading or writing the language.

McGoldrick (1982) has offered the following advice for counselors working with families experiencing cultural conflict:

> Restoring a stronger sense of identity may require resolving cultural conflicts within the family, between the family and the community, or in the wider context in which the family is embedded. . . . Families may need coaching to sort out deeply held convictions from values asserted for emotional reasons. . . . The therapist's role in such situations, as in all therapy, will be that of a culture broker, helping family members to recognize their own ethnic values and to resolve the conflicts that evolve out of different perceptions and experiences. (p. 23)

The reader is cautioned that helping families resolve cultural conflict, generational conflict, and other sources of ethnic family stress does not necessarily mean facilitation of the assimilation process. The rate of individual and family assimilation (indeed, even the decision to adopt certain aspects of the new culture) should be left to family members.

CONCLUDING COMMENT

The purpose of this chapter is to sensitize counselors and other professional educators to the role of culture in the family and to suggest ways in which the counselor can help alleviate stresses experienced by the ethnic family. In doing so it was necessary to focus on phenomena experienced by all or most ethnic groups. A complete discussion of the unique culture and experience of each ethnic group is beyond the scope of this chapter but should be of concern to any counselor working with a minority student.

The reader should also be aware of the danger of replacing old stereotypes with new generalizations. The generalizations presented here serve to help understand the cultural context of the family. In the final analysis each person and family has its own unique combination of values, stresses, and experiences to which the counselor should attend.

REFERENCES

Atkinson, D. R., Ponterotto, J. G., & Sanchez, A. R. (1984). Attitudes of Vietnamese and Anglo-American students toward counseling. *Journal of College Student Personnel, 25,* 448–452.

Hines, P. M., & Boyd-Franklin, N. (1982). Black families. In M. McGoldrick, J.K. Pearce, and J. Giordano (Eds.), *Ethnicity and family therapy* (pp. 84–107). New York: Guilford Press.

Landau, J. (1982). Therapy with families in cultural transition. In M. McGoldrick, J. K. Pearce, & J. Giordano (Eds.), *Ethnicity and family therapy* (pp. 552–572).

Linton, R. (1945). *The cultural background of personality.* New York: Appleton-Century.

McGoldrick, M. (1982). Ethnicity and family therapy: An overview. In M. McGoldrick, J. K. Pearce, & J. Giordano (Eds.), *Ethnicity and family therapy* (pp. 3–38). New York: Guilford Press.

Smith, M. E. (1957). Progress in the use of English after twenty-two years by children of Chinese ancestry in Honolulu. *Journal of Genetic Psychology, 90,* 255–258.

Smith, M. E., & Kasdon, L. M. (1961). Progress in the use of English after twenty-two years by children of Filipino and Japanese ancestry in Hawaii. *Journal of Genetic Psychology, 99,* 129–138.

Sue, D. W., & Sue, D. (1977). Barriers to effective cross-cultural counseling. *Journal of Counseling Psychology, 24,* 420–429.

Yu, W. (1985, September 11). Asian-Americans charge prejudice slows climb to management ranks. *The Wall Street Journal,* p. 37.

Chapter 19

COUNSELING CHILDREN AND FAMILIES IN THE SCHOOLS

LARRY B. GOLDEN

School teachers, administrators, counselors, nurses, and psychologists are very much aware of the importance of including families in the task of helping children adjust to the demands of school. There is ample support for the position that professionals who have brief but significant contacts with families should intervene to help families manage maladaptive behavior in children (Golden, 1984; Nicoli, 1984; Palmo et al., 1984). The family is in a powerful position to support or sabotage our best efforts on a child's behalf.

It is proposed that if an accurate discrimination can be made between functional and dysfunctional families, the school can offer effective services to both. The school professional's time, energy, and expertise are regarded here as precious commodities that must be wisely distributed. The intent of this chapter is to offer instruction in a method of assessing families that promises to conserve that precious capability. Subsequently, the goal of brief family interventions is to enable families that are assessed as "functional" to gain control of problematic behavior with only minimal reliance on an outside professional. Consequently, they will bring an expanded repertoire of problem solving skills and renewed self-confidence to the next disruptive episode in their lives.

ASSESSING FAMILY FUNCTIONALITY

For this discussion, we discriminate between two types of families, the dysfunctional and the functional. This assessment can help school personnel make good decisions about how to work with a family.

What is the difference between a functional family, here defined as one with whom school personnel can work with productively, versus a dysfunctional family, one which does not possess the prerequisite capability? It is proposed that the functional family will score "high marks" on each of these criteria: (a) Parental resources, (b) Time frame of problem behavior, (c) Boundary characteristics and patterns of communication, (d) Hierarchy of authority, and (e) Relationship with school personnel. Each of these criteria is discussed below.

Sources of information about a particular family include anecdotal records, teacher reports, and interviews with the child. However, the best source is a structured family interview. At such an interview, family members are encouraged to talk with each other about the child's behavioral problems. What would account for the child's problem? What changes in the child's behavior are desired? What will happen if nothing changes? Who wants things to change the most? What solutions have already been tried? Responses to these probes can shed light on family dynamics.

Parental Resources

A relatively simple decision must be made: Can these parents provide for the child's basic needs? A strong marriage, supportive extended family, gainful employment, financial solvency, and a high degree of education or skill are characteristics that suggest a large capacity for parents to respond as full working partners with school personnel. On the other hand, the young, immature, single parent may have fewer resources at his or her disposal. Extreme poverty over several generations, criminality, alcoholism, and child abuse are conditions that confront us with crises that obviate the need for "brief family interventions." We are well advised to be modest about the potential of counseling to resolve all of the world's ills. Call in the social workers, legal authorities, and governmental agencies!

Time Frame of Problem Behavior

Is the child's misbehavior of short or chronic duration? Consider two familiar diagnoses from the **Diagnostic and Statistical Manual**, Third Edition, or **DSM-III** (American Psychiatric Association, 1980). The **DSM-III** defines an Adjustment Disorder as, "A maladaptive reaction to an identifiable psychosocial stressor, that occurs within three months of the onset of the stressor" (p. 167). A Conduct Disorder is, "A repetitive and persistent pattern of aggressive conduct in which the basic rights of others are violated" (p. 29). While these are **individual** diagnoses, they have implications for family functioning. The Adjustment Disorder portrays circumstances that bode well; the Conduct Disorder, the opposite.

As seen above, the **DSM–III** refers to "psychosocial stressors." Typical stressors in a child's experience include such events as the birth of a sibling, marital discord, the death of a beloved pet animal, a move to a new school, or the onset of illness in self or another family member. Stress may provoke a variety of problematic behavior including enuresis or encopresis, disruptive classroom behavior, antagonistic peer relationships, or decline in academic performance. The presenting problem is of little relevance in evaluating family functionality. Without the perspective of many years of living, a child is prone to act out in bizarre ways that may be disproportionate to the actual cause. Of far greater significance is chronicity.

A parent's response such as, "She's always been a difficult child and I can't understand it for the life of me!" indicates a less favorable prognosis than, "I lost my job in October and its been hard on all of us; his grades have fallen sharply since then." Ask about previous contacts with mental health professionals. The fact that a behavioral problem has existed for a long time tells us something important about the competence of the parents to manage the current crisis.

Boundary Characteristics and Patterns of Communication

Family systems theory is concerned with the boundaries that separate individuals from each other. Minuchin (1974) describes three types of boundaries that separate individuals in a family. The **diffuse** boundary fails to provide opportunity for individuation. Children in these enmeshed families may be denied privacy and be overprotected; their development in the area of autonomy is obstructed. The **rigid** boundary blocks communication and creates distance. This closed system is maintained by yelling, blaming, sarcasm or, more ominously, silence. The following interaction illustrates elements of both rigid and diffuse boundaries:

> COUNSELOR (To child): Tell your parents how much spelling homework you would do during the week to earn Saturday morning television privileges.
>
> FATHER (Angrily interrupting, to counselor): She would have to change her entire attitude!

MOTHER: It seems to me that the teacher is the one who needs a change of attitude. It is abnormal to expect a child to do hours of homework after being in school all day long.

With his critical response, the father in this exchange ensures that a meaningful dialogue with his daughter will be avoided. The mother reinforces her daughter's dependency by speaking on her behalf against the teacher.

The **permeable** boundary allows for both healthy individuation and deep interpersonal involvement. The permeable boundary is, of course, characteristic of relationships in functional families.

Boundary characteristics are evident in the ebb and flow of communication. If family members cannot talk to each other, they may not be able to help one another.

Hierarchy of Authority

It is useful to imagine an organizational chart that illustrates family structure. Parents in functional families hold an executive decision making position within the family organization. This is not to say that children do not have **age-appropriate** opportunities for having their opinions heard and respected. In dysfunctional families, however, children have undue power because of parental default. Children in such families appear out of control and their parents seem helpless.

Parents who are successful in asserting authority are likely to agree on basic principles of child rearing that help them to "hang tough" when confronted with a child's manipulations. When the hierarchy of authority is disturbed, parents will be unable to agree on effective measures of control.

Relationship with School Personnel

Can parents and school people work as a team? Dependability is central to the issue. Do these parents return phone calls? Do they show up for meetings at school? The real test, however, is follow-through; the functional family does its homework. For example, there may be agreement that the mother will help the child with spelling on Wednesday evening and that the father will telephone the teacher on Thursday afternoon to make sure the assignment was submitted. There is a good probability that a functional family will complete these tasks, whereas the dysfunctional one will fail for any number of reasons.

School people tend to be highly verbal and psychologically sophisticated. Rapport is most easily established with parents who "speak the language." Parents who feel intimidated by school authorities will need special encouragement. Hostile, litigious parents may be almost impossible to work with because school authorities will feel pushed into a defensive stance. Positive energy is drained by the need for meticulous documentation.

INTERVENTIONS

Based on an assessment of functionality, how can we best work with a particular family? Just as school personnel are accustomed to think in terms of an Individual Educational Plan (IEP), perhaps they should consider an "FEP" or Family Educational Plan.

The goal is a team effort to shape up a child's behavior. There is always a temptation to focus our energies on the child, conveniently captive to our good intentions. The parent may be seen as a nuisance to be circumvented or, at best, may be trusted not to interfere. However, an accurate assessment enables the school professional to make an appropriate commitment to parent involvement.

Interventions with Dysfunctional Families

If the assessment indicates a highly dysfunctional family, the best options are to offer the child "in-house" services, such as individual and small group counseling and structured classroom management. It would be a mistake to expect a dysfunctional family to follow through on a plan to reward or punish school behavior at home.

Just as we prescribe structure for troubled children, so, also, for troubled families. If a parent conference is arranged, stick to the conference time frame. Be formal, professional, and affirm a shared interest in helping the child. Elicit parental permission for the school's "in house" plan.

When parents are unavailable or incompetent, play therapy may become the treatment of choice. In her influential book, **Play Therapy**, Virginia Axline says, "... while therapy might move ahead faster if the adults were also receiving therapy or counseling, it is not necessary for the

adults to be helped in order to ensure successful play therapy results"
(1947, p. 66). Axline (1969) describes "Eight Basic Principles," para-
phrased below:

1. The therapist develops a warm relationship with the child, in which
rapport is established as soon as possible.

2. The therapist accepts the child exactly as she is.

3. The therapist establishes a feeling of permissiveness in the relationship so that the child feels free to express feelings completely.

4. The therapist reflects the feelings the child is expressing in order to
help the child gain insight into her behavior.

5. The therapist maintains respect for the child's ability to solve her
own problems. The child is responsible for change.

6. The therapist does not direct the child's actions or conversation.
The child leads; the therapist follows.

7. The therapist does not hurry. Therapy is a gradual process.

8. The therapist establishes only those limits that are needed to anchor
the therapy to reality and to make the child aware of her responsibility in
the relationship.

There are some cautions regarding play therapy. Firstly, play therapy,
other than in some abbreviated format, is too time consuming to be used
by most school counselors. Secondly, with its intense focus on the therapist-
child relationship, the role of the family in the therapy process may be
ignored. A troubled marital relationship may go unrecognized (Golden,
1985).

The power of play therapy is in its explicit recognition of the need to
help children express feelings and the contents of their powerful imagi-
nations through verbal and nonverbal means. Play therapy provides us
with a special language and materials that can serve as a springboard for
communication and for building rapport.

The school mental health professional should weigh the capabilities of
the school, itself, to follow through with a treatment plan. The criteria
for assessing family functionality could easily be applied to evaluating
the school. Previously, chronicity was seen to reflect negatively on the
competence of parents. A behavior problem that continues from year to
year tells us something about the capabilities of the school, as well.
Today, not only parents, but school personnel, are experiencing a crisis
of authority. It is essential that the child or adolescent be blocked in any
attempt to pit parental and school authorities against each other.

If a referral for psychotherapy is advisable, parents should be made aware of the seriousness of the problem and the advantages of prompt action. Inviting the family to imagine a crystal ball that shows them how the situation will be three years hence if nothing changes can be a strong motivator. It is also helpful to be able to recommend specific agencies or practitioners with confidence (Amatea and Fabrick, 1984).

Interventions with Functional Families

It is proposed that a school counselor or other mental health worker can help a **functional** family gain control of childhood misbehavior in as few as three face-to-face family conferences (Golden, 1983; Golden, 1984). This process is best described by a literal example of what might be said to a family. In this case, the child presents a problem of intermittent truancy.

> I am interested in working with your family for a limited period of time to help you get this problem straightened out. I think you can manage this situation with only a minimum of help from me but if it develops that there is a need for another type of approach, I will bring that to your attention. There is cause for optimism. Your son has a previous record of good attendance prior to his truancy this year. As parents, you have shown that you are willing to work with your son to get this problem resolved. My goal will be to help you, as parents, in your efforts to get your son go to school every day. We won't talk about past grievances; we will focus on the present problem.

It is likely that the family will want to know about the time commitment. Failure is indicated when brief interventions exceed six family conferences without resolution of the problem. The conferences themselves should be limited to about 30 minutes, with the exception of the initial interview, which may well last an hour. Note that contacts with the family are termed as "conferences," not "sessions," because of the therapeutic associations of the latter term. It is important to clarify to the family that it does not need nor will it receive "therapy" from the school mental health professional.

Many of the best laid plans are defeated by ambivalence. Our motto should be, "Go for it!" Continuation of problematic behavior may result in a negative and habitual style of coping with stress. The school counselor should organize a concentrated effort to get the problem resolved and be willing to coordinate the efforts of parents and other school personnel.

Open Lines of Communication. According to Satir (1972), there is a tendency to close down communication during periods of stress. Frightened, anxious people tend to blame, withdraw, or to adopt any strategy that will diminish the experience of painful realities. Unfortunately, it is precisely during these periods of stress that open communication is most crucial. At the start, the school counselor should challenge the family's feelings of helplessness. Leavitt (1982) advises prompting to recall the family's resourcefulness in handling stressful situations in the past.

In a functional family, a gentle and respectful application of basic, active listening skills (e.g., paraphrasing, reflection) will usually suffice to get people talking. These facilitative skills have been discussed in the professional literature, notably by Brammer (1979), Carkhuff (1969), and Rogers 1980), and therefore are not presented here.

Support the Hierarchy of Parental Authority. In stressful times, even competent parents are quick to relinquish authority to outside professionals. Haley (1980) emphasizes the importance of putting parents in charge of managing the child's behavior problems. The distressed child is making a plea, albeit indirect, for parental control. Out of feelings of guilt and confusion, parents may permit the child more freedom than is appropriate.

Encourage parents to take control of resources that could serve as reinforcers. For example, an adolescent who is "independently wealthy," sporting a big allowance and a room full of electronic equipment, is in a position to "blow off" his parents' demands for behavioral change. In this case, the child's allowance should be reduced to zero. He earns money the old-fashioned way, by behaving responsibly!

The artistry in this approach lies in supporting the authority of the parents without alienating the child. It helps to reframe the child's apparently negative motives and hold out hope for the future. For example, here is a counselor response to fifteen year old Cindy who has attempted to run away from home only to "crawl" back, unable to support herself: "Cindy, the most important job you have to do is making a plan for leaving home on your own two feet. What resources will you need to do the job right? How can your parents help you prepare?" The process of preparation for this crucial life task can be ego-enhancing for both parent and adolescent (Haley, 1980).

Implement a Plan. According to Haley (1980), parents must agree on three issues if they are to work together to manage their child's behavior: (a) The specific behaviors that are desired from the child, (b) The mechanism by which the parents will know if their child has behaved in the desired way, and (c) The specific consequences for behavior or misbehavior. It is essential that both parents agree on each of these points. If marital discord surfaces, parents should be encouraged to work toward agreement for the good of their child and deal with their marital problems at some later time.

In most cases, the "plan" will consist of the teacher sending home daily reports about the child's behavior and parental reinforcement of positive performance. For example, the teacher may write that the child remained in his seat during one of the two half-hour reporting periods. The parents then permit the child to color one spot on a giraffe. Eventually, when all the spots are colored, the child has earned a trip to the zoo.

The plan is treated as an "experiment" so that the family can more easily accept the risk of failure. The family is encouraged to brainstorm about ways a plan could be sabotaged. For example, the child could "lose" the teacher's report or the child could threaten to run away or commit suicide and thereby panic his parents into giving up on the plan.

Meanwhile, the counselor attempts to build an influential relationship with the child in order to reinforce goal behavior. The counselor must convince the child that he or she cares enough to get involved. To that end, home visits and classroom observations can be useful. A telephone call or a postcard from the counselor can be very special reinforcers for some children.

Brief family interventions can work with single-parent families as well as with the traditional nuclear family. The process can be crippled, however, if one of the parents the child normally lives with is absent from the conferences. This is more significant if the parent's absence reflects disinterest or opposition than a bona fide difficulty with scheduling.

Case Study

This case was contributed by Diane Johnson, an elementary school counselor in San Antonio. Ben Y. was a capable second grader who came to the attention of the school counselor when his mother called to complain that Ben was not getting his school work done. Mrs. Y. said that school papers were not being brought home, that when confronted, Ben would lie or "clam up," and that Ben had told her that he hated school.

Mrs. Y. used deprivation of television to punish misbehavior and engaged Ben in two hours of nightly drill on school work. She tried using favorite foods as rewards for good behavior but without success.

The classroom teacher described Ben as a slight, fragile child who was not working to potential and showed facial tics, thumb sucking, and tugging on collar and shirt tail and minimal eye contact when speaking. The teacher was also worried about Ben's lack of friends, unusual content of art work (i.e., Ben depicted Santa Claus as a monster), and repeated exposures of his body in the boy's bathroom (pulled down pants and underwear).

An only child, Ben lived with his mother and father. Mrs. Y. is a homemaker and Mr. Y. is employed as an auditor.

When asked what he would wish for if he had a magic wand, Ben replied, "I'd have a great big rocket ship and go to the moon." His favorite activities at school were recess and lunch. He most disliked, "working." When quizzed, "Who is best at getting you to do what you are supposed to do?" he answered that it was his mother.

All three family conferences were attended by Mrs. Y. and Ben. Mrs. Y. said that her goals for Ben were that he do his schoolwork and to tell the truth. She reported that her husband was not as worried by Ben's misbehavior as she was. Ben said that he wanted to invite friends over to play. Mrs. Y. couldn't understand why Ben needed friends when he had her, "I'm his friend and we've always been buddies." Ben's one neighborhood friend was two years his junior.

Ben's teacher had already told Mrs. Y. that two hours of drill per afternoon was excessive. The counselor reiterated this and Mrs. Y. agreed to the following contract: (a) Drill sessions would be limited to fifteen minutes, (b) Ben could play each afternoon when his school work was complete, (c) With five days of complete work in a row, Ben could invite a friend to stay for the night.

Mrs. Y. reported that Ben looked forward to the family conferences which were scheduled at two week intervals. Ben was helped to communicate feelings with his mother. During one session, he hit a punching bag while talking about things that made him angry.

During the six weeks of intervention, Ben made good progress in getting classwork completed with the benefit of a lot of special help on the part of the classroom teacher. Ben earned his "friend-over-for-the-night" reward. His teacher also observed increased class participation and improved penmanship.

Shortly after the last conference, classwork began slipping. Mrs. Y.

reported that Ben was going downhill and added that she was, too. She no longer had the use of a car and felt isolated at home. At this point, the counselor encouraged her to make an appointment with a psychologist but Mrs. Y. declined.

Near the end of the school year, Mrs. Y. was upset with Ben's poor report card and requested that he be retained in the second grade. However Ben's grades did not justify retention and the teacher was reluctant to act on the parental request. Finally, Mrs. Y. sought out a psychologist and followed his recommendation that Ben not be retained. The family continued in therapy.

With reference to the criteria for family functionality, it appeared that the Y. family was a poor candidate for brief interventions:

Parental Resources. These parents possessed sufficient material resources to meet Ben's basic needs.

Time Frame of Problem Behavior. Not finishing work was reported as a new problem. However, when probed, Mrs. Y. told of much earlier behavioral deviations. Ben did not cry as a toddler; he raged with no tears. A pediatrician had stressed the need to encourage Ben to cry to give vent to his feelings.

Boundary Characteristics and Patterns of Communication. Mrs. Y.'s reluctance to encourage outside friendships for her son and her inclination to have him retained in second grade would suggest that normal individuation was being obstructed. Information about parental communication was minimal since the father did not attend the conferences.

Hierarchy of Authority. The lines of authority were unclear with Mrs. Y. vacillating between friend and parent to her child. Mrs. Y. reported that her husband sabotaged the reinforcement plans by taking Ben to a shopping mall to choose any toy of his choice.

Relationship with School Personnel. The counselor was impressed with the strength of Mrs. Y.'s desire to cooperate with school personnel in helping her son.

Although the Y. family was responsive to initial interventions, the degree of dysfunctionality became increasingly apparent. Given the disturbed hierarchy of authority, a sustained effort was impossible.

IMPLICATIONS FOR COUNSELING PROFESSIONALS

In order to test the practical implications of this model, it was tried in a school setting. The participants were four elementary school guidance counselors. These counselors received training in the family assessment model and in brief family intervention methods. Subsequently, they received five group supervisory sessions while they worked with families.

Children were referred either by teachers or parents and were part of each counselor's normal case load. Families who were invited to participate were described by counselors as being "functional" according to the specified criteria. Referrals ranged in age from six to twelve and were evenly distributed across elementary grades. "Brief Family Interventions" were defined as cases in which counselors had at least three face-to-face contacts with a parent. Three counselors reported four cases each and one reported five for a total of seventeen cases.

These seventeen case studies of "brief family interventions" support some tentative but interesting conclusions.

A. Ongoing supervision of counselors during the time they attempt to implement new techniques should be part of any effort to change the way counselors work.

B. Counselors should give themselves permission to decide which cases to work with and which to refer. The data support the view that the more functional a family is to start with, the less of the counselor's time will be consumed and the more positive the final outcome will be.

C. Counselors should try to determine if the hierarchy of parental authority is intact. The data support the view that firmly established parental authority contributes more to behavioral change than good communication in the family, problem solving skills, or short duration of problem behavior.

D. Counselors should expect to spend about four hours on a "brief family intervention" with a functional family.

E. There is a sequence of counselor interventions that seems to be effective—(1) Include parents, teachers, and the child in devising a plan that specifies goal behaviors and consequences; (2) Encourage parents to follow through with consequences; (3) Encourage the child to try adaptive behaviors; (4) Phase out the plan with intermittent reinforcement.

F. Some counselor interventions are seen to be ineffective—(1) Taking a "Wait and See" instead of a "Go for It" attitude is probably a mistake. Since school personnel can be overwhelmed by the demands of their work, there may be a tendency to opt for "a little bit of this, a little bit of that," and then to give up when cure proves elusive. As one counselor stated rather poetically, "The counselor slacked off the teacher, the teacher slacked off the student, the student slacked off!" (2) Counselors who misdiagnose and attempt to organize a highly dysfunctional family have let themselves in for frustration. In fact, such a family is effectively organized against the threat of change.

It should be noted that the case study method employed has the limitation that it does not yield conclusive data. Without a control group, it is impossible to isolate therapeutic mechanisms of change (Barlow & Herson, 1984). However, the carefully constructed case study can yield descriptive pre-post data that sheds light on a clinical phenomenon and may generate new hypotheses (Barlow & Herson, 1984).

REFERENCES

Amatea, E. S. & Fabrick, F. (1984). Moving a family into therapy: Critical referral issues for the school counselor. *School Counselor, 31*, 285–294.

American Psychiatric Association (1980). *A quick reference to the diagnostic criteria from DSM-III*. Washington, DC: Author.

Axline, V. M. (1947). *Play therapy*. Cambridge, MA: Houghton Mifflin.

Axline, V. M. (1969). *Play therapy*. New York: Ballentine.

Barlow, D. H. & Herson, M. (1984). *Single case experimental designs: Strategies for studying behavior change* (2nd ed.). New York: Pergamon.

Brammer, L. M. (1979). *The helping relationship: Process and skills* (2nd ed.). Englewood Cliffs, NJ: Prentice-Hall.

Carkhuff, R. (1969). *Helping and human relations*. New York: Rinehart & Winston.

Golden, L. (1983). Brief family interventions in a school setting. *Elementary School Guidance & Counseling, 17*, 288–293.

Golden, L. (1984). Managing maladaptive behavior in ill children through family interventions. *Journal of School Health, 10*, 389–391.

Golden, L. (1985). A critical case study of play therapy. *Journal of Child and Adolescent Psychotherapy, 2*, 286–290.

Haley, J. (1980). *Leaving home: The therapy of disturbed young people*. New York: McGraw-Hill.

Leavitt, M. (1982). *Families at risk: Primary prevention in nursing practice*. Boston: Little, Brown.

Minuchin, S. (1974) *Families and family therapy*. Cambridge, MA: Harvard University Press.

Nicoli, W. G. (1984). School counselors as family counselors: A rationale and training model. *School Counselor, 31*, 279–284.

Palmo, A. J., Lowry, L. A., Weldon, D. P., & Scioscia, T. M. (1984). Schools and family: Future perspectives for school counselors. *School Counselor, 31*, 272–278.

Rogers, C. A. (1980). *A way of being*. New York: Houghton-Mifflin.

Satir, V. (1972). *Peoplemaking*. Palo Alto, CA: Science and Behavior Books.

NAME INDEX

259

SUBJECT INDEX